NIXON'S GOOD DEED
Welfare Reform

NIXON'S GOOD DEED

Welfare Reform

/VINCENT J. and VEE
BURKE

Columbia University Press
New York & London 1974

Library of Congress Cataloging in Publication Data

Burke, Vincent J., 1919–1973.
  Nixon's good deed.

  Bibliography: p.
    1. Public welfare—United States. 2. Guaranteed
annual income—United States. 3. Nixon, Richard
Milhous, 1913— I. Burke, Vee, joint author.
II. Title.
HV95.B77   362.5   74–3393
ISBN 0–231–03850–X

For Vince

who caused the sun to shine
upon me
for eleven thousand
days and nights

CONTENTS

FOREWORD
by Abraham Ribicoff

IT WAS too good to be true. In 1969 President Richard Nixon proposed a welfare plan which rivaled all the programs of the war on poverty of the early 1960's in its concern for the poor. It would have tripled the incomes of impoverished whites and blacks in some states of the South, ended the state-by-state welfare non-system which splits families, demeans them, and encourages them not to work. It would have made the welfare system a federal rather than a state responsibility. All this from a president who was supposed to be a conservative Republican—a man who believed in returning power to the states rather than accumulating it in Washington. It was truly Nixon's good deed.

But somewhere between conception and birth the Family Assistance Plan foundered. Most participants in the development and legislative process surrounding the Family Assistance Plan had differing ideas of what it could and could not accomplish. To some it was a harsh workfare program; to others a give-away guaranteed income program.

Its defenders in the administration attempted to sell it as a liberal guaranteed income package to liberals and as a workfare plan with tough work requirements to conservatives. FAP tried to be both liberal and conservative but few understood that the welfare and workfare aspects were intricately entwined. The program attempted to make it more profitable to work than stay on welfare. This would be accomplished by allowing those working to retain a larger portion of their earnings without having their welfare payments reduced. But it also meant that more people would be eligible for the program and costs would mount.

Vince Burke followed the tortuous history of FAP from its beginning. He understood its ramifications when government officials did not. He talked with all the participants and knew what motivated them. Day after day and year after year he sat in hearings—sometimes exciting, sometimes tedious—following congressional developments.

Vince Burke was my friend. But he questioned and probed us, ferreting out facts which escaped other reporters. He was a reporter in the best sense—a true professional investigative reporter. Only he could have written a book that goes behind the public pronouncements on FAP and gets the true story of its rise and fall—both within the administration and Congress.

Tragically, Vince was struck down by cancer before he had a chance to finish his book. He worked on it to the end. As a fitting memorial to him, his loyal and loving wife, Vee, carried the project through to completion. Her dedication and knowledge should not go unnoticed. She has done a masterful job in completing Vince's work.

No study of the Family Assistance Plan would be complete without a careful reading of *Nixon's Good Deed*.

And no tribute to Vince would be as convincing as the enactment of a meaningful welfare reform program.

PREFACE

This preface should be the work of the two of us, like the rest of the book. But I must write it alone, because Vince died of cancer one year ago.

It was on April 20, 1969, that Vince revealed in the *Los Angeles Times* what he had deduced by close reporting and analysis: "The Nixon administration is considering a dramatic proposal to provide federal cash for the first time to fathers who work full time but don't earn enough to support their families."

Because it was his hardest and most far-reaching scoop, it was the most satisfying among many in Vince's long Washington newspaper career, and ultimately it led to our decision to write *Nixon's Good Deed*. We undertook the book after Richard Nixon advanced the Family Assistance Plan (FAP) in August 1969 because we were curious to know exactly what had produced such a startling development and why. We both had studied history at the University of Chicago, and Vince had observed Congress at close hand since 1947, when he joined the Washington bureau of United Press; so we recognized FAP as a dramatic instance of a quantum jump in American politics.

Vince was in an ideal position to explore this issue more thoroughly —and from more angles—than anyone else, for he had long been a specialist in legislative reporting and he had daily responsibility in Washington for *Los Angeles Times* coverage of welfare news. His reporting activity revealed the many perspectives towards FAP that had developed within both houses of Congress, in the massive HEW bureaucracy, in the White House, among state and county welfare officials, among organized lobby groups, among economists.

At the outset we had to design a procedure for accumulating and organizing the material that this book required. Our procedure employed chronologies, interviews, memos, coverage of congressional action, and historical and field research.

Chronologies

We began by constructing two chronologies. One, drawn from the *New York Times* index and other public sources, listed events on the record that were relevant to FAP. The other, drawn from Vince's own notes, by-line stories, and interviews, chronicled the development of FAP itself from November 1968 onwards. Before long we realized that we needed also a pre-Nixon chronology, for we learned that the roots of FAP stretched back to Lyndon Johnson's poverty war.

Interviews

We are grateful to the many participants in this story who helped us reconstruct the evolution of FAP by searching their memories, consulting their calendar pads and diaries, sharing their memos and notes, and commenting on our draft efforts. We typed interviews in duplicate so that one copy could be cut apart by the date (and issue) concerned. The interview strips then were taped into position in a looseleaf notebook. This process showed up gaps and, sometimes, discrepancies. We cross-interviewed, seeking corroboration from at least two witnesses for statements that we quoted, and often we obtained more. As we dug more deeply into the subject, reinterviewing, and as the story lengthened in Congress, the FAP chronology overflowed into a second notebook. Those whom we interviewed—many of them repeatedly—included:

Taggart Adams	aide to Senator Abraham Ribicoff
Martin Anderson	aide to Arthur F. Burns
Robert M. Ball	Commissioner of Social Security
Paul Barton	Department of Labor policy planning staff
Worth Bateman	former deputy assistant secretary of HEW
Hyman Bookbinder	Washington representative, American Jewish Committee
Arthur F. Burns	counselor to President Nixon
Phillip Burton	member of Congress

Lewis Butler	assistant secretary of HEW
John W. Byrnes	member of Congress
Joseph A. Califano	attorney and former aide to President Johnson
Howard A. Cohen	deputy assistant secretary of HEW
Wilbur J. Cohen	former secretary of HEW
John D. Ehrlichman	assistant to President Nixon
Clint Fair	legislative representative, AFL-CIO
Robert H. Finch	secretary of HEW
Mitchell Ginsberg	dean of the School of Social Work, Columbia University, and former administrator of Human Resources Administration, New York City
William Gorham	former assistant secretary of HEW
Fred Harris	U.S. senator
Robert Harris	executive staff director, President's Commission on Income Maintenance
Charles Hawkins	special assistant to the administrator, Social and Rehabilitation Service, HEW
Stephen M. Hess	deputy assistant to President Nixon for urban affairs
Allen C. Jensen	special assistant for human resources, National Governors' Conference
Tom Joe	special assistant to the undersecretary of HEW
Tom C. Korologos	administrative assistant to Senator Wallace Bennett
Melvin Laird	secretary of defense
Leonard Lesser	general counsel, Center for Community Change
Russell B. Long	U.S. senator
Norman Lourie	deputy executive secretary, Pennsylvania Department of Public Welfare
James Lyday	analyst, Office of Research, Plans, Programs and Evaluation, Office of Economic Opportunity
Richard Lyng	assistant secretary of agriculture
Michael Mahoney	aide to HEW Deputy Assistant Secretary Bateman

Theodore R. Marmor   special consultant, President's Commission on Income Maintenance

Eugene McCarthy   U.S. senator

Wilbur D. Mills   member of Congress

Edward L. Morgan   attorney for President Nixon

Jack Moskowitz   legislative representative, Common Cause

Daniel P. Moynihan   executive secretary of the Urban Affairs Council

Richard P. Nathan   assistant director of the Budget Bureau

Robert Patricelli   deputy assistant secretary of HEW

Geoffrey Peterson   aide to Senator Abraham Ribicoff

John R. Price Jr.   staff assistant to President Nixon for urban affairs and, later, executive secretary of the Domestic Affairs Council

Abraham Ribicoff   U.S. senator

Elliot Richardson   secretary of HEW

Alice Rivlin   former assistant secretary of HEW

Jerome Rosow   assistant secretary of labor

Donald Rumsfeld   director of the Office of Economic Opportunity

Sidney Saperstein   bill draftsman, HEW

George Shultz   secretary of labor

Michael Stern   Senate Finance Committee staff

James R. Storey   assistant to Richard Nathan and, later, HEW analyst

Alair A. Townsend   special assistant to executive director Harris of the President's Commission on Income Maintenance and, later, HEW analyst

Thomas Vail   Senate Finance Committee staff director

John G. Veneman   undersecretary of HEW

Betty Vinson   legislative representative, League of Women Voters of the United States

George Wiley   executive director, National Welfare Rights Organization

Our thanks go to all.

Action in Congress

We covered legislative hearings on FAP and lobbying and maneuvering for changes in the bill during 1969–72. We watched the House twice pass FAP and the Senate finally kill it. We followed the rise and triumph in Congress of Supplemental Security Income, which has offered all needy aged, blind, and disabled Americans a minimum cash income from the federal Treasury since January 1, 1974. We saw Congress establish a national income guarantee in the form of food stamps for *all* needy Americans, including the fully employed but poor fathers who would have been major beneficiaries of FAP.

Historical research

In our initial outline we assigned a modest role to "background history," but we learned that even to state the issues in the welfare debate one had to understand the past—and the special vocabulary of welfare workers and welfare data. This sent us to history books, welfare textbooks, the law, old congressional hearings, and to the files and regulations of the Department of Health, Education, and Welfare. To clarify some points, we corresponded with those who had made earlier welfare policy.

Field research

During the course of his assignment as an urban affairs and social welfare specialist for the *Los Angeles Times,* Vince occasionally investigated the situation outside Washington. He always returned with the news that we had to tear up some paragraphs already written because "welfare doesn't work the way Washington regulations say" in Pennsylvania or in Mississippi or elsewhere.

Many persons helped us determine the facts of this story, but we are responsible for their selection and interpretation. Much that we learned is unsaid for lack of space. However, we tried to present enough detail to tell this true story in a clear manner and to provoke thought about the dilemmas it raises.

His whole professional life prepared Vince for this book. He knew Congress intimately, he was an expert on tax and social security legislation, he knew and understood lobbyists, and he loved to find the presidential policy decisions hidden in the federal budget. He always looked behind political rhetoric for the reality, and he had a scholar's zest for mastering a topic. His judgments were his alone; no dogma ever inhibited him.

Writing this book was hard work and great fun. During the terrible last weeks of Vince's life, it was a comfort besides. May the book contribute to a better understanding of welfare and help achieve a more fair resolution of its dilemmas.

Vee Burke

May 1974

CHRONOLOGY OF WELFARE REFORM

1969

<table>
<tr><td>May 6</td><td>President Nixon sends message to Congress on hunger and malnutrition, proposing a guaranteed income in the form of food stamps equal in value to the cost of an adequate diet.</td></tr>
<tr><td>August 8</td><td>On nationwide television Nixon proposes a "Family Assistance Plan" to provide a federal floor under incomes of all families with dependent children (at the rate of $1600 for a family of four persons). He also proposes that states be required to pay a federally prescribed minimum sum to the aged, blind, and disabled on their welfare rolls.</td></tr>
<tr><td>August 11</td><td>Nixon sends message to Congress on welfare reform.</td></tr>
<tr><td>October 3</td><td>Administration sends "Family Assistance Act of 1969" to Congress. Bill includes a $90 per person minimum standard for state welfare payments to needy adults.</td></tr>
<tr><td>October 15–November 13</td><td>House Ways and Means Committee holds 18 days of hearings on FAP and on proposed "Social Security Amendments of 1969," a bill providing benefit increases and future automatic adjustments for</td></tr>
</table>

higher living costs. Social Security provisions get most attention at hearings.

1970

March 5
House Ways and Means Committee approves (21 to 3) FAP.

March 11
House Ways and Means Committee reports "Family Assistance Act of 1970,"
H.R. 16311 (House report No. 91–904).
Bill includes $110 per person federally
prescribed minimum for needy adults on
state welfare rolls.

April 16
House passes (243 to 155) H.R. 16311 under a rule barring amendments.

April 29–May 1
Senate Finance Committee opens hearings
on H.R. 16311, rejects bill as drafted, and
sends proposal back to administration with
directions to devise an "overall plan" that
takes account of other benefits also available to poor families.

June 10
Administration submits revised FAP proposal to Senate Finance Committee.

July 21–September 10
Senate Finance Committee holds 18 days
of hearings on H.R. 16311.

October 13
Administration submits additional revisions to Senate Finance Committee.

November 20
Senate Finance Committee votes (10 to 6)
against FAP.

December 11
Senate Finance Committee reports conglomerate bill, H.R. 17550 (Senate report
No. 91–1431), which includes Social Security, Medicare and Medicaid, and foreign trade provisions. FAP supporters
hope the family plan can be added to the
bill on the floor, but a filibuster ensues.

December 28
Senate votes (49 to 21) to recommit the
bill to committee with instructions to re-

port back only Social Security, Medicare, and Medicaid provisions.

December 29   Senate passes Social Security benefit increase.

December 31   House refuses to go to conference on the Social Security measure. Thus, both FAP and the Social Security bill die with the 91st Congress, but Rep. Wilbur D. Mills, Ways and Means Committee chairman, pledges early action in the new Congress.

December 31   Congress passes food stamp amendments, after adding a requirement that able-bodied recipients work, to assure all needy Americans (in participating counties) an "adequate" diet. The penniless are to receive free stamps; others are to pay no more than 30 percent of their income. Essentially, this is Nixon's May 1969 proposal.

1971

January 22   In the 92d Congress, Rep. Mills and Rep. John W. Byrnes, senior Republican on the Ways and Means Committee, introduce H.R. 1, "The Social Security Amendments of 1971." H.R. 1 includes FAP (with the guarantee level raised to $2400 for a family of four—to compensate for elimination of recipients' eligibility for food stamps).

May 17   House Ways and Means Committee votes (22 to 3) approval of FAP.

May 26   House Ways and Means Committee reports H.R. 1 (House report No. 92–231). Bill proposes a new federal income program (Title III) for needy aged and for the blind and disabled of any age (pro-

	viding $130 per individual and $195 per couple to those with no countable income).
June 22	House defeats (234 to 187) a motion to delete FAP (Title IV) from H.R. 1, then passes (288 to 132) H.R. 1.
July 27–August 3	Senate Finance Committee holds four days of hearings on H.R. 1.
August 15	President Nixon defers effective date of H.R. 1's proposed welfare reform by one year, saving budget funds.
October 28	Senator Abraham Ribicoff introduces a more generous reform bill co-sponsored by 18 other senators.
December 14	Congress passes Talmadge amendment requiring welfare mothers with no child younger than six to register for work or training. Bill provides penalty for noncompliance by states.

1972

January 20–February 9	Senate Finance Committee holds 15 days of hearings on H.R. 1.
April 28	Senate Finance Committee votes (10 to 4) to reject FAP in favor of Chairman Russell Long's "workfare" plan: to withdraw federal welfare aid from mothers whose youngest child is six and to instead guarantee them a job at $1.20 an hour. Plan also provides wage supplements for those who take low-paying private jobs. For low-paid family breadwinners at jobs covered by Social Security, plan provides a tax credit (maximum credit: $400 a year).
June 22	Nixon announces that he will not compromise with Ribicoff forces, but will insist upon H.R. 1 as passed by House.

August 29	Senator George McGovern, Nixon's Democratic opponent in the presidential race, abandons his proposal to give every American $1,000 a year and proposes a plan that aids only the poor already on welfare.
September 26	Senate Finance Committee reports its version of H.R. 1, "Social Security Amendments of 1972," (Senate report No. 92–1230), including Long's welfare plan for families and the federal guarantee for the aged, blind, and disabled, now named Supplemental Security Income.
October 4	Senate rejects (52 to 34) Ribicoff's compromise version of FAP.
October 15	Senate-House conferees delete FAP from H.R. 1.
October 17	House and Senate pass H.R. 1, minus the Family Assistance Plan, but including Supplemental Security Income.

NIXON'S GOOD DEED
Welfare Reform

1.

STRANGER THAN FICTION
(An Overview)

ANYONE WHO had predicted that Richard Nixon would be the first president to propose a guaranteed income for families, coupled with wage supplements for poor fathers, would have been dismissed as mad.

He would have been held doubly mad if the prophet had also forecast that during the heat of the 1972 campaign Nixon's Democratic rival for the presidency would delete help for the working poor from his own welfare platform.

More important than what this tells us about Mr. Nixon and Senator George S. McGovern is what it says about the American public, the American political process, and the difficulty of reforming any American institution no matter how discredited.

President Nixon's welfare reform plan for the first time forced the nation to confront welfare's discrimination against poor fathers who stay with their families and work at low wages. Welfare's incentives to produce broken families had worked—only too well. By 1972 one of every nine American children under eighteen was on the welfare rolls, the vast majority living in female-headed families. Intact families of working fathers were barred from federally subsidized welfare, regardless of how meager their income, on the erroneous assumption that a man's full-time job would meet their income needs.

Mr. Nixon's welfare reform tested the conscience and intelligence of America. Both failed. Americans cherished the work ethic and family stability, but not sufficiently to pay the price of larger relief rolls.

In welfare, it is true that "if you're not part of the solution you're part of the problem," and those who are part of welfare's problem include some of America's most self-righteous "limousine liberals," as well as George Wallace's blue-collar army.

In a broad sense the American public IS the welfare problem, because it does not understand the problem and impedes those who do. Most Americans nod their heads approvingly at all three of these statements:

—We should provide adequate welfare for those who cannot work.
—Those who can work should do so.
—Welfare rolls should not be increased.

Senator Lloyd Bentsen, Texas Democrat, used that formulation in defeating for the U.S. Senate a Republican congressman who voted for Mr. Nixon's Family Assistance Plan. Candidate McGovern used a variation of that formula when, on August 29, 1972, he retreated to a welfare position less bold than Nixon's. And Mr. Nixon himself, after advancing the Family Assistance Plan on August 8, 1969, tried to play it safe by always stressing that FAP was "workfare," ignoring that workfare, by definition, meant *more welfare.*

Tested by opinion polls as politically safe, the three welfare platitudes are heard often on the political stump. As welfare policy they are absolute gibberish. They constitute the great evasion of welfare's dilemmas.

These platitudes assume that families can be divided into two mutually exclusive groups: those who work versus those on welfare. The statements ignore that, as a matter of national policy, we have defined welfare mothers (with school-age children) as employable and we have decreed every working welfare mother to be entitled to a wage supplement until her income far exceeds her basic welfare benefit (how else motivate her to "work her way off" welfare?). For welfare mothers "workfare" was first enacted in 1967 and took effect on July 1, 1969. The real question is whether wage supplements (welfare payments) are to be provided to poor families headed by working *fathers.* In killing the Family Assistance Plan on October 17, 1972, Congress answered no to that question, but the question was not silenced. Because it reflects a socially destructive inequity, the question will persist. (Indeed, after some poor families split to qualify for welfare, they surreptitiously pool their income and thus already receive wages plus welfare. But this is underground "workfare.")

Throughout the FAP debate Congress ignored the conflict, reconcilable only at astronomical cost, between guaranteed benefit levels and work incentives. This conflict means that welfare is not logically susceptible to the traditional cry of Democratic liberals for "more." More of which? More benefits or more incentives? Evading this dilemma, many liberals issued their reflexive demands for "more" in general. Their irresponsible posing on behalf of the poor was harmful to the poorest of the poor: 1) the broken welfare families of the South, who received very low relief payments; and 2) intact families of working poor fathers throughout the nation, whose presence in the home barred their wives and children from AFDC (Aid to Families with Dependent Children).

Our story reveals that sloppy analysis of welfare and evasion of its dilemmas is promoted not only by politicians but also by welfare bureaucrats. They have invented a specialized vocabulary for the complexities of welfare that misleads everyone, including some of its initiates. Most citizens do not examine the matter, for they have no fear of joining the casualties on welfare rolls although they pay the immense costs.

Our tale takes us behind the scenes in the Johnson and Nixon administrations. It reveals that McGovern's 1972 running mate, Sargent Shriver, was the real godfather of Nixon's welfare reform, and that Nixon's running mate, Vice-President Spiro T. Agnew, tried to kill the plan.

Also revealed is the incredible story of how holdover Democrats took Shriver's leftover plan for fighting poverty (which Lyndon Johnson had rejected) and sold it as welfare reform to Mr. Nixon. Excluded from the conspiratorial strategies that helped propel the plan to Nixon's White House was Daniel P. Moynihan, who later was erroneously credited as the plan's "architect."

This book tells why a conservative Republican president proposed to expand the welfare state of Franklin Delano Roosevelt. It examines the three-year struggle over family welfare, which left Congress persuaded that it was politically perilous to attempt to deal rationally with the problem.

Although Congress rejected a federal income guarantee for America's children on October 17, 1972, it, at the same time, enacted ederal income guarantee for all other groups society feels should not be obliged to work. These groups—the elderly, the blind, and the disabled—won in the new law an unqualified right to a minimum income from the U.S. Treasury. Since January 1, 1974, these needy Americans, estimated to total six million, have been eligible for special new golden checks, called "Supplemental Security Income," from the Social Security Administration, whether or not they ever paid Social Security payroll taxes.

Had Republican Nixon not won the presidency in 1968, America almost surely would not have adopted a federal income guarantee for the aged in 1972. Not only was this revolutionary concept missing from the Democratic agenda; the party's leaders and professionals were embarrassed by welfare and loath even to discuss the matter. Nixon put welfare on the desks of a reluctant Congress by proposing, in August 1969, a sweeping income guarantee for families with children and a modest little welfare reform for the aged, blind, and disabled. Out of the latter plan evolved our first guaranteed income.

Why did the same Congress that denied an income guarantee to children grant one to the aged, blind, and disabled? It was not simply because of America's long tradition of giving less to its poor children than to its poor aged—a group deemed worthy of help and possessed of political power. Ignorance and neglect also aided passage of Supplemental Security Income (SSI), while publicity and debate helped to doom the Family Assistance Plan (FAP). Most important, SSI solved a problem for key politicians—the defense of the Social Security wage-related "insurance" system against encroachments by welfare. In contrast, FAP created problems for politicians, and hence it failed. In order to justify a vote for FAP (which was Title IV of H.R. 1), one had to 1) defend doubling "welfare" rolls, and 2) risk the anger of organized and predominantly nonworking northern welfare mothers, who feared that FAP would benefit the working poor at their expense.

The two proposed income guarantees had much in common. Both the Family Assistance Plan and Supplemental Security Income provided for the transformation of "welfare," hitherto basically a state and local responsibility, into a direct federal benefit, operated by the federal government on standard rules. Because of their more liberal eligibility rules, both FAP and SSI would have vastly enlarged the number of persons getting "welfare," and would have given maximum help to the poorest at heavy cost. FAP's federal payments would have cost an estimated $6 billion annually at the outset, about one-third more than the initial cost of SSI payments.

But, after twice passing the House, FAP floundered and died. The congressional struggle over FAP made pawns of two groups of needy families, the poorest and the less poor. It pitted liberal against liberal, conservative against conservative. Nixon's plan would have benefited both components of the poorest of the poor—working poor families who were denied federal welfare cash everywhere, and the South's welfare poor, whose payments were lowest.

One group of the poor, welfare families of the North, already received more than the federal floor Nixon was proposing to establish. Their lobbyists and allies, from social workers to church leaders (liberal Protestant), vowed to block passage of help for the poorest unless existing higher benefits were guaranteed. Their price was a guarantee lacking in existing law.

When the showdown came, leaders of both parties, President Nixon and Senator George McGovern, each in his own way and each for political reasons, turned his back on the working poor.

Richard Nixon deserted his own program in deference to the general hostility to enlarging family welfare rolls. Already in 1972, one of every three black children under eighteen years old was on welfare, and 43 percent of welfare families included an illegitimate child. Smouldering with resentment against huge welfare rolls and the taxes to support them, the American public assumed that to "reform" welfare meant to cut welfare numbers—or at least to stabilize them—certainly not to enlarge them.

This book, in addition to telling a dramatic and unlikely story about how the political system really works, aims to provide a solid factual basis for thinking about the dilemmas of welfare, poverty, and the American family. Until these dilemmas are candidly faced and rational choices are made, welfare will continue to injure the work ethic and family stability. Until these dilemmas are resolved, poverty cannot be overcome.

The fight over welfare reform offers many lessons:

—A conservative Republican president has more power than a liberal Democratic president to initiate bold policy. His conservative cloak protects him. On the other hand, a liberal Democratic president could no more have recommended a guaranteed family income than he could have opened a dialogue with the People's Republic of China.

—America has a high tolerance for irrationality and injustice; the status quo arouses passionate defense from those whom it benefits. But change becomes possible when the status quo begins to threaten groups with political power (in this case, governors whose budgets were squeezed by rising welfare costs and local property taxpayers outraged by county welfare levies).

—Liberal ideologues can be more destructive to social progress than conservative ideologues. All or nothing was demanded by some liberals, willing to forsake a federal income guarantee for the nation's children, willing to abandon the children to the mercies of the states, rather than to accept a guarantee that represented a long overdue new principle, but whose monetary terms they disliked (even though they could have worked to raise their levels in the future).

—The primary force that motivates the politician is a desire for political credit. Hence, form and rhetoric can be more important to him than substance.

—The analyst and the politician are natural antagonists. The analyst insists that when values conflict, society must understand that every choice sacrifices one good for another. (For instance, within a given cost, the higher the FAP guarantee the lower the work bonus; that is, the more adequate the guarantee, the smaller the work incentive.) But the politician tries to cover up such conflicts; his rhetoric deliberately evades dilemmas and inconsistencies. It is not so much that the politician wants to have his cake and eat it too. Rather, he knows that some voters want to have it and some want to eat it and he wants to please them all.

Passage of the income guarantee for the aged gives no promise of a universal cash income guarantee in the future. The circumstances that enacted SSI are lacking for other needy groups: families with children, childless couples, singles. However, in the federal food stamp program America already has an income guarantee open to all these needy.*

* About 800 counties failed to offer food stamps in the summer of 1973, when Congress (in the farm bill) ordered states (and Puerto Rico, Guam, and the Virgin Islands) to extend food stamps to every political subdivision by July 1, 1974.

2.

CAMOUFLAGE AND A SKIRMISH WITH POVERTY

"Oh! We are overwhelmed with lies, and there is no worse lie than a problem poorly stated"
—GEORGES BERNANOS, *La Liberté pour quoi faire?*

IMAGINE A Social Security "system" that paid five times more to a New York family than to a corresponding Mississippi family; that reduced benefits in almost half the states in a period of rising living costs; * that penalized those whose behavior offended the community; that could be abolished overnight by the state legislature.

Such a federally subsidized system was enacted by Franklin D. Roosevelt's Social Security Act of 1935. Public assistance has been the shameful half of our social security law. One critic has called it "social insecurity," and so titled his first book on the matter (Gilbert Y. Steiner, 1966).

From the beginning states' rights dominated the new welfare program. States decided whether to provide any welfare and, if so, how much and to whom, and then submitted a specified portion of the total bill to the U.S. Treasury for payment. Before enacting FDR's 1935 bill, Congress erased a welfare provision that would have

* Because states were free to set payment levels for federally subsidized welfare, or even to abolish the program altogether, there was no federal guarantee of cash. Despite rising prices 21 states reduced basic benefits in at least one of the years, 1968–71, to spread funds over the growing number of families on Aid to Families with Dependent Children (AFDC). As of July 1971, ten states were paying smaller checks to penniless AFDC families than in January 1969 when President Nixon took office.

required states to furnish sufficient aid to provide "a reasonable subsistence compatible with health and decency," a stipulation of the old-age relief laws of Massachusetts and New York, because suspicious southern members feared that it might give Washington authority to compel states to give poor blacks as much as poor whites. Edwin E. Witte, executive director of FDR's bill-drafting committee, however, wrote (1962, p. 144) that it never occurred to his group that the "Negro question" would come up in connection with welfare payments.

Witte's comment reflected the white racism of that time, so pervasive that Harry Hopkins, arch-liberal and chief of Roosevelt's Works Progress Administration, approved use of WPA funds to subsidize the writing of a book that displayed contempt for the Mississippi Negro. *Mississippi, A Guide to the Magnolia State* (1938, p. 30) told the nation: "Seated in the white man's wagon, and subtly letting the white man worry with the reins, the Negro assures himself a share of all things good. Once a landlord was asked if the Negro really had a soul. 'If he hasn't,' the landlord replied, 'it's the first thing that a white man ever had that a Negro didn't share if he stayed with him long enough.' "

In the early days of the new state-federal welfare program, it was customary in some areas to offer smaller payments, if any, to blacks than to whites. The rationalization was that blacks could get by with less.

In the very month (January 1935) that President Franklin D. Roosevelt, denouncing the dole as a "narcotic," turned his anti-Depression program from relief to public works, he planted the seeds of the welfare problem of the 1960s and 1970s. The seeds were federal funds offered to states by the Social Security Act to encourage them to make welfare payments to two groups of the needy who everyone agreed should not work, even if jobs were available. They were persons over 65 years of age and members of broken families— dependent children and their mothers who had been deprived by death or other cause of a male breadwinner. These programs of public charity, it was thought, would largely wither away, unneeded, once Social Security began paying out retirement and survivor benefits and once unemployment insurance took hold for the jobless.

Instead the little-noticed federal program of aid for broken families, launched in 1935, grew into a monster. By providing welfare funds for fatherless families (and later, beginning in 1961, for families of jobless fathers), yet denying funds for families headed by working poor fathers, Congress inadvertently encouraged creation of mother-headed families.

"The tacit assumption was that the institution of the nuclear family, the taboo on illegitimacy, and the ethic of paternal responsibility were too strong to be affected by financial incentives," wrote Professor James Tobin (1968, p. 96) in *Agenda for the Nation*. This turned out to be, as Tobin suggested, a "serious miscalculation." The best paychecks within the hope of many poor fathers were smaller than the welfare checks, geared to family size, paid upon their desertion. The median number of children in welfare families was three; if a family stayed together the father's paycheck would have to cover five persons.

In 1940, 2 percent of American children were on welfare. From 1940 to 1962 the proportion doubled; in the next eight years it doubled again, and by 1972 it reached 11 percent. Eight out of ten welfare children were on the rolls not because their fathers were dead or disabled, the original premise of AFDC law, but because they had left home.

The massive movement of mothers onto welfare rolls in the 1960s reflected both (a) continuous growth in the pool of eligible persons * and (b) rapid swelling of the proportion of eligibles who were willing to seek—and were successful in seeking—welfare. More mothers

* The number eligible was enlarged by the continuing migration of "surplus" unskilled manpower from South to North and West, where welfare rules were more generous; and by rising benefit guarantees, which automatically expanded eligibility in states that paid full "needs"—most major industrial states. Many states increased AFDC payment levels after the federal government in mid-1966 first offered to pay at least one-half of whatever total sum the state paid to AFDC families, provided the state offered Medicaid (in 1973 only Arizona lacked Medicaid). This option permits states to bill the federal government for 50 to 83 percent of total *cash* welfare payments (the Medicaid reimbursement formula) and eliminates maximums on average grants eligible for reimbursement.

without husbands applied for welfare in the 1960s, not just because there were more of them, but also because it had become easier to get, was less stigmatizing, and—especially after 1966 when free medical care (Medicaid) was added—was more valuable. Attitudes of both the giver and taker of relief were transformed, in part, by federally funded workers in the "war" against poverty, including Community Action groups, who popularized the doctrine that welfare was an entitlement, like Social Security, not a handout to be begged. Anti-poverty lawyers helped the poor obtain this right.

Maryland's lieutenant governor, Blair Lee III, complained in November 1971, that Baltimore caseworkers had become "wholly un-cooperative" in trying to weed out ineligibles. "In recent years social workers have become missionaries trying to increase welfare rolls," Lee said. "They just don't like to do eligibility checks."

The welfare explosion followed logically upon the huge uprooting of 3.5 million blacks and other rural poor, who were driven by agricultural mechanization and farm production control programs out of the rural South from 1940 to 1970, and who were attracted by the greater opportunities of the North. Unskilled and poorly educated, they poured northward into the big cities; but here, too, mechanization was eliminating unskilled jobs. Those who found work often were paid less than their wives and children could obtain in welfare upon their desertion.

Politicians blinked at this reality, attributing welfare's surprise growth to fraud, careless administration, and massive indolence. Help for the helpless and work for the able-bodied—the popular slogan—was a corrupting falsehood because it evaded the problem.

Lyndon Johnson's "war" on poverty perpetuated this lie, refusing to face the poverty against which jobs were helpless—the poverty of the large family and of the low-paid worker. In fact, LBJ's "unconditional" war against poverty was so constrained in both funds and philosophy that it amounted to little more than a skirmish. His "Great Society" was built on a timid and conventional economic base.

Although Johnson's poverty program gave the poor revolutionary tools of judicial challenge and community organization, it withheld the most basic aid—money. Instead, most of the program's limited funds were paid to middle-class teachers, consultants, and other professionals to provide schooling, counseling, and other services of highly variable effectiveness to upgrade the skills of poor people and their children.

In contrast, the Family Assistance Plan proposed by Republican Nixon in August 1969 was a radical thrust against poverty. For American children it proposed a federally paid and federally administered right to minimum income; for the needy aged, blind, and disabled a companion postscript to FAP proposed that, for the first time, the states be required to pay a specified welfare minimum.

Thus, Robert H. Finch, Nixon's secretary of health, education, and welfare, was justified in his boast that Mr. Nixon was proposing a "real war" on poverty—direct income support through welfare cash and food stamps that would overnight wipe out 59 percent of the nation's poverty income gap.

True, had there been no Democrats, Nixon would not have made his move. Political competition from the majority party in Congress compelled Nixon to act on food stamps, which Johnson had refused to do. And, although its origins were long kept a secret, the Family Assistance Plan was actually designed by leftover Democrats in the executive branch who had earlier repeatedly tried to persuade Johnson to adopt a similar scheme as a weapon against poverty.

The Skirmish

At the outset of the poverty war the government knew little about poverty; it did not even know who was poor. Initially, the Council of Economic Advisers gave a misleading report to the president. CEA said (1964 annual report, p. 57) that aged persons headed one-third of the nation's *poor households* (defined as having less than $3,000 in annual income, regardless of size!),* but later acknowledged that children were the most numerous group of poor persons (43 percent of the 1964 total) and that the aged had been only 16 percent of the 1964 poor population (1966 annual report, p. 114).

* CEA said it had not been possible to refine the cutoff by indicators of family need, but that its simple measure was a "valid benchmark" for assessing the anti-poverty task (p. 58). In March 1964, Chairman Walter Heller told the House Education and Labor Committee that the $3,000 standard tended to understate the poverty of children.

The high incidence of poverty among American children had first been shown in 1963 by a government statistician who toiled among piles of computer print-outs in a dingy room at the Department of Health, Education, and Welfare. Mollie Orshansky, whose name later was given to the official poverty index, based her count of poor children on food costs. Miss Orshansky (1963, p. 3) calculated that poor children, measured by the Agriculture Department's economy diet,* totaled 17 million; measured by the low-cost diet, 23 million (in 1963)—in all, from one-fourth to one-third of children! Yet CEA's 1964 report estimated that only one child in six was poor (p. 59).

Miss Orshansky, herself a child of poverty and the first in her family to receive a college diploma, also helped explode the myth that no family with a full-time breadwinner could be poor. On the hypothesis that a job was no guarantee against poverty, as she knew from her father's untiring efforts as tinsmith, repairman, and small grocer, Miss Orshansky studied the work record of the poor, using a special Census Bureau tabulation of family income. Her findings (1965, p. 5) were startling: in almost 30 percent of the families identified as poor in 1963, the breadwinner had worked full time.

"I thought it would be an impressive number—the poor families headed by the year-round workers, the 'working poor,' the guys who do everything we tell them to, work hard, yet can't make it," she said later in an interview with the authors, "but I don't think anyone realized how impressive the number would be. We should have known. After all, the minimum wage then was only $1.25 an hour. You didn't really need to have a poverty 'line' to know that $2,600 before taxes in 1963 was poverty income."

In its 1964 report, the CEA made a naive declaration about the ease and cost of overcoming poverty. "Conquest of poverty is well within our power," it said (p. 77). "About $11 billion a year would bring all poor families up to the $3,000 income level we have taken to be the minimum for a decent life. The majority of the Nation could simply tax themselves enough to provide the necessary income supplements to these less fortunate citizens."

* Miss Orshansky said that the economy food plan would provide "adequate nutrition" for less money than the low-cost plan and that both plans were "by no means subsistence diets," although each assumed that the housewife would shop carefully and skillfully prepare all the family's meals at home (1963, p. 8).

After a moment's reflection, any $60-per-week dishwasher or bus boy could have told the prestigious White House economists that their cost estimates had omitted the human dynamic. If the government guaranteed everyone a minimum income of $60 per week, but gave nothing to those *earning* $60, why work for $60? There would be massive withdrawals from work by those toiling at low-paid, unpleasant jobs. Who would work for no monetary gain? Only those few who found psychological pleasure, a sense of worth, or community status in their jobs.

Professor Robert J. Lampman, University of Wisconsin economist who had served the previous year on the staff of the Council, was appalled that CEA would disseminate the delusion that the poverty income gap could be closed by an appropriation equal to it. Six years later, after the poverty income gap had been reestimated at $10 billion, Lampman still was trying to refute the misconception.

"It is a major disservice to rational discourse to suggest, as many have done, that the United States could eliminate poverty if we were only willing to transfer an additional $10 billion to the poor," Lampman (1970, p. 16) told the American Economics Association in December, 1969. "There is no way to get that $10 billion into the hands of the poor without spending far more than that."

To close any income gap through unconditional payments would always cost far more than 100 percent of the deficit. If payments equalized conditions for the poor by bringing them all up to some minimum income level, many low-wage earners would quit work, since for them the income floor would be an income ceiling. Once adopted, the no-poverty target would recede, and the cost of reaching it would grow.

Of course, one could try to sustain work by providing payments *above* the chosen level of income guarantees. If, for example, the guarantee were $3,000 a year, 50 cents (instead of one dollar) might be subtracted from the guaranteed payment for every dollar earned. That would give the bus boy an inducement to keep working; he then could boost his total income to $4,500—$3,000 from work and $1,500 from government payments.

The lower the earnings, the higher would be the government payment, the reverse or "negative" of the positive income tax, which increases taxes with income. This concept of a guaranteed income with a built-in work incentive was advanced by conservative economist Milton Friedman, publicized in the 1964 election as "Goldwater's economist." Among economists the concept became known as the "negative income tax."

To eradicate a poverty income gap of $10 billion with a negative income tax mechanism so as to preserve financial gain from work would cost much more than $10 billion, possibly as much as $25 billion.

New Field: Poverty Analysis

Johnson's poverty war created the Office of Economic Opportunity and charged it with the unprecedented task of helping the poor, a hidden and unknown group that heretofore lacked representation in Washington. Assigned the poor as its constituency, OEO had to find out who was poor and why, and to what extent they were or could be helped by government programs. This poverty agency assembled economists and others who became specialists in the new field of poverty analysis. At HEW, similar work was begun. William Gorham, that department's assistant secretary for program coordination, appointed a group to evaluate Social Security and welfare, not for their administrative efficiency, but rather for their impact against poverty.

In their report (U.S. HEW, 1966), prepared by Otto Eckstein, Harvard University economics professor and a former member (1965–66) of the Council of Economic Advisers who had presided over a White House task force on income maintenance, and by Robert Harris of Gorham's staff (who in 1968 became staff director for President Johnson's Commission on Income Maintenance), the program analysts challenged the current system of income transfers. They said that 60 percent of the needy got no help from public assistance or from Social Security (p. 13), that the aged poor, whose total incomes averaged 10 percent below the poverty line, fared better than poor children, whose total family incomes averaged 44 percent below the poverty line (p. 3).

They found that large general increases in Social Security had relatively small impact on poverty: for example, only 14 cents of every dollar in extra benefits from a 35 percent increase would help reduce the income deficit of the poor; the other 86 cents would go to the non-poor (p. 24).

The analysts found that the welfare practices of many states virtually precluded work by recipients. In major industrial states, which then paid a welfare family's full "needs," * a welfare mother was discouraged from working by a 100 percent tax on *net* earnings,† subtracted from her welfare check. Only if the mother could earn substantially more than her welfare check (in which case her family was dropped from welfare) could she increase total income by work. An unpublished study made for HEW (Leonard Hausman: "The Use of Monetary Incentives in AFDC and AFDC-UP") indicated that 70 percent of AFDC mothers could not possibly earn more than their welfare checks. The solution, said the analysts, was to let welfare recipients boost their total income considerably above the assistance level by exempting "a substantial part" of their earnings from offsetting cuts in their relief checks. The analysts warned that unless this were done, any other liberalizations of welfare (such as raising basic benefits or admitting working poor families to welfare) would further damage financial work incentives.

The Eckstein-Harris report, finished by the analysts ‡ in August 1966, went to Undersecretary Wilbur J. Cohen for publication clearance. Fearing that the report's criticism of across-the-board increases in Social Security would threaten the system's maturity and impede

---

* In theory each state established standards of "need" for welfare recipients by adding up costs of basic items in a "budget" for an individual or a family. But in practice needs standards were derived more frequently from social and political judgments than from living costs and then were compromised by fiscal restraints.

† In 1965 states were permitted to disregard $50 a month of earned income of an AFDC child (up to $150 per family); but most states withheld this benefit from welfare families. Also, states were allowed to disregard sums set aside for "future identifiable needs" of children.

‡ James Lyday, OEO, and Worth Bateman, HEW, who later were to draft Nixon's Family Assistance Plan, had a part in the Eckstein-Harris 1966 report. Lyday served as OEO's representative on the formal program analysis group, and Bateman worked some with Harris on the analysis.

benefit gains, Cohen failed to respond. (At the time benefits lagged behind price increases, but from 1967 to 1973 they were to rise twice as fast as the consumer price index!) Theodore R. Marmor, a young political scientist who was gathering material for a book, *The Politics of Medicare* (and who became a special consultant to the President's Commission on Income Maintenance in 1968–69) worked as an assistant to Cohen at the time. He recalls that Cohen scoffed, "That's what your friends (analysts in Assistant Secretary Gorham's office) come up with!" and thinks Cohen threw the 83-page report in the wastebasket. At any rate, Cohen never returned the report. In order to publish it, Gorham's office had to have it completely retyped— and its art work redone. This time a photo copy went to Cohen, with a note saying that publication was planned within a week. Although the published report is dated October 1966, it was not actually reproduced until far into 1967, and it never won the signature of Wilbur Cohen.

HAVING THE POWER . . .

Before the start of the Poverty War in July 1964, Secretary of Health, Education, and Welfare Anthony J. Celebrezze appointed an Advisory Council on Public Welfare. After 23 months this panel of social workers, headed by Fedele F. Fauri, dean of the School of Social Work, University of Michigan, reported that the major problem with welfare was that it gave too little money to too few persons. Borrowing for the title of his report a phrase from President Johnson, "Having the Power, We Have the Duty," the Council exhorted America to accept a new duty: To guarantee everyone, as a matter of right, a "modest but adequate" income (1966, p. xiii). What it proposed, however, was a federal-state guarantee, administered (and partially financed) by states and localities. It gave no cost estimates but said the nation could "well afford" the guarantee. Moreover, to get full benefits from its plan, the Council said it was "imperative" (p. 76) to expand the number of social workers.

PLAN OF THE POVERTY WARRIORS

Aware that almost one-third of poor families already had a full-time breadwinner, and mindful of the limitations and inequities of existing government programs, the poverty warriors concluded that the most efficient tool for alleviating poverty would be the one that Milton Friedman had designed expressly for that purpose: a negative income tax. This was a plan to provide a minimum guaranteed income, varying with size of family and reduced by only a fraction of each dollar earned so as to preserve work incentives. Friedman's own words are best for explaining the idea of the negative income tax. Below are excerpts from his article, "The Case for a Negative Income Tax," published in 1968 in *Republican Papers* (pp. 207–9), edited by Representative Melvin R. Laird:

> I have termed this device for helping the poor a *negative income tax* in order to stress its identity in concept and operation with the present income tax. The essential idea is to extend the income tax by supplementing the income of the poor by a *fraction* of their unused income tax exemptions and deductions.
>
> Under present law [1968] a family of four is entitled to exemptions and deductions of not less than $3,000 (precisely this sum if the family uses the standard deduction). If such a family has a total income of $3,000 it pays no tax. If it has a total pre-tax income of $4,000 (and uses the standard deduction), it has a *positive* taxable income of $1,000. At the current tax rate for that bracket of 14 percent, it pays $140 a year in taxes, leaving it with $3,860 in income after taxes (see table). If such a family had a total

Example of Income Tax Incorporating 50 Percent Rate on Negative Taxable Income

(Family of four; existing exemptions and standard deduction; existing rates on positive income)

Total income before tax	Exemptions and deductions	Taxable income	Tax rate	Tax	Income after tax
0	$3,000	$–3,000	50%	$–1,500	$1,500
1,000	3,000	–2,000	50%	–1,000	2,000
2,000	3,000	–1,000	50%	– 500	2,500
3,000	3,000	0			3,000
4,000	3,000	+1,000	14%	+ 140	3,860

pre-tax income of $2,000, it would have unused exemptions and deductions of $1,000, or in other words, it would have a *negative* taxable income of $1,000 ($2,000–$3,000). Under present law, it gets no benefit from those unused exemptions and deductions. Under a negative income tax, it would be entitled to receive a payment, the amount depending on the tax rate.

If the tax rate were the same as for the first bracket of positive income, or 14 percent, it would be entitled to receive $140, leaving it with a post-tax income of $2,140. If the tax rate were 50 percent, the highest rate that seems to me at all feasible, and the one I have used for illustrative purposes, it would be entitled to receive $500, leaving it with a post-tax income of $2,500.

If the family had a zero pre-tax income, it would have a negative taxable income of $3,000. With a 50 percent rate, it would be entitled to receive $1,500 leaving it with a post-tax income of $1,500.

For each size of family, this plan defines *two* incomes: the *break-even* income, at which the family pays no tax and receives no payment—in the example, $3,000—and the *minimum guaranteed* income—in the example, $1,500. For different sizes of families, these incomes are different, both the break-even income and the minimum guaranteed income being higher, the larger the size of the family.

Earlier, in *Capitalism and Freedom* (1962, p. 192), Friedman had summarized the "positive case" for the negative income tax:

It is directed specifically at the problem of poverty. It gives help in the form most useful to the individual, namely, cash. It is general and could be substituted for the host of special measures now in effect. It makes explicit the cost borne by society. It operates outside the market. Like any other measure to alleviate poverty, it reduces the incentives of those helped to help themselves, but it does not eliminate the incentive entirely . . . Finally, it treats all members of the community alike, with a single impersonal means test for all, the same for those who in a particular year pay taxes and for those who in that year receive benefits.

John Kenneth Galbraith, a liberal economist, lauded Friedman's negative income tax as "one of the two or three new ideas in economics in 25 years." Galbraith said the negative income tax was an exception to his general rule that brilliant and innovative ideas come from the left.

National Antipoverty Plan

Before OEO's first birthday it developed a secret five-year plan of jobs, cash, and services "designed to end poverty in the United States, as we know it today, within a generation." Key feature of the "National Antipoverty Plan" was a negative income tax for all Americans, under which a penniless family of four, for example, would receive payments, or guaranteed income, totaling $1,738 per year (58 percent of the poverty escape line). For each dollar it earned, the family would lose only a portion of the payment. OEO director Sargent Shriver said the plan was designed to fill only *part* of a family's poverty income gap because to close the gap immediately "would have deleterious effects upon incentive and structural elements of our economy." (1965, p. 4–5). He wrote that by about 1985, however, all capable of "raising themselves" above poverty would have done so and that it should then be possible to guarantee a minimum nonpoverty income to all. One of the key architects of this negative income tax (NIT) plan was OEO economist James Lyday, who later was to help draft a different version that became Nixon's Family Assistance Plan.

In a memorandum recommending the plan to the president's budget director on October 25, 1965, Shriver argued (1965, p. 8), "Introduction of a negative income tax at this time is equitable because the last two tax cuts have gone almost entirely to the non-poor. The income tax cut of 1964 was only for positive taxpayers and the excise tax cut was primarily on items not used by those below the poverty line."

A negative income tax, Shriver wrote, is needed to reach "all the nooks and crannies where other programs have not reached." In particular, it would reach millions of children poor despite their fathers' jobs, the working poor who were barred from federal welfare cash.

Shriver was won to the negative income tax by economist Joseph Kershaw, OEO's director of Research, Plans, Programs, and Evaluation. "Shriver and the top staff were fascinated by the five-year plan and indeed interest was fairly high throughout the government," Kershaw's successor, Robert Levine, later recalled in his book about the poverty war. "In command performances, Kershaw briefed Vice-President Hubert Humphrey, Budget Director Charles Schultze,* and

* In a memo to Kershaw, Levine (1965) reported that at a September 7 meeting of the White House task force on income maintenance, it was decided to present an alternative each of a universal negative income tax system and a children's negative tax system. Levine wrote that Budget Director Charles Schultze "doubted that it would be politically possible to put through a universal system which paid money to 'able-bodied employable males.' He made it quite clear that he was talking about the politics, not his own viewpoint."

newly appointed Presidential Assistant Joseph Califano. . . . In September 1965 all this changed—it changed sharply, abruptly, and very traumatically" (Levine, 1970, pp. 60 and 62).

Levine blamed the loss of interest in OEO's National Antipoverty Plan on escalating fiscal demands of the Vietnam War and on complaints at the White House against OEO from Democratic mayors angry because OEO-financed community action groups were organizing the poor against city hall. However, it is hard to conceive of Johnson ever asking Congress to expand welfare except, possibly, as a grand gesture in his second and final term. Organized labor, which exerts influence on policies of Democratic presidents, opposed the negative income tax, arguing that wage supplements for the working poor would subsidize low-paying employers. Moreover, many voters would have been alienated by the expansion in "welfare" resulting from the guaranteed income feature of a negative income tax.

Despite lack of White House encouragement, over the next three years OEO's Office of Research, Plans, Programs, and Evaluation became the national headquarters for design of the negative income tax, a concept so new that it had scarcely reached university lecture halls. Hoping to tempt the Johnson White House, Shriver's zealots each year turned out a new NIT model that they incorporated into OEO's program memoranda of 1966, 1967, and 1968. These proposed five-year plans, never accepted by the White House, were kept secret from Congress.

The 1966 model, OEO's most ambitious, proposed to eradicate poverty in ten years. "With this program," said OEO (U.S. OEO, p. IV–3), "we can celebrate the 200th anniversary of political independence with a new freedom from want."

By 1977, under this plan, every American would be guaranteed a minimum income at the poverty line, adjusted for intervening price inflation. Everyone would be out of poverty, the minimum wage would be unneeded (p. IV–1), public "welfare" would no longer exist

---

During the Johnson presidency there were annual White House Task Forces on Income Maintenance, chaired by a member of the Council of Economic Advisers and including Budget Bureau people. But NIT never got a serious hearing at the White House at the political level under LBJ. It took a change in administration to accomplish this.

(p. IV–2) and the U.S. Treasury would be paying $17 billion a year in "negative tax payments" to households comprising 59 million adults and children, about one-fourth of the anticipated population (p. IV–31).

NEGATIVE INCOME TAX EXPERIMENT

Giving money to the working poor would reduce pressure on them to work. Friedman had suggested that to maintain work incentive the supplement should be reduced by no more than 50 cents for each earned dollar. But no one knew how recipients would react to such a plan. Would they go on working as before if they had the cushion of a government payment at zero earnings, a cushion that would be "taxed" away at 50 cents per wage dollar? Would work effort be altered if the "tax rate" were set at 30 cents? Or at 70 cents?

To test reaction to alternative income-support levels and work-incentive rates OEO researchers designed a bold experiment: a demonstration project on a negative income tax. Urging an immediate start, Levine told OEO Director Shriver in a May 6, 1967, memo: "We will be able to point to the fact that while others stood around debating in a vacuum OEO acted to determine the facts in this important innovation in public policy."

"I'm all for the experiment," Shriver scrawled his approval and directed that OEO's director of congressional relations, George McCarthy, be "clued in." McCarthy was appalled. He thought the experiment would be political suicide. "If Levine is looking for a research and demonstration plan on how to 'effectively kill legislation' . . . this will do the job," he wrote. OEO then was fighting for its life, seeking its annual one-year extension, and hostile Senate investigators had charged that poverty war funds had financed establishment of a "hate-Whitey" school.

Shriver dismissed the warnings, and the experiment went forward among some New Jersey families. To make it less offensive, the project was renamed the "Graduated Work Incentive Program," which, Shriver told LBJ, is "a more descriptive phrase for what is frequently called the Negative Income Tax." Later similar experiments were launched by HEW in Gary, Seattle, and Denver.

Several hundred low-income families took part in the New Jersey project, in which they were guaranteed a minimum income, a specified portion of which was withheld for each wage dollar. Control groups received no cash benefits. Participants were not required to work.

The experiment, which ran for three years, showed only small effect on work of prime-aged husbands and a more substantial effect on work of their wives. The tax rate (the maximum tested was 70 percent) appeared to have no clear effect on work effort, and the analysts concluded that the sample size for each of the eight NIT plans tested was too small to reflect differential response to varying tax rates.

Experimental findings (Garfinkel, 1974) included: 1) negative income tax male recipients worked about two hours less per week, but received higher average hourly wages than control group members; * and 2) wives whose families received benefits worked about 36 minutes less per week (15 percent less) and earned $1 less than wives in the control group, but only 30 percent of the control group wives ever worked.

Also there were indications that some male recipients used the guaranteed income as a base of security on which to shop around for better jobs (U.S. HEW, 1973).

LBJ's Response to the Analysts

Despite the evidence that Social Security benefit increases were a poor means of combating poverty, the only major distribution of federal cash to the poor seriously proposed by LBJ during his four-year war on poverty took the form of larger Social Security checks.

In January 1967 Johnson proposed a 10 percent increase in general Social Security benefits, plus a 59 percent increase in the minimum benefit, that paid to those with a minimal Social Security wage record. The latter was intended to help the poor, but a substantial fraction of its beneficiaries had worked only sporadically or part-time at

---

* A word of qualification. Participants all knew the NIT experiment would end in three years. Further, control group members had an opportunity to receive non-wage income from a state-operated program. These factors normally would not be present.

covered employment and were not needy. They included retired government workers and even former members of Congress, who were drawing pensions; as well as housewives and foreigners who had worked temporarily in the United States.

No matter how the benefit rises were skewed, it was costly and inefficient to rely on a Social Security increase to combat poverty, since only 16 percent of the poor were aged. It calls to mind the story of the little boy, down on his hands and knees, peering at the ground under a street light:

"What are you looking for?"

"A nickle."

"Where did you lose it?"

"Over there—in the bushes."

"Why not look over there?"

"Because it's dark over there!"

Higher Social Security benefits were shining under the bright light of political reward, which could not be dimmed by any cost-effectiveness study. But needy children were hidden in the dark bushes.

Under pressure from organized labor for government-guaranteed jobs, Johnson told Congress in January 1967 that he planned to establish a commission to examine the many proposals then under discussion for guaranteeing minimum incomes, ranging "from a 'negative income tax' to a complete restructuring of Public Assistance to a program of residual public employment for all who lack private jobs." However, the matter was so unimportant to LBJ that he waited a year before naming the commission, whose chairman was Ben W. Heineman, Chicago Democrat and head of Northwest Industries, Inc., an industrial conglomerate.

Johnson asked Congress in January 1967 to make two legislative changes in welfare:

First, to aid broken families already on welfare, he proposed that Congress require all states to pay 100 percent of the gap between a family's income and its state-determined need, as most major welfare states then did.* It was the first time a president proposed federal

---

* Although Congress rejected this proposal, it did require states that had not recently raised their needs standards (used as eligibility limits) to make a one-time upward adjustment to reflect higher living costs, effective July 1, 1969. However, some states subverted the law's intent by no longer basing eligibility upon full "needs," but rather on a percentage of the needs standard.

intervention to increase state welfare levels, and the White House knew there was no chance for enactment, for the proposal would have imposed heavier welfare costs on at least thirty states. (A dozen states would have been compelled to more than double their AFDC payments; Mississippi to quintuple payments, Alabama and Florida to triple theirs.)

Second, to make it worthwhile for welfare mothers to work, LBJ proposed a modest work bonus—disregard of $50 monthly in net earnings, even if that sum raised total income above the state's eligibility limit. Eager to get welfare mothers into jobs, Congress welcomed this cautious proposal and expanded it into a generous work incentive formula that constituted our first nationwide negative income tax plan.

Welfare Amendments of 1967

Johnson's second proposal was warmly received by the House Ways and Means Committee,* whose members were under growing pressure from voters to stop the welfare explosion, to get welfare mothers off welfare rolls and onto payrolls.

During the 1960s, while unprecedented numbers of mothers moved onto welfare rolls, unprecedented numbers of other mothers moved into jobs. Most of these new workers were middle-class mothers of *young children*, and they worked to increase family income.

From 1961 to 1968 the number of women in the labor force grew at a rate triple that of men. By March 1968 one-half of all women with school-age children were working; among all two-parent families with children of preschool age, three of ten mothers worked. American women were rejecting the old adage that mothers belonged at home. Increasingly the working mother asked why she should pay taxes so that the welfare mother could sit home with her children.

* Historical accident gave jurisdiction over public welfare to the House Ways and Means Committee and the Senate Finance Committee. In order to strengthen prospects for enactment of his controversial Social Security payroll tax plan in 1935, FDR included it in a measure that provided grants for state relief of the needy aged, a popular proposal. Because payroll taxes were to finance Social Security, the omnibus measure was sent to the tax-writing committees, which thus became responsible for welfare also.

Over the years the Ways and Means Committee had listened ad nauseum to businessmen complain that high taxes stifled individual incentives and initiative. Thus, the members appreciated the criticism that confiscatory taxes kept mothers on AFDC rolls.

In high-benefit states with the nation's largest and fastest-growing AFDC rolls, it did not pay a welfare mother to work. In these "welfare-versus-work" states, earnings merely supplanted welfare dollars, keeping net income constant.

However, in more than half the states, including all but one southern state, it already paid a welfare mother to work. These states applied a "welfare-plus-work" policy, paying an AFDC family less than the full "needs" budget and then allowing a mother to fill the income gap by work. She was permitted to keep all or part of her earnings without welfare deduction until total income reached the state's needs standard. Most of these states imposed flat dollar limits on welfare checks, giving the same maximum to those of unequal need.* However, several paid a specified percentage of unmet need and then deducted the same percentage of any net earnings from the welfare check. (This amounted to a variant of Friedman's negative income tax, with the needs standard serving as the point of "breakeven" income, at which earnings reduced the welfare payment to zero.)

Nowhere, North or South, could a welfare mother boost her net income *above the state's needs standard* by work and still remain on welfare.

Congress changed this situation in December 1967 by approving a plan devised by the Ways and Means Committee to put welfare mothers to work. The Ways and Means Committee plan heeded the call of the Eckstein-Harris report for financial incentives in family welfare. Michael Stern, who later joined the staff of the Senate Finance Committee, Joe Corbett, and Worth Bateman, all of HEW, did staff work on this plan for the House committee. The new law included "tax" relief for working AFDC mothers, reducing the 100 percent

---

* In most states whose needs standards exceeded actual welfare payments to the penniless, the standard merely determined who was eligible for aid. The needs standard could be set high to qualify "worthy" (and usually white) persons with some income of their own, such as part-time wages, insurance payments, Social Security checks, even rentals. Then to avoid the heavy cost of paying full needs of the penniless, a low arbitrary limit was imposed on payment. Hence, recipients with greatly different "unmet" needs received the same maximum payment.

tax on their net earnings in excess of the needs standard. Instead of merely exempting the first $50 in monthly earnings from any welfare deduction, as LBJ had recommended, the new law gave immunity to the first $30 in monthly earnings *plus one-third of the rest*. After July 1, 1969, when the law was to take mandatory effect, AFDC mothers in all states would find it profitable to work.

So it happened that Congress enacted a negative income tax for welfare mothers while economists still debated the political feasibility of the negative income tax and poverty warriors tried in vain to persuade Lyndon Johnson to accept it as the best weapon against poverty. The AFDC negative income tax law had a "tax" rate of two-thirds for earnings above $30 monthly.

Because the new welfare benefit was administered by state and local welfare officials, not by the Internal Revenue Service, as Milton Friedman had recommended; because it was restricted to AFDC parents and not universal, as Friedman recommended; and because it had different guarantee levels in each of the 50 states, it was generally unrecognized as the first national negative income tax in America.*

The idea of letting all welfare mothers keep part of their earnings was widely praised. Except for a few economists, no one seemed to realize that since this was not a universal benefit, it introduced another major inequity into welfare, an additional penalty against a poor family headed by a man.

At the time no one warned that Congress was opening a welfare loophole that would authorize relief payments to some mothers who earned as much as $8,000, $10,000, even $12,000 or more. This should have been obvious to those who made or administered AFDC rules.

The "loophole" stands as an indictment of the House Ways and Means Committee and its chairman, Representative Wilbur D. Mills, Arkansas Democrat; the Senate Finance Committee and its chairman, Senator Russell B. Long, Louisiana Democrat; and the Department of Health, Education, and Welfare, and its secretary, John W. Gardner.

In reports accompanying the work incentive bill, the committees (Senate Finance, 1967, p. 158; House Ways and Means, 1967 p. 17)

---

* Actually, Congress earlier had enacted a negative income tax formula for another group of welfare recipients—the blind. Since 1962 states were required (and since 1960 permitted) not to count against relief checks of the blind the first $85 in monthly earnings, plus one-half the remainder.

said that by going to work under the new rule an AFDC mother could boost her total income by the first $30 plus one-third of remaining earnings per month. However, in both text and examples the reports were wrong, and so Congress misunderstood the law it was passing. The reports failed to take into account a 1962 law that already provided that states must disregard "any expenses reasonably attributed to the earning of income," counting only a welfare mother's *net* income. Thus, the actual effect of the new law was to permit welfare mothers to increase their total income through work by $30 plus one-third of remaining earnings monthly *plus work expenses.**

Federal regulations signed by outgoing HEW Secretary Cohen on January 18, 1969, just before Nixon's inauguration, set *no* limits on what expenses could be deducted, and required states to disregard mandatory payroll deductions—such as federal and state income taxes, Social Security taxes, and union dues—and "other work-related" expenses. The regulations explicitly named "grooming, transportation, and extra food" as allowable expenses. All these costs were to be fully reimbursed by the welfare grant. Within a few years the neglected, or suppressed, factor of "free" work expenses was to produce the occasional horror story of AFDC families who received incomes of $10,000 or more from a combination of work and welfare. Some states even disregarded monthly installment payments on automobiles used for work. After the 1967 law was enacted, Pennsylvania's Department of Public Assistance allowed unlimited deductions for auto payments until early 1971, when complaints that some welfare recipients were buying new cars in the luxury class—fully financed by the welfare grant—caused the department to limit the auto payment allowance to $30 monthly.

Their erroneous 1967 reports reflected the committees' neglect of welfare. Since welfare policy remained the prerogative of the states—

---

* HEW regulations adopted to implement the new law required states to "count" against a recipient's AFDC benefit only that sum of earnings left after 1) deducting the first $30 monthly plus ⅓ of remaining earnings *from gross income, rather than from net;* and then 2) deducting work expenses. Thus, recipients could keep, in addition to full welfare, $30 earned monthly plus ⅓ of remaining earnings (equivalent to $20 monthly plus ⅓ of *total* earnings) *plus work expenses.* Recipients would not go off welfare until earnings equalled 1½ times their basic benefit plus $30 monthly plus 1½ times their work expenses.

with federal law confined largely to cost-sharing provisions—the committees gave welfare low priority in building their staffs. Prior to 1968 neither committee employed a permanent welfare expert, relying instead on the Department of Health, Education, and Welfare for welfare expertise. (To help them shape federal tax policy, on the other hand, both committees had strong staffs of tax specialists, backed up by experts at the Treasury Department.)

Ways and Means and Finance Committee reports on the 1967 welfare amendments were drafted by HEW officials, subject to editing by the committee staffs. Either because of incompetence or design, HEW failed to include mention of the work expense allowance in the reports. Wilbur D. Cohen, HEW undersecretary at the time, rejected the latter possibility (letter to the authors, July 15, 1971). "As I recall the matter of work expenses in 1967," Cohen wrote, "this was not a controversial item, so that there would not be in my opinion any reason to have neglected to mention it specifically."

Charles Hawkins, HEW legislative expert, said later that department officials mentioned the 1962 expense rule during closed-door drafting sessions with the congressional committees.*

However, in public testimony Cohen told the Senate Finance Committee that existing law allowed "no earned income exemptions" for AFDC parents. (Senate Finance hearings, 1967a, p. 260). It is possible that HEW was trying to sneak through Congress a windfall benefit for some welfare mothers.

Chairman Mills said later that the Ways and Means Committee simply forgot the 1962 law. Senate Finance Committee clerk Tom Vail said that his committee also was under the impression that it was approving an "exclusive rule"—safeguarding only the first $30 plus one-third of earnings from offsetting cuts in welfare payments.

NEW INEQUITY

The new law discriminated against nonwelfare working mothers and fathers, as can be illustrated by three families living in a state that paid its full needs standard of $200 a month to an AFDC mother with three children.

* In an interview, asked why the reports neglected to mention work expenses, Hawkins seemed incredulous. He said he was certain they did. But after paging through the House committee report, he exclaimed: "You're dead right! There's not a word there about work expenses!"

Mrs. A and Mrs. B each had three children but no husband. Mrs. A's only income was a $200 AFDC check. Mrs. B, who never had been on welfare, worked full time for $240 and netted $190 after expenses. Mr. C also had three dependents, his wife and two children. He worked beside Mrs. B and also netted $190 from a $240 full-time job.

Now suppose the welfare mother took a job beside Mrs. B and Mr. C on the same terms. Prior to 1962 Mrs. A's family would have been dropped from welfare, as her gross income would have exceeded the needs standard (eligibility limit). Under the 1962 rule for disregard of work expenses, she would have stayed on welfare, collecting $10 in AFDC (only her $190 net income would have been charged against the welfare benefit).

However, the 1967 disregard made it much more advantageous for Mrs. A to take the job. Under the new law she could collect, in addition to her $240 paycheck, a welfare supplement of $110 (only $90 in "counted" income would be deducted from the AFDC check: the $240 paycheck would be reduced by $30 to $210 and then by one-third to $140, from which the $50 work expenses would be subtracted).

Mr. C's family could not qualify for welfare because he lived at home, was able-bodied, and worked full time.

What about Mrs. B? Couldn't she reduce her earnings to qualify for welfare and then, once on AFDC, boost them back to $240 and, like Mrs. A, draw a $110 welfare supplement?

Concerned lest this happen, the House Ways and Means Committee said in its report: "the bill provides that individuals who deliberately reduce their earned income or terminate their employment . . . will not qualify for the earnings exemption" (Ways and Means Committee report, 1967, p. 107).

Conceding that it was being unfair to Mrs. B, the committee defended its decision with the argument that its bill was "designed to get people off AFDC rolls, not put them on." The committee was wrong. Although its aim was to "get people off" AFDC rolls, the new law's design made it harder to get people off and, in fact, lured new persons on.

In the past, when an AFDC mother found a job paying more than welfare she usually took the job and went off welfare. Every month some families had gone on the rolls and others had left, the median stay approximating two years.

Henceforth, assuming work expenses of only $50 a month, no AFDC mother entitled to $200 in welfare (like our Mrs. A above) could work her way off welfare unless she earned at least $405 a month ($4,860 annually). For many welfare mothers the income level for welfare cutoff was much higher, since some had welfare guarantees above $200 and many had work expenses in excess of $50. A $10 increase in either the basic welfare guarantee or the work expense total raised the income cutoff for welfare supplementation by $15.

During the first year in which the new rule applied nationwide (the year ending June 30, 1970) AFDC rolls expanded by 25 percent, faster than ever before. In an attempt to move mothers from welfare rolls onto payrolls, Congress had not only compounded welfare's inequities but had accelerated the enlargement of AFDC rolls. Now many welfare mothers could never earn enough to get off welfare.

SUBTERFUGE

Fathers working full time remained ineligible for federal welfare cash no matter how scanty their pay. However, by subterfuge of welfare workers, some working poor fathers received AFDC payments. New York, New Jersey, Pennsylvania, Hawaii, and a few other states used their own funds to pay welfare supplements to needy fathers with full-time jobs. Administrators of these programs had a budgetary incentive to attempt to squeeze their working poor fathers into AFDC, for which the federal treasury paid at least half the costs.

For example, Pennsylvania welfare workers sometimes asked a poor working father applying for state aid: "Do you wear glasses?" and if the answer were yes, placed his family on AFDC on grounds that the father's "total and permanent disability" deprived the children of support (interview with social worker, spring, 1971).

Because he was classified as disabled even after he returned to work, one father in Green County, Pennsylvania, received welfare to add to his monthly earnings of $1,800 ($21,000 annual rate of income). The family of 14 was admitted to welfare on July 1, 1970, when the state welfare department said its only income was a monthly $15 contribution from a son. The state authorized a monthly AFDC payment of $692 to the family (basic guarantee of $707 minus $15).

Later when the father, who had been ill, returned to his job as a construction worker, he was kept on AFDC and given the benefit of the disregard of the first $30 plus one-third of earnings, plus the expense exemption. Against the $707 welfare guarantee the welfare department "counted" only $441.56 of his earnings of $1,821.10 during the month, plus the $15 contribution; and hence paid the family an AFDC check of $250.44. Altogether, the family had monthly cash income of $2,086.54, plus Medicaid, and it was eligible for the minimum food stamp allotment so long as it received a federally aided welfare check (data from Green County Board of Assistance).

Disregarded monthly income totaled $1,379.54, as follows:

First $30 in earnings		$30.00
⅓ of remainder (⅓ of $1,791.10		597.03
Expenses:		
U.S. and local taxes	325.10	
Union dues, including back payment	169.90	
Car payment	110.00	
Transportation cost, 7¢ a mile	147.51	
Total expenses		752.51
Total disregarded		$1,379.54

Actually, under the 1967 formula this family could have received some welfare until its income reached $2,196 per month—the sum of $30 per month, plus 1½ times its net welfare guarantee of $692, plus 1½ times its work expenses of $752.51!

(In June 1973, HEW Secretary Caspar Weinberger asked Congress to end AFDC's unlimited disregard of work expenses, but the Ways and Means Committee took no action.)

Hiding Income—By Lexicon

Welfare bureaucrats at the Department of Health, Education, and Welfare employed a highly specialized vocabulary that exaggerated the poverty of AFDC families. Whether by design or thoughtlessness, they were guilty of those worst "lies" deplored by Georges Bernanos —misstatements of a problem. Their unorthodox use of common terms, such as "net income," "unmet need," "unemployment," misled readers of HEW periodic reports, including authors of welfare textbooks, fellow social workers, presidential speechwriters (for Nixon's Family Assistance Plan), and even volunteer researchers for the League of Women Voters.

HEW reported (U.S. HEW, 1972, table 41) that monthly needs for AFDC families in 1971 averaged $242.34 per family (four persons), but that families received only $179.76 in cash welfare plus $32.86 in "net non-assistance income," leaving $29.72 as recognized "unmet need."

This is grossly misleading. First, it omits actual net income (averaging $15.10 per family) received and retained by AFDC families (table 71) but not "counted" under the work incentive rules. Second, it omits the food stamp bonus (averaging about $50 in value) available to AFDC families in most of the nation's counties (and obtained by about one-half of them in 1971).

Thus, AFDC families actually had an average net cash income of $227.71, plus the right to another $50 in food stamps: a total of $277.71, which was $35.37 *above* "needs." Their gross income was higher than net by an average of $16.62 monthly (spent for work expenses, child care, etc.).

In testimony submitted to the Senate Finance Committee (1972, p. 1281) Mrs. Elizabeth Davey, board member, League of Women Voters of Michigan, presented a table about AFDC families' income. Based on data from the Michigan Department of Social Services, the table showed that a sample Michigan AFDC family of four that earned $400 a month would have a "net" earned income of only $171. To this would be added $134 in AFDC cash and $48 in food stamps, for a total "net" income of $353. The money actually retained by the family as a work incentive bonus (the first $30 plus one-third of the remaining earnings), a total of $153 per month, was totally ignored, treated as though it were an illusion. By this reasoning a Michigan family with actual net spendable income of $506 per month had only $353!

Year after year, HEW published meaningless monthly statistics about welfare payments that misled many who read them. These data showed "average" payments made to recipients of welfare and were useful only to the accountants who calculated from them the amount of reimbursement due the state. But students of social welfare erroneously interpreted them to indicate the relative generosity of states to welfare recipients and tried to detect historic trends in the figures. Their error can be seen by examining the old-age data of Rhode Island for April 1971. That month Rhode Island old-age relief payments averaged $55.10 per recipient (U.S. HEW, 1971a, table 4), *third smallest* in the nation. But the state's guarantee to an aged needy person without other income was $164 per month (U.S. HEW, 1971b, table 1), *eleventh highest* in the nation. The explanation was that so many of the aged Rhode Islanders already had significant income (chiefly Social Security) that only a small relief supplement *per average recipient* was needed to bring the income of all up to the state's guarantee level. By definition, average payments always were smaller than the maximum payments made to the penniless. But this difference was not understood by the speechwriters who prepared Mr. Nixon's welfare reform address of August 8, 1969. They compared the prevailing state *average* payments with the proposed federal *maximums* and thus exaggerated the impact of the proposed federal guarantee.

(The authors protested HEW's failure to publish actual maximum state benefits along with average payments. Eventually, in April 1971, HEW began adding a cautionary note to its monthly "Public Assistance Statistics," DHEW Publication No. 72–03100, stating that "these [average] payments do not represent the total average amount of income an individual or family has to live on.")

Although the full-time jobs of fathers, no matter how low-paid, disqualified their families for federally aided welfare, "unemployment" could make them eligible for aid in those states (about half the total) that offered AFDC-UF (Aid to Families with Dependent Children of Unemployed Fathers). This was an emergency anti-recession program first authorized for one year in 1961 (originally called Aid to Families with Dependent Children of Unemployed *Parents*—AFDC-UP), then extended and, in 1967, made permanent. The work-incentive bonus of the 1967 law (disregard of the first $30 plus one-third of remaining earnings) required states to supplement earnings of an AFDC mother even when her wages exceeded the state's needs standard. But even though his wages were below the needs standard, no welfare supplements could be paid to a father who worked full time. Thus, if an AFDC-UF father got a full-time job, his family was dropped from welfare. But what if he couldn't find full-time work? Should welfare discourage his part-time work? No! The answer to this problem was an administrative ruling that stretched the definition of "unemployment" to make it possible for a father to take a job and yet receive supplemental AFDC-UF welfare, plus Medicaid and food stamps, so long as he worked only part time.*

As a result, in New York City, fully employed welfare workers, whose regular work week by union contract was set at 35 hours (and reduced to 30 hours in the summer) were certifying AFDC payments to families of "unemployed" fathers who worked up to 35 hours a week.

This ironical situation was corrected in October 1971 by HEW Secretary Elliot Richardson, who lowered to 100 hours per month the maximum that an "unemployed" father might work without losing eligibility for AFDC.†

---

* Twenty-five days after Nixon entered the White House a California private security guard, father of 10 children, filed suit against the new Republican secretary of HEW, charging discriminatory welfare. Juan Macias complained that when he went from a part-time to a full-time job, his income fell because of loss of his welfare supplement from AFDC-UF. The antipoverty lawyers who prepared the suit on behalf of him and another father—Francisco Tarin, who lost income by going from actual unemployment to full-time work—protested the federal policy as a "Don't Work (full-time)!" rule. The U.S. Supreme Court in November 1970 unanimously ruled against them without comment, leaving their work-versus-welfare dilemma for solution in the legislative arena that had created it.

† The original Family Assistance Plan bill of October 1969 required all states to offer AFDC-UF. This created an incentive in some states for low-paid fathers to quit full-time jobs (eligible for the federal FAP wage supplement only) and become "unemployed" (working up to 35 hours weekly) so as to qualify for a state welfare supplement in addition to FAP. Debate over FAP exposed the irrationality of the 35-hour unemployment week of HEW regulations. At Senate Finance Committee hearings (Senate Finance, 1970, p. 576) Senator Herman Talmadge, who had just read that New York City electrical workers had negotiated contracts for a 20-hour week, asked HEW Secretary Elliot Richardson why the welfare system should not have a "more realistic definition" of unemployment. Richardson agreed that it should. Talmadge asked whether it should not be corrected "now" by regulation. "I think it should, and I shall follow that up," Richardson promised. The HEW secretary changed the regulation 15 months later.

Carrot and Sticks

The Social Security Amendments of 1967 asserted for the first time some federal control over the calculation and conditions of benefits paid by state welfare programs. The object of this federal intervention into state policy was to curtail AFDC rolls.

The work incentive bonus, the "carrot" of the new law, was accompanied by two "sticks." One stick required "appropriate" members of AFDC families to work or take job training when requested to do so, on pain of losing welfare benefits. The other stick limited the number of illegitimate (and otherwise father-abandoned) children for whom states could claim federal reimbursement. Like King Canute commanding the waves, Congress declared a halt in the rising tide. By 1967, three out of four AFDC children got welfare because their able-bodied father was "absent" from home. Congress decreed that it would not finance a rise in the proportion of such children in any state.

No one objected to the work-incentive carrot which, as we have seen, was more succulent than advertised. But liberals protested that the sticks would club welfare policy back into the Dark Ages. Civil rights organizations, welfare clients, labor leaders all assailed the legislation as a vengeful attack on defenseless children and their mothers, and Senator Robert F. Kennedy of New York led the unsuccessful Senate fight against the AFDC freeze and the work rule.

The new law established a work training and job placement program for AFDC recipients called the Work Incentive Program. (The proper acronym, WIP, was discarded for the less-offensive WIN.) Refusal to obey the work-or-train rule was to halt welfare cash, but the rhetoric was more harsh than the reality. Under the new law no state could compel a mother to work or train without providing free day care, an impossibility in most areas, which lacked enough day care centers even for children of mothers who *volunteered* to work.

Moreover, the threat to compel welfare mothers to work was vitiated by regulations issued just before Richard Nixon's inauguration. HEW Secretary Cohen ruled that a state that did not want to force a welfare mother to work *need not* do so to qualify for federal welfare cash and that a state that wanted to force a mother to work *could not* do so, even in the unlikely event that child day care were available, unless it first summoned to work unemployed fathers from welfare families (those who received AFDC-UF), AFDC children 16 years or older not in school, and volunteer mothers. Under the regulations the mandatory work-or-train rule applied only to unemployed fathers and to school dropouts at least 16 years old.

The AFDC freeze on the proportion of federally aided children whose fathers were neither dead nor disabled never took effect. It was thawed by heated protests from governors, whom it would have compelled either to increase state welfare outlays or to slash AFDC benefit levels. Congress first postponed the freeze and then, at President Nixon's request (1969b), repealed it outright. (President Johnson's final budget, however, affirmed the AFDC freeze—to save federal dollars.)

Congressman Mills insisted later that he knew all along that his committee's freeze never would go into force. He said that its purpose was to shock the states, which were accustomed to setting basic welfare policy, into obeying the other new AFDC rules to promote and require work from recipients.

Forget the Working Poor!

In the spring of 1968, after welfare law was changed to offer wage supplements to all working welfare mothers, analysts at the Department of Health, Education, and Welfare urged Wilbur J. Cohen, who had just succeeded John Gardner as secretary of the department, to recommend welfare supplements to needy families of fathers working at low wages. Denial of such aid to intact families of the working poor provides an incentive for families to split up, they argued—a terrible and perverse inequity.

Forget the inequities, Cohen told them; *inequities produce social change.* Cohen considered the analysts naive and ignorant of political and legislative limits. The president had just refused (January 1968) to ask Congress to require all states to offer welfare to needy families with *jobless* fathers.* Imagine LBJ's reaction if anyone dared suggest that welfare be extended to fathers *who had jobs!* Even if by some miracle LBJ could be persuaded, so what? Congress wouldn't buy it. "Little Wilbur" (Cohen) saw no use in proposing legislation that would not even get a hearing from "Big Wilbur" (Mills), chairman of the House Ways and Means Committee, which had original jurisdiction over welfare measures.

As William Gorham, an assistant secretary of HEW, recalled: "In those days welfare policy was made by three men—Cohen, Mills, and the president. And sometimes you had the feeling that the president wasn't included."

Cohen, an original member, resigned from the President's Commission on Income Maintenance after he became HEW secretary in April 1968. In September, Commission chairman Heineman invited Cohen to outline his recommendations for "income maintenance" at a closed commission hearing in Washington. In advance of the hearing, Alice Rivlin, an assistant secretary of HEW, and Worth Bateman, her deputy, urged Cohen to endorse help for the working poor through a negative income tax.†

"He [Cohen] thought it wasn't feasible," Mrs. Rivlin said later (interview with the authors, Dec. 1, 1970). "He thought it would be impossible to get through Congress, that labor unions would oppose it because of fear that it would undercut wages, and that it would have no appeal for Wilbur Mills."

At the hearing, which was barred to the press and the public, Cohen

---

* A recommendation that Congress require all states to offer welfare to needy families of unemployed fathers, advanced by the Department of HEW, was cleared by Johnson men in the White House and Budget Bureau (who assumed Johnson's consent), and printed in the President's annual budget, which outlined his 1968 legislative program. By the time LBJ learned of his administration's proposal for mandatory AFDC-UF, the budget was on its way to Capitol Hill. LBJ "vetoed" the proposal, which would have expanded welfare rolls in half the states, by forbidding HEW to send the draft legislation to Congress. This was one of the rare times when legislation proposed in a president's budget message was, by secret presidential decree, erased from his legislative program.

† Cohen turned down Commission testimony prepared for him by Bateman and asked Social Security Commissioner Robert M. Ball to draft a statement on improvements in Social Security. This he presented.

suggested ways in which Social Security could be liberalized, after which there was this exchange:

Heineman: "Divorcing yourself from congressional expertise and your knowledge and feeling of political feasibility, what would you recommend as desirable with respect to the poor who are employable?"
Cohen: "I don't have any such recommendation."

"BETTER OFF WITH NOTHING"

During Johnson's last summer in the White House, in 1968, a team of administration experts, headed by Merton (Joe) Peck, of the Council of Economic Advisers, was assigned to develop proposals for income maintenance that LBJ might bequeath to Congress in his final budget message. Peck's group recommended that Johnson ask Congress to repeal the AFDC "freeze" scheduled to take effect on July 1, 1969, to require all states to offer welfare to needy families of jobless fathers (AFDC-UF) and, for the first time, to impose a "means" test in Social Security, limiting to the needy a proposed new $100 minimum benefit (up $45 from the prevailing Social Security minimum benefit, paid to all with minimal Social Security wage records, regardless of need).

HEW Secretary Cohen opposed Peck's antipoverty plan and offered the White House a politically attractive alternative that would funnel most of its cash to the middle class rather than to the poor: a general increase of 10 percent in Social Security benefits and a minimum Social Security benefit of $100 for *all* retired workers, rich or poor.

It was an article of faith with Cohen that programs only for the poor are "lousy, no good, *poor* programs" and that the American public would not long support a program with "nothing in it for the middle and upper class" (Cohen and Friedman, 1972, p. 55). (However, the Medicaid program for the poor has turned out to be more generous, often, than Medicare for the middle class. Medicaid recipients receive free and unlimited hospitalization and, in most states, free eyeglasses, dental services, and out-patient drugs.)

Peck was furious when the White House summarily rejected his plan and chose Cohen's. "Neither (of Cohen's proposals) does much for the poor," Peck protested to Joseph Califano, Johnson's chief of domestic policy (in a memo after a November 29, 1968 meeting in Califano's office). "I think that we might be better off with nothing than with proposals that could be criticized as doing little for poverty and being inflationary."

"Abolish poverty in 10 years!" Cohen exhorted America in a long declaration of social goals as he prepared to leave Washington, upon the inauguration of Richard Nixon, to become dean of the School of Education at the University of Michigan. Cohen's list was so exhaustive, said *Washington Post* reporter Eve Edstrom, that no matter what the Nixon administration proposed in the field of health, education, and welfare, Cohen probably would be able to claim paternity.

Eve Edstrom was wrong. So was Mrs. Rivlin, Democrat, who felt that the climate at the start of the Nixon era was adverse to any major welfare advances. Several weeks after Nixon's inauguration Mrs. Rivlin, preparing to make way for a Republican successor, was astonished at the responsive attitude of the new HEW administration.

"I couldn't believe that I was sitting there talking to a Republican administration that seemed eager for this new solution [negative income tax] that six months before I hadn't been able to convince Wilbur Cohen was the right thing to do," she said later.

Democrat Worth Bateman, who had been told by Democrat Cohen to forget the working poor, was likewise astonished.

"A change of administration is a very promising time," Bateman said later. "All the lines are cut for a few seconds, and they will listen to you for a while."

3.

CONSPIRACY FOR THE POOR

"This is a Negative Income Tax plan for families with children but it could be called by a different name"
—WORTH BATEMAN

WHEN Richard Nixon won the 1968 presidential election, he inherited not only Lyndon Johnson's Vietnam War, but also his Poverty War. By that time, because of Johnson's steadfast opposition—and surely Nixon would be no less hostile—the poverty agency had abandoned hope for adoption of a negative income tax, its master weapon against poverty.

This is a form of income guarantee that covers both the working and the nonworking. For those without other income it provides a specified payment from the government. For those with earnings, it provides a smaller government payment, one that declines as earnings rise. However, the decline in the payment is not so sharp as the rise in earnings, as that would eliminate all incentive to work—that would be a 100-percent earnings tax for those on welfare.

The poverty warriors' master proposal, which Sargent Shriver, director of the Office of Economic Opportunity, took to Johnson, had been a negative income tax scaled to wipe out "poverty" in ten years. The plan was to begin by guaranteeing everyone 50 percent of the gap between his actual income and the sum that would remove him from poverty and then, year by year, to raise the guarantee until after a decade (1977) it equalled the poverty escape line.

As the costs of the Vietnam War climbed ever higher, Johnson rejected the master plan against poverty and modified variations of it. He clung instead to cheaper and more conventional methods of attacking poverty, such as training the poor in hopes of thereby up-grading their earnings, although most of this effort proved ineffective.

The Task Force

The explosion in family benefit recipients put welfare, a subject typically shunned by the White House, on the agenda of President-elect Nixon. In the decade of the 1960s the proportion of children on relief more than doubled, from 3.5 percent of those under 18 in 1960 to 6.8 percent in 1969 and to 8.7 percent in 1970. The welfare explosion angered taxpayers and put severe pressure upon state treasuries, especially in such states as Illinois, California, Pennsylvania, and New York. Their Republican governors wanted relief from Washington and from their party's president-to-be.

A few days after his November 5th election Nixon's headquarters established a task force to make policy recommendations on welfare and poverty. Selected as chairman was a young Republican, Richard P. Nathan, 33, a research associate at the Brookings Institution, who had distinguished himself as chairman of a preelection Nixon task force on intergovernmental fiscal relations.

For welfare advice Nathan picked three experts: Marion Folsom, a secretary of health, education, and welfare in the Eisenhower administration, who had helped draw up FDR's Social Security bill; Wilbur Schmidt, secretary of the Wisconsin Department of Health and Social Services, and Mitchell I. Ginsberg, a nationally known pioneer in liberal welfare reform, who was chief of New York Mayor John Lindsay's Human Resources Administration, the superagency that ran the nation's largest welfare program. The composition of this task force virtually assured a report that would not disturb the basic structure of welfare, but would merely propose more for those within it.

The Plan

At its first meeting Nathan's welfare panel defined the central problem as the intolerable variations in state welfare benefits. At the high extreme in these payments, runaway costs imperiled state budgets;

at the low extreme meager welfare checks mocked the needs of poor children and mothers receiving AFDC (Aid to Families with Dependent Children).

At that time a welfare family of mother and three children received a *maximum* of $50 monthly in Mississippi, of which $41.75 was provided by the federal government. If the same family moved to New York and qualified for welfare, it could receive $278, of which $139 would come from Uncle Sam.

The states decided where to set benefit levels and then sent the federal government a bill for partial reimbursement.

To help simultaneously the most troubled state treasuries and the poorest welfare recipients, the Nathan group designed an ingenious remedy: establishment of a nationwide minimum floor for welfare beneficiaries, to be *fully paid* by the federal government. At one stroke this would raise income of recipients in the lowest-benefit states, concentrated in the South and governed generally by Democrats, and save funds of state and county treasuries in higher-benefit states, most of which were headed by GOP governors. In such states as New York, Illinois, and Pennsylvania, recipients would receive no extra money, but the all-federally-paid minimum would replace state funds (and in New York, county funds, too) that hitherto had to match every Washington welfare dollar.

Under the Nathan plan the states would continue to administer welfare, but the federal government would pay $30 per month of *average payments* per AFDC recipient plus one-half of any additional payments (up to a maximum of $70 per recipient). All states would be required to provide AFDC benefits averaging at least $40 a month (of which federal funds would pay $35).

The plan would have raised *average* * payments to AFDC children in Mississippi by $31.50 per month, from $8.50 to $40.00 (with the federal government paying $27.75 of the increase and Mississippi $3.75).

---

* Note that average Mississippi payments ($8.50 per child) were not equal to *maximum* payments ($25 for the first child, $15 for the next, $10 for the third)—a matter misunderstood later by President Nixon's advisers and some speechwriters. Their ignorance led to exaggerated claims for the largesse of the Family Assistance Plan. Average payments include those made to persons with some other income and hence are always lower than maximums paid to those who lack other income.

In New York, where monthly benefits then averaged $70 per recipient (half paid by Uncle Sam), the federal government's payment would have been boosted to $50, saving the state and local governments $15 per recipient.

In a corollary plan for those on old-age relief, the Nathan plan proposed that states be required to provide benefits averaging $65 per month, of which Uncle Sam would pay $57.50. From this modest beginning was later to evolve America's first guaranteed income.

Three days after Christmas 1968, Nathan dropped his 63-page welfare-poverty report into a Washington mail box. Understating its own boldness, the report assured Nixon that minimum payments standards would be only an "incremental" step. Nothing drastic. No big deal. Actually that "incremental" step would reverse the direction of Republican welfare doctrine. Dwight D. Eisenhower, the last Republican president, had held welfare to be a state and local duty from which the national treasury should gradually withdraw. On the contrary, the Nathan task force (p. 10) urged Nixon not only to make welfare a *national* duty for the first time, but even to move *"toward complete federal financing of welfare."*

Would Nixon do this?

Robert H. Finch, 43, the man chosen to be Nixon's secretary of health, education, and welfare, would help to answer that question. Unlike some of his Cabinet colleagues, Finch could easily reach the president, as the two shared the mutual trust and cameraderie of friends who have weathered good and bad together.

Finch came to Washington in 1947 as staff aide to a veteran California congressman and became friends with freshman Congressman Richard Nixon in the adjacent Capitol office. When Nixon became vice-president in 1953, Finch became his chief aide; when Nixon sought the presidency in 1960, Finch was his campaign director. During the 1968 presidential campaign, Finch, by then lieutenant governor of California, traveled with Nixon as an adviser.

Offered his choice of Cabinet posts after Nixon's election, Finch selected HEW as the place "where the action is." Finch welcomed the welfare blueprint of the Nathan task force as a political treasure, a bold innovation with universal appeal. Federal welfare standards would help both the poor of the South and taxpayers everywhere.

Northern taxpayers would applaud higher welfare payments in the South, since they would retard the flow of unskilled poor to the North's welfare rolls.

Moreover, the proposed federal floor, a $30 average payment, would help answer the protest made by the Reverend Ralph D. Abernathy during the Poor People's Campaign in June 1968, that the United States paid only $9 a month to a starving Mississippi child while it paid more than $13,000 a month to the Mississippi plantation of U.S. Senator James Eastland so that he would not grow food or fiber.

Finch not only recommended the Nathan plan to Nixon but began himself to promote it. Two weeks before the Nixon inauguration, Finch broached the idea during a courtesy call on President Johnson, but the outgoing president, after remarking that his own HEW secretary, Wilbur Cohen, also favored federal welfare standards, diverted the conversation to his administration's health achievements. To LBJ welfare was so unpleasant a word that he sometimes referred to HEW as "my department of health and education." Finch used the steps of the Johnsonian White House as a platform to champion minimum welfare standards, telling reporters on his way out: "Obviously we can't continue to live with the great disparities (in payments) among states."

PRESS LEAK

On January 8 the 250 academicians, specialists, and others who had served on a score of Nixon task forces gathered at New York's Hotel Pierre to brief Nixon's Cabinet designees on their reports. As host at a black-tie dinner the next night, Nixon thanked the volunteers for their work, remarking with a grin that he suspected that most of them had voted for his Democratic rival, Hubert H. Humphrey.

During the dinner, Dick Nathan was shocked to learn that his report was no longer secret. The Sunday newspapers across the country carried the news, leaked by a partisan who hoped that publication would arouse support, that a Nixon task force recommended a welfare scheme that would cost the federal treasury $1.4 billion a year. Nathan feared that the disclosure might cost him a high federal post that he had been promised, but the next days brought a rash of editorials favorable to the Nathan plan and, to Nathan's relief, nobody in the Nixon camp seemed upset.

President-elect Nixon was angered, however, by another item in that Sunday paper. Beginning a series on alleged corruption in the city's Human Resources Administration, a *New York Times* headline shouted across three columns on page one: "Millions in City Poverty Funds Lost by Fraud and Inefficiency." (Mitchell Ginsberg, a member of Nathan's task force, was alerted to the newspaper series by telephone during the task force dinner.)

Outraged by the newspaper charges, the incoming president told aides that welfare should be investigated. On January 15, five days before his inauguration, he dictated an angry memorandum to Finch and three others: John N. Mitchell, attorney-general designee, who had been his campaign director, (and who resigned the attorney-generalship in spring 1972 to again be campaign director); Bryce Harlow, to be his chief of congressional liaison; and Daniel P. Moynihan, to be his urban affairs adviser. Nixon said:

> This New York welfare mess is probably typical of a problem which exists all over the country. I want a thorough investigation made with all the resources that we have at our disposal so that we can set the stage for what we have to do later in cutting some of these purely political programs. . . .
>
> The American people are outraged, and, in my view, they should be.
>
> I would like Harlow to discuss this with appropriate legislative leaders on our side to see if they can get cooperation from some good investigating committee to look into this whole matter . . . Possibly John McClellan [Arkansas Democrat, chairman of the Senate's permanent investigations subcommittee] might appoint a special subcommittee to investigate the welfare program.
>
> I do not want this swept under the rug or put aside on the ground that we want to have an "era of good feeling" with the bureaucrats as we begin. This whole thing smells to high heaven and we should get charging on it immediately.

The angry tone and content of Nixon's memo alarmed Moynihan, who had not signed on for the Republican voyage to crusade against poor welfare recipients. By January 31, deadline for reply, Moynihan was to find a way to employ the New York "welfare mess" as an argument for the Nathan plan.

On the first day of the Nixon presidency Republicans paraded and danced.

On the second day the new president persuaded Dr. Arthur F. Burns, 64, nationally known economist and a long-term close associate of Nixon, to be his chief adviser on domestic policy. Earlier Burns had declined the White House post, saying that he would move to Washington only as chairman of the Federal Reserve Board, a position that did not open for him until January 1970, upon expiration of the term of William McChesney Martin.

Burns said later of his capitulation: "The president literally didn't give me a chance to say a word. He talked of 'your responsibilities.' I didn't have any responsibilities. He showed me the Cabinet room. 'This is your chair.' He waved aside my protests."

On his third day in office President Nixon created and convened a new organization to demonstrate his commitment to bettering urban conditions. The president's new Council for Urban Affairs was composed of the president, vice-president, and seven Cabinet officers; and organized by subject matter into nine subcommittees with overlapping memberships. This was orderly. For every major urban problem there would be a Cabinet-level subcommittee; each subcommittee would bring proposed solutions to the full Council, where Nixon would preside and ultimately decide. One subcommittee, headed by Finch, would study welfare.

Enter: Moynihan

The executive secretary of this Council was a Democrat, Daniel P. Moynihan, 41, a sub-Cabinet officer in the Kennedy-Johnson administrations and, more recently, a professor at Harvard University, where he directed the Harvard-Massachusetts Institute of Technology Joint Center for Urban Studies. Urban expert Moynihan would be the "White House liberal" in the Nixon administration.

Moynihan was a maligned prophet of the welfare explosion. Four years earlier, as assistant secretary of labor in the Johnson administration, he had written a confidential report: "The Negro Family: The Case for National Action," later published by the Labor Department

(1965) and sold by the U.S. Government Printing Office. Its thesis was that the poor Negro family in urban ghettos was breaking down, the victim of "three centuries of injustice by white America." To counter this family breakdown, Moynihan proposed that the nation adopt the goal of stable Negro families and its corollary, jobs for black men. "The object should be to strengthen the Negro family so as to enable it to raise and support its members as do other families," his 1965 report said: "After that, how this group of Americans chooses to run its affairs, to take advantage of its opportunities or fail to do so, is none of the nation's business."

After this report leaked to the press, Moynihan was vilified as a racist by some blacks and by some white liberals. They charged that no white man had a right to set standards for black families. By the time he left the Johnson administration in 1966, Moynihan had become a controversial figure among liberals.

For many years Moynihan had urged the nation to adopt a children's allowance and to provide more job opportunities for fathers so as to strengthen the American family. (He had proposed federal payments for every family, rich or poor, of $12 monthly for the first dependent child and $8 for each additional child, at an estimated cost of $9 billion annually.)

But once Nathan's plan was drafted to help the poorest welfare families, Moynihan joined its enthusiasts. Later, chided for deserting children's allowances to embrace the limited goal of minimum welfare payments, he told the authors, "My God! I didn't think any Republican administration would go for any more than that!"

In a 12-page reply to the president's welfare memo, Moynihan urged him to attack the welfare "mess" by sending the Nathan plan to Congress and by naming an investigatory commission. Moynihan said that welfare must be changed, that the president was right to denounce the existing system. "The fact is the more one knows about welfare the more horrible it becomes," wrote Moynihan, (1969a, pp. 10–11) "but not because of cheating, rather because the system destroys those who receive it, and corrupts those who dispense it."

He capitalized his main recommendations (1969a, p. 9): "I BELIEVE THE SINGLE MOST DRAMATIC MOVE YOU COULD MAKE WOULD BE TO SEND A MESSAGE TO CONGRESS CALLING FOR NATIONAL MINIMUM STANDARDS

IN WELFARE. THIS SHOULD BE ACCOMPANIED BY THE APPOINTMENT OF A
NATIONAL COMMISSION TO FIND OUT WHAT IS GOING ON. CERTAIN MINI-
MUM FEDERAL REQUIREMENTS FOR STATE PARTICIPATION SHOULD BE PRO-
POSED, PRINCIPALLY THAT ALL STATES ADOPT THE AFDC-UP PROGRAM,
INSTITUTED IN 1961, WHICH ENABLES FAMILIES WITH AN UNEMPLOYED
MALE HEAD TO RECEIVE BENEFITS."

The "White House liberal" cited four advantages of the national
minimum welfare standard proposed by the task force:

> 1. It will give money to women and children who desperately need it,
> mostly in the South. Mississippi provides $8.50 per month to support a
> child.
> 2. It will give financial relief to large cities that are now providing de-
> cent enough welfare payments, but at great costs to their taxpayers. [This
> was an error; the fiscal relief would go to states, plus those counties that
> shared nonfederal welfare costs. The only major city to get help would
> be New York City, which performed the functions of the five counties of
> which it is comprised.]
> 3. It will help the Negro poor. Half the children on AFDC at present
> are black. [This implied that *all* AFDC recipients would gain from the
> national minimum welfare standard, but in the North, where at least 60
> percent of black recipients lived, benefits generally would not rise. Gains
> would go to the welfare poor of the South—black and white.]
> 4. It will be received by the white middle and working classes as a mea-
> sure that will impede northward migration. I have some doubts whether
> it actually will, but it will be taken as such, and that is a plus. I.e., that is
> a good reason for Northern congressmen to support such a measure.

A TYPICAL TASK FORCE

The typical task force, as Nathan Glazer put it so well in *Public
Interest* (1969, p. 43), is a group of outsiders from which "no one
stays behind to fight for anything; it is pure input with no liability."

Often there is nothing worth fighting for; many task force reports
fatuously urge that problems be confronted by applying more resources with greater imagination and more efficiency. Of course, to
be called upon to advise a man who may become president satisfies
the ego, even if you suspect that you are being used to improve
the candidate's image, as Franklin D. Raines has suggested was in part
the case in 1968: "The [Nixon] task forces were looked upon by the
Nixon staff as being intellectual exercises for academics and had been

formed partially to give the appearance of support by intellectuals for the administration." Raines, a White House summer intern in 1969, made the observation in a paper written as a senior honors thesis at Harvard in the spring of 1971 under supervision of Professor Edward Banfield, who was chairman of Nixon's task force on urban affairs.

Unlike the typical advisory report, the Nathan task force report proposed a specific blueprint at a costly but feasible price. Further, its chairman became an insider and "stayed behind" to fight for it. Nathan entered the new administration as assistant director of the Budget Bureau in charge of human resources, a post that gave him budgetary purview over several departments and agencies, including Finch's vast domain at HEW. In this job Nathan could try to soften any Budget Bureau opposition that might develop to his welfare proposal.

Thus, the prognosis for the Nathan plan was favorable. In a campaign speech the President had endorsed "greater standardization" of welfare payments. The Nathan scheme had powerful champions in the White House, HEW, and the Budget Bureau.

Its strongest foe was Arthur F. Burns, who, at the president's request, had reviewed all of the task force reports. Burns already had warned Nixon that spending must be restricted to bank the inflationary fires inherited from LBJ. When the budget permitted new federal initiatives, revenue-sharing would be at the top and welfare near the bottom of Burns' priorities.

THE PUSH BEGINS

Finch and Moynihan wanted to get the Nathan plan on the agenda of the new Urban Affairs Council quickly so that the president could hear the debate and resolve the issues. Because the plan first needed approval of his group, Chairman Finch immediately scheduled a meeting of the Urban Affairs Council welfare subcommittee for February 6, 1969. For that meeting the Nathan plan was condensed into nine pages under Moynihan's direction and elevated to the status of "White House staff paper." Its youthful editors, Nathan and John Price, 30, Moynihan's counsel and a founder of the Ripon Society (a studious Republican youth group, which in April 1967 endorsed a negative income tax plan "to help the poor"),* confidently described the paper as "the basis for discussion for a program to be announced in mid-1969 to take effect on Dec. 31, 1969." Their paper revealed that the plan would give $300 million in enlarged checks to welfare recipients and $1.1 billion in fiscal relief to states and counties.

Before the meeting Finch gave his copy of the paper to the man who would make welfare policy for him: California state assemblyman John G. Veneman, 43, a strapping six-foot-two peach-grower from Modesto, California, whose appointment as HEW undersecretary soon would be announced. (California governor Ronald Reagan opposed the appointment, not only because it rewarded his ideological foe, but because it jeopardized the Republican Party's one-vote control of the California assembly, requiring a special election—in a normally Democratic district—to fill Veneman's seat.) A liberal Republican first elected to the California legislature in 1962, Veneman had won reelection with growing majorities. He had managed Finch's winning campaign for lieutenant governor and served *de facto* as Nixon's California campaign manager in 1968 while Finch, who held the title, traveled with the candidate.

Chairman of the legislature's committee on revenue and taxation and an expert on California welfare and health programs, Veneman had challenged Reagan's opposition to tax withholding and had blocked Reagan's attempt to cut back Medicaid benefits.

Several hours before the welfare subcommittee met, Veneman handed his copy of the welfare paper to *his* chief welfare expert, the California state assembly's senior research specialist on welfare, Tom Joe, 34, who had come to Washington to assist Veneman. Because he was blind, Joe had the paper read to him, and then he dictated a critical analysis for his friend, Veneman. Joe's principal objection was the distribution of the plan's money—only about one

---

* The Ripon Forum, in a six-page research paper, urged the Republican Party to commit itself to a negative income tax and to make the commitment the "cornerstone" of an effective alternative to the War on Poverty. Within a year, at a small dinner in January 1968, Price told presidential hopeful Richard Nixon that both liberal and conservative wings of the Republican Party could agree on two proposals—a negative income tax and a volunteer army.

dollar would go to the poor for each $3.67 to states and local governments.

Tom Joe, who had received welfare as a child in Hawaii, would never forget how it was to need money. When he was graduated from the Oakland, California Technical High School in June, 1954, a thin blind youth of 19, he stood sixth in his class. Yet social service authorities, because he lacked a precise career plan, balked at his hopes for college and tried to appease him with training to fold pillowcases. Gifted with keen mental perception, Joe "saw" more than the average person with eyesight. Persisting in his ambitions, he obtained scholarships, acquired a B.A. and then an M.A. in political science at the University of California at Berkeley, and now he was on the threshold of a PhD. and one of the nation's leading experts on welfare. In California he had shown the state how to expand its social services severalfold for present, former, and potential welfare recipients by taking advantage of a new funding feature in federal law, overlooked by most states.

THE SETBACK

The Nathan plan suffered a surprise setback at the February 6, 1969, meeting of the UAC welfare subcommittee, whose members were Finch, Labor Secretary George Shultz, Agriculture Secretary Hardin, Attorney-General Mitchell, and Commerce Secretary Maurice Stans.*

Except for Finch, who already favored the plan, the Cabinet officers responded to Nathan's oral presentation with questions that were hostile, searching, critical, or irrelevant. Some of the questions Nathan could not answer. Although the group planned to talk again about the proposal at a later meeting, it set up no study machinery. Nathan concluded that his plan must be extricated from the Cabinet-level group, which had neither time nor appetite for it, and assigned to a lower-level task group that could gather experts to perfect it.

The next day Tom Joe, disappointed that Veneman hadn't brought up his criticisms at the subcommittee meeting, went to Nathan's office to voice his complaints. Pleased that one of Finch's people cared

* Mitchell and Stans in 1973 were indicted on charges of perjury and of attempted interference with a Securities and Exchange Commission investigation of financier Robert L. Vesco, and in April were acquitted.

enough to discuss his plan, Nathan told Joe that the blueprint needed to be improved by experts like him. Why not have HEW and Budget Bureau staff experts work together on this under a new sub-Cabinet task force? Nathan asked. When the plan was perfected, the task force could take it back up to Finch's Cabinet subcommittee. Joe agreed to recommend this procedure to Veneman.

"In government," Nathan later told the authors, "when your ideas are attacked, the solution sometimes is to create another committee."

Neither Nathan, who proposed it, nor Veneman and Finch, who agreed to it, dreamed that the creation of the sub-Cabinet task force would lead to the sudden demise of the Nathan plan and the hidden birth of a guaranteed-income plan for all families. Ironically, Nathan, who set the stage for it, would be excluded from this drama, and so would Moynihan, who would have relished it.

Nixon's Decision

Now there was an "inside-outside" lobbying operation underway on behalf of a federal floor for existing welfare recipients. Finch, Moynihan, and Nathan worked on the inside; governors and editorial writers were building pressure on the outside. Governor Nelson Rockefeller, New York, obtained an appointment with Nixon to press for maximum New York savings from the welfare plan. Afraid that the president might be stampeded, Arthur Burns wrote Nixon a memo on the eve of Rockefeller's arrival warning him not to make any welfare promises without a crash investigation. "Our welfare system is in serious trouble," Burns wrote. "The desire to do something—such as setting up national welfare standards—should be resisted until we have a clearer idea of what the results may be. . . . The American people . . . want and expect you to provide the leadership toward effective reform—that is, a reduction in the number on welfare rolls."

Burns was too late. The next day, February 12, 1969, at a meeting with Burns, Finch, and Moynihan, President Nixon remarked that he wanted to establish national standards. This was bad news to Burns, no news to Finch, who had assumed it for weeks, and joyous news to Moynihan. That day, to seal the triumph, a jubilant Moynihan wrote down, in a memo replying to Burns' warning, what the president had said. Moynihan later confided to Price: "You have to seize such opportunities with a president!"

THE ATTACK

Five days later the Nathan plan came under an attack from which it was never to recover. The man responsible was a young economist, an outgoing HEW official who expected to have no influence with the Republican administration. He was Worth Bateman, 30, HEW deputy assistant secretary for program analysis (who later became a vice-president of the Urban Institute).

Bateman criticized the Nathan plan and suggested a bold alternative in a paper written for Tom Joe, who was assembling an overall review of policy questions facing Finch. Joe included the Bateman paper in a thick looseleaf policy book that was presented to Finch and Veneman on February 17, 1969.

"Many persons consider a national standard in Public Assistance a step in the right direction," wrote Bateman. "However . . . such a change would intensify present inequities in the treatment of male and female headed families and provide increased financial incentives to break up intact households, particularly those low income families headed by a man who works."

He gave examples: A male with a wife and two children who works full-time and earns $3,000 would receive no supplementation, whereas a woman with 3 children who works full-time and earns the same amount would receive about $1,100 supplementation. If the first family split up (man living alone, wife and two children living alone) its combined incomes would be about $2,000 greater than if it remained intact.

To end discrimination against the working poor, Bateman wrote (p. 9), "you may want to trade higher payment levels in the Public Assistance program for broader coverage and propose a modest new program which is income tested but provides supplementary income to all families with children. The program could be staged in a way which could result in some State savings. (This is a Negative Income Tax plan for families with children, but it could be called by a different name.)"

Bateman wrote that anyone designing a welfare reform must confront the contradictory objectives of adequacy versus work incentive. If a guarantee is set high enough to be adequate for those who can't or shouldn't work, it raises serious work-incentive problems for some who can and should work. In order to assure that the poor receive a high proportion of the limited dollars from an income-maintenance program that lets recipients retain some earned income as a work reward, Bateman said, benefits must be set "low"; otherwise, payments extend to individuals in middle-income brackets.

The previous year Bateman had written a department analysis that strongly endorsed a negative income tax to provide coverage of the working poor; but HEW Secretary Wilbur Cohen, whose own favorite welfare prescription was to "federalize" welfare for all groups then aided (with national standards and full federal funding) refused to sign Bateman's analysis and ordered him to rewrite it. In his review of policy issues for Finch, Bateman listed the Cohen proposal of federalization and warned that it, like the Nathan plan, would increase monetary incentive for family breakup.

"It was kind of a surprise to me that Tom (Joe) didn't attempt to stop me from writing the report that I wanted to write," said Bateman of his policy paper. Bateman said he assumed that Joe had "very different ideas" from his about the desirable form of welfare reform.

THE NAME OF THE GAME

The next day brought a bigger surprise to Worth Bateman. At the first meeting of the newly created sub-Cabinet welfare "task force"* suggested by Nathan, chairman Veneman named Bateman chairman of a "working group" of technical experts—Tom Joe; Charles Hawkins, HEW veteran legislative expert who later (in July 1971) joined the staff of the House Ways and Means committee; and two of Nathan's Budget Bureau aides, Greg Barlous and Jim Storey. The working group was directed to strengthen the Nathan plan and report back to the task force.

* The task force consisted of Veneman; Nathan; Wilbur Schmidt, who had helped to design the Nathan plan; and, ex officio, John Price, all of whom wanted Nixon to be the first president to recommend national minimum welfare standards.

Veneman chose Bateman as chairman of the working group on the recommendation of Tom Joe, who was impressed by Bateman's competence. Bateman, however, interpreted his appointment as a secret policy signal. Unaware that Nathan himself had instigated creation of the Veneman task force and its working group, Bateman deduced that Finch and Veneman had established this machinery *as a means of sidetracking the Nathan plan.* Only the day before Finch and Veneman had heard Bateman criticize the structural weakness of the Nathan plan. Obviously, Bateman thought, they have read my recommendations for a negative income tax to expand welfare to the working poor (actually, they later told the authors, they had not), and they are giving me a green light.

Excited by his imagined invitation to draft a negative income tax plan covering poor families, Bateman got Veneman's approval to add a sixth person to the working group, James Lyday, thirty-eight, economist in the OEO's Office of Research, Plans, Progress, and Evaluation, leading architect of the poverty war's abortive negative income tax proposals.* (Lyday also had drafted the first NIT measure introduced in Congress—the "Income Maintenance Act," sponsored in May 1968 by Democratic Representative William Ryan, New York.)

When Bateman invited him, Lyday thought he must be dreaming. At the poverty agency he had spent four years helping to design negative income tax plans to combat poverty, all to no avail. Was it possible that the conservative Nixon administration might buy what Lyndon Johnson had spurned?

That breathtaking possibility was discussed on February 19, 1969, by four men who gathered in Bateman's office: Bateman, Lyday, Mike Mahoney (a Bateman aide), and Robert Harris, executive staff director of President Johnson's Commission on Income Maintenance (whose report would be submitted to President Nixon in November).

An incredible gathering! Here were four men from the Johnson

---

* Beginning in 1967, Lyday of OEO, Bateman and Harris, of HEW, and Nelson McClung, of the Treasury Department, each of whom had some responsibility for welfare reform analysis in different government departments, used to gather on Thursday afternoons at Lyday's house near Capitol Hill. Their "Thursday club" shared ideas and data and planned ways of promoting a negative income tax. When Harris, in 1968, joined the Heineman Commission staff as director, McClung became his deputy.

administration who were beginning to hope that the GOP administration might resurrect the antipoverty strategy killed by the president from Texas.

As Bateman perceived the situation: "It was clear to three or four of us that the name of the game was structural reform. I saw the creation of the task force as a maneuver to get key people—Price and Nathan—committed to structural reform, rather than simply the Nathan plan." With that in mind, Bateman, at the outset, secretly divided his working group into two parts, the insiders who knew what was going on and would privately develop an alternative to Nathan's plan; and the outsiders, who would be busied with assignments to perfect variations of the Nathan plan, ostensible goal of the group. The insiders were Lyday and Bateman; the outsiders were Tom Joe, Charley Hawkins, Greg Barlous, and Jim Storey.

For the time being the Nixon White House and the Nixon Budget Bureau would be kept ignorant of the welfare plan being developed by Democrats Bateman and Lyday in the working group of the Veneman task force of the Finch welfare subcommittee of the President's Council for Urban Affairs.*

LIGHT-BULB LYDAY

Working in secret, Bateman and Lyday set out to build a proposed new welfare system for the Nixon administration that would embrace millions of new persons by putting a floor under the income of every American family with children. To win consideration as an alternative to the Nathan plan of minimum payment standards for existing recipients, their broader plan could cost no more. The limit was $1.4 billion.

Under existing welfare the federal government paid at least one-half of every AFDC dollar. Under the Nathan plan AFDC's financing would change: the federal government would pay 100 percent of a new national minimum benefit, plus one-half of state supplements. To design a bigger new system without increasing federal costs, it appeared necessary to reduce either the federal income guarantee or the federal share of state supplements, or both.

On the third or fourth day of their intrigue, NIT advocates huddled

---

* Neither Bateman nor Lyday had been appointed as Democrats per se, but the new administration regarded them as holdover Democrats.

in Bateman's office, discussing this problem. Lyday stood at a black-board, chalking down figures, when Bateman pondered aloud: "Can't we set the guarantee high enough so that no state gets hurt—and then just cut loose from AFDC?"

"Wow!" Lyday jumped. "God! That's it!"

Lyday said later that it was so brilliant a solution that "I could see the Smokey Stover light bulb go on!" (as in the comic strip).

Until then the planners had been assuming a dual system: a federal floor and a federal-state financed supplementary AFDC system. Bateman's breakthrough idea—to eliminate federal dollars from the second system—would make it possible to raise the basic payment of the first! * Now the question became: How high must the federal guarantee be so that no state would have to increase its welfare spending in order to maintain existing AFDC benefits by supplements to the floor? The calculated answer (too small, it later turned out) was a federal floor of $900 for a parent-child family, $1,200 for three persons, $1,500 for four. The guarantee was to be reduced by 50 cents for each dollar earned.

But what would the new plan cost? The federal family benefits, when coupled with increased federal financing of welfare programs for needy, blind, or disabled adults, would boost federal welfare costs $2 billion. That was $600 million over the Nathan ceiling. Undismayed, our resourceful economists found a way to close the cost gap. Since they could not reduce the cost of their plan, they increased the cost of the Nathan plan.†

---

* As staff director of the President's Commission on Income Maintenance, Robert Harris also got the idea to drop federal funding for AFDC. He proposed to put the saving into the basic program. Harris' calculation showed a need for a federal floor of about $2,200 (for a family of four) to allow states sufficient savings with which to bring payments up to their existing AFDC levels at no added cost. Ultimately the staff gave the Commission two options: 1) a $2,200 federal floor, the minimum for state supplements at no added cost; and 2) a $2,400 floor. It chose the latter.

† In the budget inherited by Nixon, Lyndon Johnson had made a phony "saving" of $300 million by endorsing the congressionally ordered freeze on federal AFDC funds scheduled to take effect July 1, 1969. Even if Nixon recommended no welfare reform, Congress was certain to set aside the freeze. It was a separate issue. Nevertheless, Bateman and Lyday added to the Nathan plan's cost $300 million for "repeal of the freeze" (which the Nathan task force, too, had recommended). They then added another $300 million by estimating that the Nathan plan would have a larger impact than Nathan had forecast on "increasing the caseload."

Veneman was startled but intrigued when Bateman sketched for him the first outline of the plan, still a secret from the "outsiders" on the working group. Because he had been called away to finish a California welfare assignment, Tom Joe missed the early plotting for a guaranteed income plan. When he learned about the secret blueprint he was appalled, for he saw that it would hurt some poor AFDC familes. The proposed ceiling on federal welfare payments ($1,500 for a family of four) would be set well below levels of some states' existing AFDC guarantees. (Some states then guaranteed a penniless broken family of four $3,200—half paid by the federal government. The median state guarantee then was $2,400.) If the federal government stopped helping states make payments above the proposed federal floor, states would be under strong fiscal pressure to cut benefits, Joe fumed.

At the time Bateman and Lyday saw Joe as a disruptive nuisance who didn't share their vision of building a new and better institution.

"Screw the details!" Lyday told Joe. "You can't make an omelet without breaking an egg. You're just a bleeding heart trying to keep a lousy discredited AFDC system. Don't you care about the working poor?"

"I just want you guys to put more money into your system so you won't hurt people," said Joe.

"We can't," they replied. "It won't fly if we do."

A RED FLAG

Day by day, in Bateman's office, the secret plan took shape: a negative income tax for all families (working or not) with children; a national welfare standard for needy adults; and abolition of AFDC as a federally aided program. When the first draft was ready, Bateman and Lyday proudly took it to the next-door office of Lewis H. Butler, assistant HEW secretary for planning and evaluation (who had been a Peace Corps official and, at Stanford University, a law school classmate of John Ehrlichman; Butler left HEW in the summer of 1971 to join the faculty of the University of California at Berkeley).

"Oh no!" groaned Butler, when he saw the plan. "You've *got* to change the name." Later Butler explained: "When I opened the book the first thing I saw was 'negative income tax.' It looked like a red flag to me. I knew people were violently for and against that."

Whatever its name, the Bateman-Lyday plan for families could have been lifted, with two major changes, from Friedman's "Case for the Negative Income Tax" (see chapter 2, p. 17). The differences were that Bateman-Lyday benefits would be restricted to families with children and paid by HEW. Friedman's plan called for universal benefits paid by the Internal Revenue Service.

With Veneman's guidance, Bateman and Lyday perfected a draft to show to HEW Secretary Finch. Unless Finch supported the plan there would be no point in trying to push it through the policy-making machinery (from Veneman's task force to Finch's Cabinet subcommittee, to the Urban Affairs Council, and, finally, to the president himself).

Present at the March 3, 1969, briefing in Finch's office was a newcomer to his staff, Robert E. Patricelli, formerly on the staff of Republican Senator Jacob K. Javits, New York, a founder of the Ripon Society, and a member of the Nathan task force on welfare. (Later Patricelli became an official of Greater Hartford Process, Inc., which undertook community redevelopment in his hometown.)

Sitting on his office couch, Finch opened the report. "Mr. Secretary," said a disappointed Lew Butler. "I think you should go back and look at the title."

Finch turned back the cover and read: "Christian Working Man's Anti-Communist National Defense Rivers and Harbors Act of 1969." The title was supplied by John Brandl, one of Butler's education experts (who later became director of the School of Public Affairs at the University of Minnesota). "We'll have to call all our bills that," Finch grinned.

At the end of the presentation, Finch asked the dread question: "How are we going to explain why we have to add six million persons to the welfare rolls?" It was a question that came to haunt the Nixon administration; and, in the end, it killed the welfare plan. Within seventeen months it had grown to: "Why add 13 million to welfare? Why put one-third of the state of Mississippi on welfare?"

"Let's cross that bridge when we get to it," advised Veneman.

"It'll never sell!" the admonition from Patricelli chilled the room. "This is a negative income tax and the president will never buy it."

Bateman had a sinking feeling. This new guy is going to kill it!

"We ought to see how far we can go with it," said Veneman,

soft-spoken and relaxed. He knew that Finch would go along, for he had kept Finch advised ("plugged in," as Veneman called it) on the drafting of the secret plan. It was an approach that made sense, Veneman had told Finch. Sure, there would be a problem in justifying millions more on welfare, but the administration should get the plan up to Congress and force a debate on the problem of the working poor. The present system was unfair; it was splitting up families. From the outset Undersecretary Veneman had been determined to do more than plug up the leaks in welfare.

Months later, as he tried to recall the temper of that meeting, Butler said: "Finch was going to take Jack Veneman's advice. That (welfare) had been Jack's business in California, and Finch would do whatever he said . . . Veneman thought it was important, a major reform. I didn't know enough to know what it was. Among most of us I don't think it was thought of as a big deal. It was simply, should we push it forward? Is it good enough for taking forward to the next step?"

Near the end of the meeting Finch gave a go-ahead. "If you guys think it's workable, let's keep going," he said. "Our goal ought to be to get a plan up to Congress with the President's name on it and start a national debate."

Lyday, a Democrat attending his first big Republican policy-making conference, was astonished. He thought this was Finch's first exposure to details of the plan.

"When Finch bought it so easily I was flabbergasted," he said later. "From then on I never worried about Nixon buying it. I figured he was an opportunist and would do what was necessary and so he would buy it if we could get it through to him."

Now that Finch and Veneman had okayed the plan, the next obstacle was Veneman's task force. Nathan and Schmidt, the other two voting members, would have to be persuaded to abandon the plan they had developed before the inauguration. But how could Bateman, head of the working group, tell Nathan, Your plan is no good; we've got a better one?

"What's the best way to go about selling it?" asked Veneman.

Butler had an idea. "Don't go in there carrying that thing," he said. "We have to set this up so those guys are saying, 'If the Nathan report is that bad, what is there?' Get them to order you to produce it. Get a new name and get an authorization to produce what you've worked out."

That became the strategy.

When Veneman's task force met on March 7, 1969, to hear the report of the working group, not a word was said about the bold negative income tax plan, still a secret from Nathan's Budget Bureau colleagues on the working group. Drawing upon the work of those Budget Bureau analysts, Bateman reported that the working group had developed two variations of the Nathan plan, one to cost $2 billion, the other $2.1 billion. Both versions, he said, offered the advantages of raising benefits in low-payment states and relieving high-payment states of some welfare costs. But both would discourage family stability and work and racial unity.

"These criticisms are valid," Nathan said. "But you can't draft a plan within the cost limits that would meet those objections."

("It was so beautifully done, like it was scripted," Bateman said afterward. "Nathan piped up and said exactly what Butler wanted him to say.")

Having hooked his fish, Butler played him expertly. "You're probably right," he told Nathan, "but at least we should examine it and see."

Nathan agreed. And so the task force gave the working group the new assignment of producing the plan that already was in Bateman's briefcase: a plan to cover the working poor, with work incentives, at a cost of no more than $2 billion.

Shortly before the meeting ended, Bateman discreetly handed a note to Veneman. It read, "I nominate you for 'best director' of the year and myself for 'best actor.' "

Veneman looked at Bateman and solemnly inquired, "Well, Worth, do you think you know what to do now?"

"Yes," Bateman replied. "I think so."

The Family Security System

Now all that remained was to give the plan a less irreverent name and to wait. To wait a respectable time before taking the plan out of the briefcase and showing it to the task force, to Nathan, Schmidt, and Price.

In the interim Price got wind of the plan and, in an Italian restaurant a mile from the White House, he relayed the news to Moynihan, at first incredulous, then exultant.

"You've got it!" cried Moynihan. "That's it!" With wine and veal scallopini the two celebrated the amazing plan to guarantee incomes of all families with children.

The Christian Working Man's Anti-Communist National Defense Rivers and Harbors Act of 1969 was retitled the Family Security System and won approval of the Veneman task force. The man who provided the new name, Bill Robinson, staff aide to Nathan, was startled to learn that psychologist Kenneth Clark a year earlier had suggested that "family security" be substituted for the maligned word "welfare" (in a chapter of *Agenda for the Nation*).

"There is nothing new under the sun," Robinson told Nathan in a memo about his discovery. "I still lay claim to the term in its present context, but it's nice to know that Clark agrees."

Still earlier, Edward E. Schwartz (1964, p. 4), of the University of Chicago's School of Social Service Administration, had used the term "Family Security Program" for his guaranteed income proposal.

PRESIDENT JOHNSON'S COMMISSION

That same week Chairman Ben Heineman gave the first public hint of what his Commission on Income Maintenance would recommend. At a dinner meeting of a poverty conference at the Waldorf-Astoria Hotel in New York on March 21, Heineman (1969) said he favored a guaranteed income for all of America's poor.

Arthur Burns had perceived the Heineman Commission of Lyndon Johnson as an impetus to a Nixon welfare initiative, but had been unable to persuade Nixon to dismantle it. However, on April 14, 1969, Commission Chairman Heineman received a telephone call from John Ehrlichman telling him that the Commission should cease operations as an independent body and, instead, should report to the welfare subcommittee of the Urban Affairs Council. Since the president had set up his own welfare reform machinery, said Ehrlichman, an independent body would not be needed.

Alarmed at this directive to, in effect, abolish the Commission, Heineman told Ehrlichman that HEW secretary Finch, who had met with him and Commission staffers that very day, seemed to have a different idea of the value of the Commission. Then Heineman and his staff director, Harris, notified Moynihan and Finch of the Ehrlichman move, and they went to the defense of the Commission. Within a day Ehrlichman phoned Heineman and reversed the order. "I guess the right hand had better find out what the left hand is doing," he told Heineman.

Moynihan, who had close liaison with the Commission from the start of his own Nixon welfare assignment—and who often called upon the staff of Lyndon Johnson's Commission for data and memos—later used the impending Commission report as an argument within the Nixon administration for speedy action on the Family Security System. Unless FSS were sent to Congress directly, he told the president on June 6 (1969e, p. 2), the Nixon administration would lose the lead to *"President Johnson's* Commission on Income Maintenance" (the italics were Moynihan's). Moynihan said the Commission was drafting a system "very much like Family Security, but somewhat broader."

Urban Affairs Council Subcommittee Blockade

In advance of the March 24, 1969, meeting of the Cabinet-level welfare subcommittee, members received a report (from the Veneman task force) that recommended the Family Security System but offered a slightly modified Nathan plan as a "less preferred option." (Bateman called this a "fallback position.") Both plans provided a $1-billion food stamp program as an optional extra.

Since the subcommittee had been cool to the relatively moderate Nathan plan, Moynihan feared that it would be horrified by the proposal to double welfare rolls with an unconditional guaranteed income for all families with children, working or not, deserving or not. Girding himself for the offensive, he slapped the table moments after the session began and declared: "I want to say this is a great historic plan. I think we should go to the president with it immediately. If we worked on it for five years I don't think we could come up with a better plan."

Representing Dr. Arthur Burns, his chief aide, Dr. Martin Ander-

son, young conservative economist from Columbia University, sprang
to the attack. Anderson said that FSS should not be taken to the
president at all. It was a bad plan; it was a negative income tax; it
was contrary to the president's campaign pledge to reduce welfare
rolls; it was the "Speenhamland" plan of eighteenth-century England;
it was too costly; it would be a political liability.

"I believe in calling a spade a spade," said Anderson, reiterating
that FSS was nothing but a negative income tax.

"I agree with Oscar Wilde," said Moynihan. "Anyone who insists
on calling a spade a spade should be forced to use one."

Commerce Secretary Stans convulsed with laughter. Anderson
flushed. Moynihan wasn't trying to answer his arguments.

Moynihan added that Anderson was right; FSS was like Speenhamland, which "offered one loaf of bread a month to each family."
More laughter.

Whatever Candidate Nixon may have said, Moynihan argued, is
less important than what President Nixon wants. At the very first
Cabinet meeting, Moynihan said, the president called for a solution
to the welfare problem, and now he wanted a plan by April 15. This
was *the* solution. True, the plan was costly, but not in relation to
the gross national product and the problems of the people concerned.

"We are the only industrial democracy not to have a family allowance system," Moynihan said, repeating a theme familiar to him.
Before he entered the White House Moynihan had often complained
of the nation's lack of a children's allowance. Now he made a personal conversion in terminology. Others could call FSS a negative
income tax for families with children. Moynihan, the children's allowance advocate, liked to think of it as a "family allowance" plan
for the poor.

As Eisenhower's budget director a decade before, Stans had urged
Congress not to approve a modest increase in the federal share of
welfare costs. Now he was appalled to hear Democrat Moynihan
urge that the Republican administration propose that the federal
government guarantee family incomes.

Secretary of Agriculture Clifford M. Hardin was being pressed by
Congress for an antihunger program, and he wanted the president to

act quickly on food stamps. He insisted that food stamps should not be delayed until action on FSS.

Attorney General John N. Mitchell, who would emerge as the most powerful man in the Cabinet, puffed his pipe and listened.

Finch asked Mitchell what he thought. The president, Finch reminded him, wants a welfare plan by the 15th. "Can't we take FSS to a full Cabinet meeting before then?" Finch asked.

No, he would have to know more about it, said Mitchell.

Stans agreed. Anderson beamed.

Mitchell, looking at his watch, said he had to leave, but added: "I think you're on the right track, but I'd have to have some answers to a great many more questions."

Although Finch scheduled another Urban Affairs Council welfare subcommittee meeting the next week, there seemed little hope that FSS could advance through that channel. The subcommittee had balked at even taking FSS to the Cabinet for discussion.

Two days later Moynihan brought up the subject of FSS in a memo to the president:

> The essential fact about the Family Security System is that it will abolish poverty for dependent children and the working poor. The cost is not very great. Because it is a direct payment system. The tremendous costs of the poverty program comes from services. I.e., year-round Head Start costs $1,000 per child. Almost all this money goes to middle class teachers, and the like. Ditto Community Action.
>
> The Family Security System would enable you to begin cutting back sharply on these costly and questionable services and yet to assert with full validity that it was under your Presidency that poverty was abolished in America.

DOMESTIC WEEKEND

It was the tenth week of Nixon's presidency, and his domestic legislative program was embarrassing by its absence. The target of growing criticism from newspaper columnists and Democrats for this neglect, Nixon finally turned from foreign and defense policy to internal affairs. He asked Burns, Finch, and Moynihan to submit their domestic proposals to him at Key Biscayne, Florida, during the Easter weekend (Good Friday and Saturday), April 4–5, 1969.

Both Moynihan and Finch seized the opportunity to champion the Family Security System; both hailed it as the No. 1 domestic program.

"I call your attention above all to the Family Security System," said Moynihan (1969b) in submitting a package of domestic proposals. He sent Nixon what he called the "Draft Report of the Committee on Welfare of the Council for Urban Affairs" on the Family Security System. This terminology implied that the UAC welfare subcommittee had accepted the report, but in truth it had refused even to forward it to the Council for discussion.* With an asterisk Moynihan noted that the report as yet was "not approved by the Council for Urban Affairs."

In a paper entitled, "A Nixon Alternative," Finch (1969a, pp. 3 and 7) praised the Family Security System, advising the president:

> The keystone of the domestic program . . . should be revolutionary reform of the welfare system. This is one of the most expensive of our social programs, yet it is the most poorly conceived and ineffective . . . FSS would cover families headed by both employed and unemployed fathers. . . .
>
> The political support . . . should be widespread. It should appeal to state and local governments and taxpayers. . . . It should appeal to beneficiaries and social welfare groups . . . Finally, it should appeal to many conservatives, since it provides strong incentives for work and family stability.
>
> It should be remembered that FSS is not a Negative Income Tax proposal,† since it only covers families with children and does not do away with all other income support and service mechanisms, and is not a guaranteed income program unrelated to need or the ability to work.

When the president boarded Air Force One to attend the funeral of Dwight D. Eisenhower, April 3, in Abilene, Kansas, enroute to Key Biscayne, he was well supplied with papers on domestic problems. In the Senate's recording studio that day, Robert Finch made the first public mention of the Family Security Plan by name. In taping a televised interview, the HEW Secretary spoke vaguely about

---

* Despite this rebuff, in his 1973 book, *Politics of a Guaranteed Income* (p. 545), Moynihan calls FAP "a product of the Urban Affairs Council, in ways a consequence of it." Critical to FAP was the placement of welfare on the new president's agenda, but *not* the formal machinery established for welfare policy.

† Economists Bateman and Lyday knew better; FSS was, indeed, as economist Anderson had charged, nothing but a negative income tax proposal.

a "family security program" that he hoped the president would submit to Congress soon.

At the close of that business day another airplane set out for Key Biscayne to carry Finch to his rendezvous with the president. Aboard the plane to brief Finch on details of FSS were Veneman, Butler, and Patricelli.

All through that weekend James Lyday waited for a telephone call from Key Biscayne that never came. "I knew Finch and Moynihan wouldn't be able to answer technical questions, so all the weekend I stayed around HEW or kept calling in," he said. But Nixon had no technical questions.

As Moynihan later observed, the remarkable thing that happened that weekend in Florida was that "nothing happened" to FSS. Finch and Moynihan pressed for FSS; Burns fought against it; but the president didn't say yes or no.

When Nixon did not reject it out of hand, Burns was dumfounded. He found this wholly out of character.

The argument went something like this:

Burns (protesting): You would add seven million persons to the welfare rolls!

Finch: What's wrong with Republicans providing income maintenance for seven million people?

Nixon: I understand, Arthur, that you don't like it; and I understand your reasons. But I have a problem. If you don't like it, give me another solution.

Back in the White House Monday morning Moynihan was ebullient. "A good meeting," he told Price, "a very good meeting with Nixon. The president asked me, 'Will FSS get rid of social workers?' and I promised him it would wipe them out!"

Moynihan added gravely, "The next two weeks are crucial." His staff would be hearing that comment for more than three months.

4.

BUILDING A BRIDGE

"If the substance of this meeting got out to the power center on the Hill we'd be run out of the city"
—BRYCE HARLOW at White House Cabinet meeting, April 26, 1969

THE PRESIDENT'S FAILURE to kill the proposal for a guaranteed family income at Key Biscayne in April 1969 shocked his chief domestic adviser, Dr. Arthur F. Burns, who said later, "It ran counter to everything I knew about Dick Nixon. . . . It seemed that he might do the unthinkable." Nixon seemed determined to change welfare's status quo, and so Burns, adopting Nixon's suggestion that he develop an alternative to the Family Security System, grudgingly added welfare to his agenda.

Although Nixon had said neither yes nor no at Key Biscayne, Moynihan proceeded as though the president had embraced FSS. "I will begin working on a presidential message (on FSS)," he volunteered on Easter Monday to presidential aide John D. Ehrlichman in a memo listing FSS among 15 "decisions the president made on Friday." To transform FSS into a presidential proposal more was to be required than Moynihan's chutzpah and wit. Ahead were months of argument, through which Moynihan sometimes found himself "walking on eggshells."

Three main proposals commanded the debate: FSS, a counterproposal (April 21) by Burns, and a revision of FSS (June 10) by Secretary of Labor George Shultz. Cabinet officers and other advisers poured arguments of morality, philosophy, politics, and economics into secret memos to the president, each choosing what he hoped would be decisive with him. Moynihan shunned analytic debate and played to Nixon's ego, enticing him with the promise of historic greatness and the chance to "all but eliminate" poverty. Burns warned that FSS would undermine the nation's work ethic. Finch argued that FSS made good sense and good politics. Budget Director Mayo complained that it would deepen the budget deficit. Agnew said it would convert self-reliant workers into welfare "addicts," calling to mind Franklin Roosevelt's complaint that "to dole out relief . . . is to administer a narcotic." Commerce Secretary Stans opposed even the modest Burns plan and asked why welfare recipients couldn't grow gardens, fish, and hunt (in Central Park?).

A Hair-Curler

The heart of the Family Security System, developed by holdover Democrats with the encouragement of HEW's new GOP commanders, was a federal income floor for all families with children and a work-incentive formula to reduce welfare grants one dollar for each two dollars in earnings so that welfare would continue, on a declining scale, until earnings were double the guarantee. Guarantees for families with no income were $450 per adult and $300 per child. Since a child was required to qualify a family for aid, the first-child "bonus" was $750 for a single-parent family and $1,200 for a two-parent family. No strings limited the guarantee; work was not required; need alone conferred eligibility. It would be a federal system of benefits for all poor families, *working* or *not working*.

"It would curl your hair if you knew what some people around here are proposing," Martin Anderson, Burns' aide, muttered when a reporter inquired about Nixon welfare policy.

Pressing for a quick decision, Moynihan told Nixon that FSS would give him the legislative offensive against the Democratic Congress. "If you decide to adopt the plan," Moynihan (1969c) told the president, "you should announce it soon after Congress returns [from its Easter recess April 14]. It will be the centerpiece of your domestic program—truly an historic proposal. You should put it on the desks of Congress and force them right off to begin discussing *your pro-*

gram rather than new Kennedy-McGovern issues such as hunger, or old Johnson programs such as the Job Corps."

On their desks when congressmen returned was a message from the president containing budget revisions and the promise that his domestic program would ultimately include revenue sharing, a vigorous attack on hunger, and welfare reform. "Our studies have demonstrated that tinkering with the present welfare system is not enough," Nixon told Congress. "We need a complete re-appraisal and re-direction."

Speenhamland

To the president's desk that same Monday, April 14, Arthur Burns sent a six-page document that produced consternation in Moynihan's office. In preparing the paper, Dr. Martin Anderson (1969a), Burns' chief aide, had reached back 170 years into British history for ammunition against FSS. Entitled "A Short History of a 'Family Security System,'" the paper consisted solely of excerpts from Karl Polanyi's historical work, *The Great Transformation*, prefaced by a quotation from Santayana, "Those who cannot remember the past are condemned to repeat it."

The quoted excerpts (italicized sections represent underlining by Anderson) included:

> The justices of Berkshire, meeting at the Pelikan Inn, in Speenhamland, near Newbury, on May 6, 1795, in a time of great distress, decided that subsidies in aid of wages should be granted in accordance with a scale dependent upon the price of bread, so that *a minimum income should be assured to the poor irrespective of their earnings.*
>
> The magistrates' famous recommendation ran: When the gallon loaf of bread of definite quality "shall cost 1 shilling, then every poor and industrious person shall have for his support 3 shillings weekly, either procured by his own or his family's labor, or an allowance from the poor rates, and for the support of his wife and every other of his family, 1 shilling, 6 pence; when the gallon loaf shall cost 1/6, then 4 shillings weekly, plus 1/10; on every pence which the bread price raises above 1 shilling he shall have 3 pence for himself and 1 pence for the others."
>
> The figures varied somewhat in various countries, but . . . very soon it became the law of the land over most of the countryside. . . .

Under Elizabethan Law the poor were forced to work at whatever wages they could get and *only those who could obtain no work were entitled to relief;* relief in aid of wages was neither intended nor given. *Under the Speenhamland Law a man was relieved even if he was in employment, as long as his wages amounted to less than the family income granted to him by the scale.*

Hence, no laborer had any material interest in satisfying his employer, his income being the same whatever wages he earned. . . .

In the long run the result was ghastly. . . .

Little by little the people of the countryside were pauperized. . . .

Neither the rulers nor the ruled ever forgot the lessons of that fool's paradise.

PLUMBING THE LITERATURE

Asked by the president for comment, Moynihan undertook a frantic effort to learn what had happened to British yeomen almost two centuries ago. While his young aides researched the libraries, Moynihan telephoned England and discussed for 45 minutes the Old Poor Law with Dr. J. H. Plumb, of Cambridge University. From it all Moynihan distilled a two-page double rebuttal: Speenhamland did not do the damage attributed to it by Polanyi and, furthermore, because it discouraged work by a 100 percent tax on earnings, Speenhamland was not a "Family Security System." To Anderson's Polanyi Moynihan counterposed another authority, Mark Blaug, who had scoffed at "what all the books say" about Speenhamland in a paper published in the December 1964 *Journal of Economic History*.

Moynihan wrote (1969d) the president: "It seems absurd to trouble you with controversies concerning the post-Napoleonic economic history of Britain, but if you like. . . . The essential point is: Polanyi's thesis on the effects of the Speenhamland system has been rejected by economic historians. . . . Certainly one would not wish to see Speenhamland recreated in America at this time, as it imposed a 100% tax on earnings. . . . The Family Security System, to the contrary, has only a 50% tax rate and provides a positive incentive to earn."

HEW's Mike Mahoney (April 25), aware of Moynihan's call to the expert Doctor Plumb, could not resist a pun as he drafted for Finch's signature a reply to Anderson's Speenhamland memo: ". . . Having *plumbed* the relevant literature, Dr. Moynihan notes that the inference drawn by Polanyi and accepted by Anderson must be rejected" (italics added). The president was denied the punning memo; Butler, an assistant HEW secretary, intercepted it, deciding it was time to put Speenhamland to rest.

Because he felt his honor impugned, Anderson could not let Speenhamland rest. At his request, a Columbia University historian surveyed the literature. Anderson (1969b) sent the result to Burns: Of 17 authors who dealt with the matter, all but Blaug supported Polanyi's thesis that Speenhamland damaged the productivity of the poor. "Perhaps the president should not be bothered with this," said Anderson, "but I would not like to leave him with the impression that I had selected a particular historian whose thesis had been rejected generally by economic historians."

Moynihan had won this round.

Counterattack

On April 21, 1969, the major battle was joined. Burns sent a rival plan to the president and the central issues emerged: Should welfare be extended to families of poor working fathers? Should work be required of welfare parents? FSS said yes to the first question, no to the second; Burns' plan said the opposite.

In barring aid to working poor fathers, Burns (1969a) resorted to a unique glossary. He saw the working poor as millions of self-reliant people, "a good proportion of whom do not even consider themselves poor." For him payment of wage supplements was "placing . . . people in a state of dependency"; and to make eligible for welfare was "to thrust by law onto welfare rolls."

To summon the president back to orthodoxy, Burns invoked two authorities: Candidate Nixon and the American voter. He recalled Candidate Nixon's warning that a guaranteed income or a negative income tax would harm America's productive capacity without ending poverty. He stressed the "purely political fact" that most Americans oppose income guarantees, citing a recent Gallup poll in which 62 percent expressed opposition.

Brushing aside Finch's sophistry, Burns noted, "The so-called Family Security System is a plan for guaranteeing incomes of people. In its technical form it is simply a specific application of the negative income tax, as formulated by Milton Friedman." If FSS became law, Burns said, political pressure probably would expand it to universal coverage and raise the income guarantee; ultimately, it might add to welfare rolls 25 million, 50 million, or even more persons.

Because of its cost, its all-federal welfare floor, and its admitted goal of an all-federal welfare system, Burns also had opposed Nathan's plan. But to overcome FSS, Burns had concluded that he must offer an alternative way to achieve two features of the Nathan plan to which the president seemed committed: higher welfare levels in the South and fiscal relief for hard-pressed northern states.

Remodeling the Nathan blueprint, Burns devised a clever plan to meet his objectives. Federal welfare funds would be linked to a new program of revenue-sharing, itself a presidential goal that Burns favored. Superficially bold, the plan would make a minimal break with tradition, preserving the form and much of the substance of state control over welfare policy. It offered Nixon a tempting bargain —two programs, welfare reform and revenue sharing, for little more than the price of one.

Burns advised the president that there should be federal welfare standards that states need not observe: average monthly benefits of at least $40 per AFDC recipient and $65 per adult program recipient. States that met the standards would receive a reward from revenue-sharing; but no revenue would be shared with states that paid substandard benefits. The fifteen low-benefit states would have an incentive to lift benefits to the standard, as they would gain more in shared federal revenue than they would have to pay. Yet the only increased *welfare* cost to the U.S. Treasury would be the federal share, calculated by the existing formula, of the cost of raising benefits in the latter states.

Burns' plan also called for mandatory extension of welfare to unemployed fathers (AFDC-UF) and proposed an expansion of job training programs and a nationwide network of child day care centers so that welfare mothers could be required to work or train.

A Goal in Sight

On the same day that Burns submitted his 33-page memo, April 21, 1969, the U.S. Supreme Court struck down residency requirements for welfare as a violation of the constitutional right of the poor to travel. The decision voided rules of forty states that persons must live within the state for periods of up to one year to qualify for welfare.

"This makes inevitable national minimum welfare standards," Finch told newsmen an hour later. Even Burns had surrendered on that issue. Now it seemed certain that the Nixon administration would recommend—and so how could the Democratic Congress refuse?—minimum standards. That goal, forfeited by the New Deal in 1935, was in sight at last.

But Burns' assault dashed hopes of FSS backers for help for the working poor. "All bets are off now," said a Finch aide, who grumbled that Burns had made an "end run" around the Urban Affairs Council to the president. It was the pot calling the kettle black; Finch and Moynihan had made the first end run to Key Biscayne three weeks earlier.

In a memo to the president, Finch (1969b, p. 11) hurled at the Burns plan a damning indictment (echoed the next week by Secretary of Defense Melvin Laird): that it "simply pumps more money into a system which has already failed." Using a phrase that Burns had applied to FSS, Finch said existing welfare was *corrosive to moral values*, "since it pays people not to work." Although federal aid was barred to working fathers, states could dispense it to unemployed fathers. Burns proposed to make this discretionary program mandatory, which would spread the "don't work rule" to fathers in all states.

Weeks later Burns (1969b, p. 10) confessed to the president that "a case can surely be made for supplementing the income of a poor working family, particularly so when its earnings fall below what another family of equivalent composition gets through welfare." But he rejected the case and counseled Nixon to watch and restrain the level of welfare benefits, already more remunerative than un-skilled jobs in many areas.*

Finch argued that FSS would attack the existing system's "perverse" incentives against work.

"To include the working poor is not basically a 'leftish' or liberal initiative," Finch (1969b, pp. 11–12) told the president, "but rather an essentially conservative move which, while appealing to liberals, is rooted in the concept of making work as rewarding as welfare in a system which in many states has reversed the incentives."

However, Burns' attack on FSS's unconditional income guarantee won a concession from Finch that FSS could be constructed with a compulsory work feature. Earlier Finch had proposed to rely on earnings incentives rather than compulsion. Now he was preparing to retreat to a more politically defensible position.

The Cabinet Debate

When some Cabinet officers protested that they were being excluded from the welfare debate, the president called his Cabinet to a special meeting at the White House on Saturday, April 26, 1969, for a briefing on FSS. Because the president was crowning his daughter, Tricia, azalea queen in Norfolk, Virginia, and the vice-president had an out-of-town speaking engagement, Finch presided, sitting in the president's chair. (This shocked a White House aide, who observed later, "Even Agnew had never done that! I never saw anyone do that!")

The three-and-a-half-hour meeting produced many differences:

Cash vs. foodstamps. Agriculture Secretary Hardin said FSS must be accompanied by a big expansion in his department's food stamp program. "As incomes go up, . . . rent follows; so there would be no

---

* But Burns' own plan proposed to raise the ratio of welfare to wages in the low-wage South. His minimum $1,920 annual payment to a mother with three children, almost equal to take-home pay of $1 an hour, would have been about double the going rate for domestic maids in Mississippi's largest cities. Because the action might deter migration to the North and because "government should be sensitive to human distress," Burns defended his proposal to boost welfare payments in the South.

additional money for food." ("For potato chips and coke!" someone sneered.)

Cash rather than food stamps was favored by Paul McCracken, chairman of the Council of Economic Advisers: "As to the question, will they [the poor] use it wrong, I say, wrong to whom? . . . We ought to give the individual purchasing power."

Labor Secretary Shultz agreed. "Any presidential message should put its bets on the individual."

Mayo also opposed food stamps. "This is one of our conflicts in philosophy. If we go with food stamps, do you have a model budget for food, for clothing, etc. . . . I put that $900 million [the estimated cost of food stamps] in a way-out category at this point due to our [budgetary] constraints."

Hardin caustically replied, "The government policy today is to let people starve to death a little more comfortably."

Mayo bristled. "If you want money for food stamps," he told Hardin, "why not reduce the subsidies to all those big [farm] corporations?"

Moynihan hailed the Nixon administration's emphasis on income for the poor, citing Nixon's call for repeal of income taxes on poverty-level wages. "We are turning government away from a service strategy to an income strategy," said Moynihan. "The service strategy had dubious results; it is a policy of feeding the sparrows by feeding the horses. . . . We've been putting high-paid people into the resentment business [a reference to Community Action groups]. I don't think the president likes these groups, but he can pull back on them only if there aren't poor people."

Work and training requirements. The policy question, said Moynihan, was whether training for welfare recipients should be "automatic, available, or rationed out?"

"—or mandatory?" suggested Commerce Undersecretary Rocco C. Siciliano.

Shultz considered it "not even desirable" to attempt to force welfare mothers into job training. With prescience, he remarked that if free day care were offered to working welfare mothers, other working women would complain, "What about me?"

Family breakup. Finch told of the law suit filed against him on March 14, 1969, by two California fathers, Juan Macias and Francisco Tarin, whose families lost money when they went to full-time jobs (Macias from a part-time job defined as "unemployment" by welfare rules and Tarin from actual unemployment). Unless these men gave up their new jobs or deserted, their families couldn't get welfare benefits. Tarin's job cost his family $139 monthly. (See chapter 2 for more discussion.)

"Perhaps," offered George Romney, secretary of housing and urban development, "we've got to get away from the situation where the husband has an incentive to leave home."

Burns retorted that FSS wouldn't abolish that incentive. Families could split to pool full welfare plus wages, whereas working intact families would get a smaller welfare supplement.

"It's got to be an act of faith," Moynihan insisted. "The correlation between income and family stability is absolute. As you raise family income, you increase stability."

On the reaction of congressional Republicans. Bryce Harlow, Nixon's chief of congressional liaison (who left the White House to become a Proctor & Gamble vice-president at the end of 1970, but returned in July 1973 as a presidential counselor during the Watergate probe) warned: "We haven't tried it out on anybody, but . . . the opening disposition of the Republican institution will be one of absolute horror. If you could factor in a work requirement, it would make a vast difference . . . If the substance of this meeting got out to the power center on the Hill [Capitol Hill, site of Congress] we'd be run out of the city. The Republican institution would rise in revolt!"

The need to act. Moynihan grew impassioned. "We now have terror in our cities. . . . We've got to move on this issue [poverty] or we will be recorded as the people who sat by."

Mayo agreed but voiced support for Burns' approach. "I like the idea of getting started on a welfare floor and revenue sharing. I think what Pat [Moynihan] has said is almost gospel. I fear that we may have a revolution if we don't do some of these things."

Near the end of the meeting Shultz observed that Mayo, as budget director, probably would have the last word. However, he added, "I think, if we can, now is the time to put a brand new concept [a perfected FSS] into the field."

The meeting settled nothing, the Cabinet officers agreeing only that a staff committee of technical experts under McCracken should resolve a dispute over cost estimates of the two rival plans. Except for Martin Anderson, who wrote a dissent, the eleven-member technical group subsequently endorsed FSS as superior to Burns' plan, said Burns had underestimated costs of his proposal, and dismissed his call for job training and day care on grounds that their cost would exceed welfare savings. This report likewise settled nothing.

Who's in Charge?

By-passing the policy-making machinery, Finch and Moynihan had taken their welfare plan, and Burns his, straight to the president. The debate grew as copying machines multiplied the welfare memos for distribution among Cabinet and sub-Cabinet officers, their staffs and aides, top-ranking White House advisers, and career bureaucrats. Paul Barton, a government veteran at the Labor Department, was amazed at the volume of crisscrossing memos.

"There must have been dozens of career men in agencies around town reading the memorandums to the president," Barton said. "You had GS-13's [middle-layer bureaucrats] who were working on it who had almost everything that the president had. . . . There was a tone of openness about it with Labor, HEW, CEA, and OEO all involved."

Opposition to FSS and support for Burns' plan came from Vice-President Agnew and Budget Chief Mayo. But Commerce Secretary Stans and Defense Secretary Laird (who became counselor to the president for Domestic Affairs in July 1973) in separate memos in early May advised the president to reject both plans.

Advancing his own bootstrap prescription for poverty, Stans (May 8) complained "neither plan gives recognition of the ability of the poor or the unemployed to reduce their living costs by self-help means such as growing gardens, fishing and hunting, making repairs, pooling efforts, etc., or to benefits received from family members, private charities, and other services."

With mock gravity, pro-FSS staffers privately debated the policy implications. "We need an amendment to FSS to require the poor to raise tomatoes in their window boxes," said one. "No," argued a second, "the first priority should be to outfit Harlem's welfare families with fishing poles and nets, garden spades, seed packets, and bows and arrows so they can exploit the resources of Central Park." *

Laird (May 7) warned the president that Burns' approach would "lock the Nixon administration into an affirmation of the basic philosophy of the past." On the other hand, FSS "would launch us into a sharp break that I am not certain would be politically palatable or salable in its present form." The remedy, Laird suggested, was to delay action for six months while a crash study produced a "thoroughly thought-out welfare package."

The free-ranging and open debate was valuable. By inviting a flow of criticism and advice the President broadened his knowledge. However, because no one at the White House was in charge of organizing domestic options for Nixon's decision, the debate lacked a neutral manager.

H. R. (Bob) Haldeman (in the pre-Watergate years) was the White House chief of staff, in his own words the "traffic manager," who decided what persons and papers the president would see, but he was not supposed to make substantive policy recommendations. Dr. Henry A. Kissinger was the president's national security adviser. But for domestic policy there were rival White House staffs—a formula for disorder.

On advice of the National League of Cities, whose mayors wanted urban problems elevated in rank at the White House, Nixon had created a Council for Urban Affairs, patterned after the National Security Council. If the urban council were to be a domestic counterpart to the security council, its executive secretary would be a "Henry Kissinger" for domestic policy.

But Nixon chose Democrat Moynihan for that post, calling him

* The Agriculture and Consumer Protection Act of 1973 provided that needy Alaskans could purchase hunting and fishing equipment (but not firearms, ammunition, or other explosives) with food stamps.

his adviser on *urban affairs,* and then named his conservative friend, Dr. Arthur Burns, to be his chief adviser on *domestic policy,* a post that subsumed urban policy. Since both had strong policy convictions and strong egos, neither Burns nor Moynihan was suited temperamentally to manage options, pro and con, for presidential decision. Nor did either seek the king-sized Kissinger-type staff essential for that task. Moreover, there were other aides with small staffs who had direct access to the president.

One of them, John D. Ehrlichman, ultimately the president's manager for domestic policy (until his resignation during the 1973 Watergate affair), recalled the conflicts of the early months: "All of a sudden Arthur [Burns] would surface with all kinds of presidential authority. He knew more about how to operate. He would take the contract in to the president and get it signed. Those opposed would complain. 'Listen,' they would say, 'we never got a fair hearing. Arthur presented only one side.' The president asked me to take the job of arbitrating disputes. I would have Burns in, and Moynihan in. When welfare began to crystallize, irreconcilable points of view developed. So my office got involved as a sort of middle ground."

Shultz's Assignment

Flooded with conflicting welfare memos, the president in mid-May turned for advice to Secretary of Labor George Shultz, whose judgment and gift for analysis had impressed him. Knowing that Shultz favored the general concept of the Family Security System but felt that inadequate staff work had produced a faulty blueprint, Nixon asked Shultz: What do you think I should do?

The thoughtful response of the secretary of labor was to lead to a major change in the design of FSS.

All the while Burns was expanding the attack against FSS, wooing supporters for his own plan. Budget Director Mayo and Treasury Secretary Kennedy, frightened by the cost of FSS, chose the Burns plan early; but it took a month for Burns to enlist the third member of the government's economic "troika," Paul McCracken, chairman of the president's Council of Economic Advisers. On May 24 Mc-Cracken advanced a pro-Burns "compromise." Adopt Burns' plan now as an interim measure, he advised the President, and establish a task force, as Laird recommended, to develop a more comprehensive reform for the future.

Moynihan sought allies outside Washington. He arranged to have New York Mayor John Lindsay, then a Republican, invited to the next meeting of the Urban Affairs Council, to discuss welfare. Lindsay brought with him Mitchell Ginsberg, administrator of the city's Department of Human Resources and his welfare expert, and both spoke out in support of the Family Security System. (By this time New York City's budget for cash welfare and services exceeded that for education.)

Ginsberg told the president, who was presiding, that the U.S. Supreme Court had ruled that no state could deny federal welfare cash to needy children whose mother had a paramour living in the house unless there was evidence that he helped to support her children. Yet under existing law (and under the Burns plan) no state could give federal welfare cash to needy children of two-parent families if the father worked full time.

"Do you realize, Mr. President, that the federal government is subsidizing immorality?" asked Ginsberg.

"We can't have that," replied Nixon.

Alarmed by Burns' advances, Moynihan and John Price journeyed to New York to lobby Terrence Cardinal Cooke, Archbishop of New York, David Rockefeller, chairman of the Chase Manhattan Bank, and William Buckley Jr., conservative columnist. Their trip yielded a letter to Moynihan in which the archbishop endorsed FSS's "concern to strengthen family life."

"You Will Dominate"

The most effective retort to the McCracken memo came from Moynihan himself. Brushing aside as "technical" McCracken's arguments for a piecemeal compromise approach, Moynihan told the president that he faced a decision of political leadership in which the central question was whether he should propose a "genuinely new, unmistakably Nixon, unmistakably needed program." In a June 6 memo Moynihan (1969e) told Nixon:

> ... This Congress is almost certainly going to begin the discussion of a major change in our welfare system. The 1970's will almost certainly see such a change instituted.
>
> *It is open to you to dominate and direct this social transformation.* ...
>
> In September, *President Johnson's* Commission on Income Maintenance will be coming in with a $1.5 million report that will propose a system very much like Family Security, but somewhat broader. ...
>
> Thus I would argue that if you move now, you will dominate the discussion. Congress will be discussing *your* proposal. It hardly matters what final form it takes, or how many times we change our position in the process. The end result—if you wish it to be—will be *your* change.
>
> *Timing is the issue.* I feel—I could be wrong—that this is the moment to seize the initiative. Otherwise I very much fear we will "lose" out in the sense that we sort of lost out on the hunger and malnutrition issue. Although you sent up a magnificent message, you did not get the credit for it that you deserved ... the immediate impression given by the press was that we were simply catching up with the Congress.
>
> *This is a time to be ahead of the Congress and even the country.* For they will follow. This is an idea whose time has come. ...
>
> *A final point.*
>
> I am really pretty discouraged about the budget situation in the coming three to five years. I fear you will have nothing like the options I am sure you hoped for. Even more, I fear that the pressure from Congress will be nigh irresistible to use up what extra resources you have on a sort of ten percent across-the-board increase in all the Great Society programs each year. This is the natural instinct of the Congress, and it is hard for the President to resist.
>
> If your extra money goes down that drain, I fear that in four years' time you really won't have a single distinctive Nixon program to show for it all.
>
> Therefore I am doubly interested in seeing you go up now with a genuinely new, unmistakably Nixon, unmistakably needed program, which would attract the attention of the world, far less the United States. We can afford the Family Security System. Once you have asked for it, you can resist the pressures endlessly to add marginal funds to already doubtful programs.
>
> This way, in 1972 we will have a record of solid, unprecedented accomplishment in a vital area of social policy, and not just an explanation as to how complicated it all was.

Bridge

Shultz delegated to Jerome Rosow, his assistant secretary for policy development and research, the task of evaluating FSS that Nixon had given him. "Just look at everything, particularly the work incentive," Shultz told Rosow, a former official of Esso, who later returned to the corporation.

Rosow and his aides tried to look at the Family Security System from the vantage point of a mother of three children, for whom FSS would provide a guaranteed income of $1,500 a year or $30 a week.* Under FSS's formula they saw that she would lose 50 cents of this payment for every dollar of earnings and so would lose the full $30 if she worked for $60 a week. But they calculated that the job itself would cost her $15 in work expenses and $5 in irregular (and unreported) earnings foregone to work full time. Thus, she would net only $10 a week, 25 cents an hour. They calculated similar job costs for fathers working at low wages.

"The conclusion is," Shultz (1969) reported to the president, "that work at wages of $60 per week ($1.50 per hour) or below produces too little net income and will not sustain the incentive for work."

But Shultz had a remedy. To bolster the work incentive, he said, the first $20 a week in earnings should be excluded when calculating the FSS payment. Then the $60 wage earner would have only $20 (one-half of the $40 left after the $20 exclusion) deducted from the FSS guaranteed payment, and the head of a family of four who earned $60 would get a $10 supplement from the government.

"While the system may appear complicated in Washington we can be sure that the individual will be able to figure it out in actual operation," Shultz told Nixon. "He must, and can, make rational decisions affecting his economic interests. We have seen this happen in industry with complicated piece rate systems where the workers themselves spot errors to which the management was oblivious."

Shultz estimated that his $20-a-week disregard would add $1 billion

* The original FSS design provided $1,350 for a 1-parent family of 4, $1,500 for a 2-parent family; but the Shultz paper assumed $1,500 for all families of 4.

to the cost of FSS, but he added: "It is not a welfare cost, i.e., not a payment for non-workers. Instead, it is a fundamental girder in building a solid bridge from welfare to work. Without this economic support, the bridge may collapse. As workers see earnings disappear with only the work remaining, they may cross back to welfare."

Because his aides and he were ignorant of welfare's complexities, Shultz failed to cite the best possible argument for his earnings disregard. There already existed a welfare-to-work bridge; and, in the form championed by Finch and Moynihan, the Family Security System would destroy it. Unless some version of Shultz's disregard were added, FSS would offer welfare mothers less cash incentive to work than did existing law.

Federal law enacted in the winter of 1967–68 and scheduled to take effect nationwide on July 1, 1969, only three weeks off, required that all states allow welfare mothers to boost family income through work by an amount equal to $30 a month plus one-third of the rest of her earnings plus work expenses. This provision, as was seen in chapter 2, enabled mothers in many states to earn $120 or more weekly without expulsion from welfare. Neither Shultz nor Rosow knew of the existing work-expense disregard. "At the time I thought we were inventing the wheel," Rosow sheepishly confessed afterward.

In asking Shultz to study FSS, Nixon had given him a thick book of memos that constituted the policy debate over welfare reform. But the memos were silent on the issue of the liberality of the work incentive in current law. FSS foes didn't know enough to raise it, and those few welfare experts who were privy to the administration debate, pro-FSS Finch aides at HEW, did not raise the matter because they thought it would jeopardize FSS. To incorporate an equally generous work incentive into FSS would raise the cost of the plan, and they feared that the higher its cost, the less chance that FSS would win Nixon's blessing.

This was another example of the ignorance that afflicted the Nixon administration's efforts to develop welfare reform. But the ignorance probably was constructive, for if the president at the outset had been fully informed, welfare's dilemmas and facts might have deterred him from action.

Shultz's recommendation for a $1 billion revision to FSS was sent with trepidation to the White House.

Opposed to a compulsory work or training requirement, Shultz faced frankly the possibility that FSS's income guarantee might prompt some of its poor beneficiaries to stop working. Even with the $1 billion increase in incentives, Shultz told the president, as many as one-fourth of working poor parents might stop work (moving from low-paid jobs to FSS and then on to training); if so, he said, it could add as much as $600 million to FSS costs.

The next day Finch (1969c) surrendered on the work issue, telling the president that FSS should incorporate Burns' suggestions with regard to training, daycare, and a compulsory work feature. Thus, within a day of each other, Shultz and Finch each proposed a vital amendment to the Family Security System, one to reward voluntary work better, the other to compel work.

Walking past a newsstand on his lunch hour two weeks later, Paul Barton, Labor Department analyst who had served on Rosow's FSS study committee, glanced at a headline in the first edition of the *Evening Star*. It said that the president had rejected the Family Security System. Barton shook his head. Too bad.

5.

DEBATE AND DECISION

"You really think he's going to go through with it?"
—DANIEL P. MOYNIHAN

GETTING WELFARE MOTHERS to work had not been an objective of the original architects of the Family Security System. Democrats Bateman and Lyday assumed that the purpose of supplementing incomes of working poor fathers was twofold: 1) to combat poverty, and 2) to eliminate welfare's destructive incentives. Lyday, the negative income tax purist, was appalled at Shultz's proposal to increase the work incentive by disregarding the first $20 in weekly earnings.

"It was ridiculous," Lyday said later. "It was lousy staff work by Shultz's men. We were dealing with people who already were working. You don't need an earnings disregard for them. If Nixon had an extra billion to spend, it should have been used to raise the guarantee. Shultz just missed the point." *

But with Nixon Shultz hit the mark. Nixon agreed that FSS should try to move welfare mothers into jobs, and he was impressed by Shultz's recital of how, in social engineering, "intended solutions" commonly created "unintended problems." AFDC's help for the fatherless encouraged creation of "fatherless" families; public housing for those with limited income discouraged tenants from earning more; limiting food stamps to those able to afford some minimum food budget denied food to the neediest. FSS must avoid such pitfalls,

---

* However, Milton Friedman (1969, p. 1945), father of the negative income tax (and a friend and university colleague of Shultz) praised the disregard. He said the addition of an initial zero tax bracket was an "excellent idea" that provided maximum incentive where it was most needed and yet raised the breakeven point only modestly.

Shultz said, by appealing to the self-interest of the poor, by rewarding work. Amen, said Nixon.

From the beginning the boldness of FSS's family-income guarantee had appealed to the president, but not its concept of an unconditional guarantee. Nixon felt that the government should help only those able-bodied persons who were willing to work.

Nixon's Secret

In late June the president directed John Ehrlichman to draw up a proposal for Family Security that would both require work, as Burns insisted, and better reward it, as Shultz suggested. ". . . We were sitting around [the White House] on a Saturday afternoon," Ehrlichman said later, "and he [the president] suddenly announced to me: 'I've decided we should try to advance a welfare reform proposal along the lines we've been studying. It will be expensive, but in the long run the present system will be more expensive if we don't change.' "

Because Nixon disliked telling Counselor Burns that his advice had been spurned, his decision would be a closely held secret. With warnings against disclosure, Ehrlichman gave to Edward Morgan, a lawyer on his staff, the task of drafting the legislation; Morgan enlisted "Finch's man," Robert Patricelli, deputy assistant secretary of HEW, and Patricelli was given the help of two bill drafters, Sidney A. Saperstein of HEW and Mary Lawton of the Justice Department. Every morning the three surreptitiously gathered in a room across the hall from Morgan's office in the Executive Office Building next to the White House. Every night their working papers remained behind. "It was very hush-hush, a secret," said Patricelli. "The White House didn't want others to get involved and get their backs up. Three people locked up in a room and not allowed to talk to anyone, going to work out a bill for the working poor!"

Held incommunicado from other policy makers and technicians, how could the three draft the most sweeping change in federal welfare law since it began? This is ridiculous, Patricelli kept telling Morgan.

ABM and FSS

By pressing for a costly antiballistic missile system (ABM), the president had split Republican ranks in the Senate. Unaware of the secret bill drafting and casting about for a new argument for FSS, Moynihan turned his attention to ABM. Nine of the sixteen newest GOP senators probably will vote against ABM, Moynihan advised Nixon, simply because they regard it as a "touchstone for concern about domestic versus defense priorities." In a June 30 memo Moynihan (1969f) suggested that Nixon could win votes for ABM by rushing to Congress "a genuinely historic welfare proposal." In Moynihan's view "no single thing . . . would more counteract" fears that ABM would jeopardize domestic spending.

Thrice in eight days the president had offended GOP liberals, some of them already disturbed by ABM. On June 26, in a naked concession to white supremacy, he asked Congress to let expire a federal requirement that communities with a record of disenfranchising blacks obtain approval of the attorney general before changing voting laws. Two days later Nixon capitulated to demands of medicine's Old Guard that he reject Finch's choice of Dr. John Knowles, director of Massachusetts General Hospital, as his assistant secretary for health. Five days later the administration relaxed federal guidelines for school desegregation.

Liberal Republicans in Congress protested to White House lobbyists, hoping the complaints would reach Nixon's ear. Nixon's chief congressional troubleshooter, the usually jovial Bryce Harlow, was chastened by the onslaught. "I'm told," he reported at a White House staff meeting on the morning of July 7, "that we have veered too much to the right."

By then Nixon already had decided to move to the left by sending the Family Security System to Congress the very next week, as Moynihan had advised. No longer could the decision be hidden from Burns. Crash action was required. Morgan's drafting group would have to be enlarged. A presidential message would have to be written. That afternoon Ehrlichman told a second White House staff meeting that the president had ruled in favor of FSS with a work requirement.

Anderson hurried to tell the bad news to Burns, who began rallying conservative allies to try to overturn the decision.

NIXON'S GUIDELINES

Nathan, Rosow, and Anderson were enlisted to help Patricelli and Morgan draw up the welfare reform bill. This "welfare working group" represented the major points of view about FSS, from the enthusiasm of Finch to the antipathy of Burns, and all relevant agencies, yet the five members were responsible to the president rather than to their Cabinet chiefs. The group lacked anyone technically expert about the negative income tax, and the analysts who had succeeded in getting their concept this far along chafed at their exclusion. Most of the actual drafting fell to HEW welfare bureaucrats.*

After consulting with Nixon and, at Nixon's suggestion, with Shultz, Ehrlichman on July 10 gave the group "rather firm guidelines" for their draft. As *New York Times* reporter Robert B. Semple, Jr. once wrote of Ehrlichman, 43, father of three sons and two daughters, there is something about him "that resembles a stern father." The stern father appeared in the Ehrlichman (1969) guidelines, admonishing the bill drafters: "Children should not just sit around the house since this leads to their becoming non-workers."

The ten guidelines reveal, in Ehrlichman's words, the thrust of the welfare reform that Nixon sought. They follow:

---

* Sidney Saperstein, veteran HEW bill drafter, who had worked on Medicare, Social Security, welfare, and health legislation, said later: "Bob Patricelli was the one who would give us directions. Charley Hawkins and Tom Joe and I and eventually some of the others would realize the implications. . . . From time to time Herb Stein of CEA came; and evenutally Bob Ball came over. . . . It was novel, and it needed help from the experts. Charley Hawkins provided the experience in the welfare end. My feeling was that I wanted to keep it simple." Saperstein said that even four years later he couldn't get over his surprise that "a Republican administration would think of something like that!"

John Price's notes indicate repeated drafts of the legislation: July 25, July 28, August 29, September 16, September 19, September 25, and September 29. In addition, HEW prepared a summary for discussion on August 7. Not until October 2, 1969 did the bill go to Capitol Hill.

Price remarked that the drafting "did not properly reflect the president's aversion to social workers, and his desire that the bill put income and therefore greater independence in the hands of poor people themselves."

1. The system should eliminate social workers' snooping which is essentially berating [*sic*].

2. A work package is necessary.

3. The factor of cost is not as material as the foregoing since the message should make clear that the cost involved is not this year's cost.

4. You should attempt to develop a descriptive name for the program which connotes a strong work element.

5. The program should include a federal floor of income, much work incentive, provisions that if there is an opportunity to work the recipients must work and the scheme must lead the recipient to be better off if in training than if he were idle and better off working than if he were training.

6. The system should provide day care for women with children except in the instance of extremely large families. The message should make clear that day care is a constructive program which contributes in the long run to cure the basic recurring encyclical [sic] problem. Children should not just sit around the house since this leads to their becoming non-workers.

We are committed to a long-run effort to get the amount of welfare down. The younger generation must be kept off welfare.

7. The "first five years of life" program can be shown to have some relationship to this day care operation.

8. We oppose a pure negative tax because it includes no work incentive.*

9. The program with work incentive, job training, etc. is counter-inflationary since it includes the productivity of the population. Putting more people in the work force is anti-inflationary.

10. The system should be explained to the [Congressional] leadership Monday morning [July 14]. It should be announced Monday afternoon and should go to the Hill on Tuesday Noon. Shultz, Finch, Rumsfeld and Moynihan will appear at the television briefing.

NIXON'S RETREAT

Burns now tried desperately to stave off Nixon's public commitment to Family Security. Urging the president to postpone the message, he warned that it would jeopardize extension of the income tax surcharge. Having barely survived its first trip through the House, the tax bill would face another House vote after Senate amendment.

"To get the surtax adopted," Burns reminded Nixon in a July 12 memo, "you have just made a firm commitment to keep the budget down. Can you come forward now, or even in a few weeks, with the costly FSS and still maintain the credibility that the nation ex-

---

* Milton Friedman would have been appalled at this error.

pects from its president and which you have brought so refreshingly to the White House?"

The president's top fiscal officers joined in the effort to block the Monday message. Echoing Burns, Treasury Secretary Kennedy warned Nixon that Republicans and southern Democrats "would feel betrayed" and might turn against the tax bill. Budget director Mayo contributed a gloomy forecast of budgetary red ink. Burns asked in his memo, "Would it be good politics to come out with Shultz's plan?"

The president retreated. No message went to Congress on Monday, July 14. Instead, at Nixon's direction Moynihan appeared before the White House press corps to announce that before Congress recessed (a month away) the president would definitely propose a total change in the welfare system.

Moynihan misled the press by skillfully suggesting that Nixon could choose the Shultz plan without rebuffing Burns. He depicted the welfare debate as shifting from liberal versus conservative (that is, Finch-Moynihan versus Burns) toward a middle-ground compromise. He said a "comprehensive" Shultz plan, which contained features of the other two, had entered the competition.

In the eyes of Arthur Burns, Shultz's plan was no compromise but a more "prodigious" FSS. Its disregard of $20 a week, or $1,040 in annual earnings, would raise income limits for payment eligibility and add to welfare 13 million persons (almost double the seven million estimate that had outraged Burns at Key Biscayne).

On July 14, fighting desperately, Burns (1969b) sent another memo to Nixon. He elaborated on his April 21 plan for revenue sharing conditioned upon state acceptance of minimum welfare standards, and proposed steps to reduce welfare numbers. Urging that the federal government "at least stop encouraging the rise in benefits," Burns proposed that the federal grant be *reduced* as a state's benefit level rose, and he suggested a financial bonus to states that reduced the percentage of children on AFDC rolls.

On July 18 the White House announced that the President would reveal his welfare plan over national television on August 8, after returning from a scheduled global trip. Now, on the eve of Nixon's departure, final decisions were imperative.

Doing the Unthinkable

Nixon came to his daring welfare decision by stages. During the first weeks of his presidency, by mid-February 1969, with the enthusiastic support of Finch and Moynihan, Nixon decided to propose a federal floor under welfare, as recommended by his preinaugural Nathan task force. But conspirators at HEW, arguing that bettering the lot of welfare families would further penalize the work of the able-bodied poor, who were barred from welfare, produced a radically new proposal to extend help to all needy families, broken or intact. When Finch and Moynihan supported, but Burns opposed, the new plan, the president himself examined the argument, becoming the first president to confront a major welfare issue.

Until that Easter weekend at Key Biscayne Burns thought he knew Richard Nixon as well as anyone could. That the president would even entertain the "unthinkable" idea of adding millions to welfare rolls shocked Burns as "counter to everything" he knew about Nixon.

But Nixon saw reason—and bold imagination—on the side of Family Security. Why not utterly repudiate the old Democratic-devised welfare system as socially destructive and unfair? Why not insist that a reformed system reward those who work more than those who could work but don't?

"He wanted a major social program, not a 'me too' Great Society," Assistant HEW Secretary Lewis Butler told the authors later. "It was truly reform, and it fitted his philosophy. It was something exciting."

On these grounds Nixon favored Family Security, but still the plan had to survive political tests to which major presidential proposals are exposed before going to Congress.

First, would the reform damage the interests of powerful groups with a political claim on the president? As a Nixon proposal, the family-income floor passed this test; but had a Democrat occupied the White House, it would have failed. Leaders of organized labor, who exert powerful influence over policies of Democratic administrations in return for their help to the party's presidential candidates, opposed wage supplements for the working poor. They feared that wage supplements would undermine the argument for legislating a higher minimum wage and would undercut wages, thereby reducing unions' bargaining power vis-à-vis employers. "Decent wages are the obligation of the employer, not of the taxpayer," growled George Meany in voicing the AFL-CIO's "vigorous" opposition soon after Nixon advanced his welfare reform. Similarly, Walter Reuther's big independent union declared (Glasser, 1969): "The United Auto Workers is opposed to bringing several million of the working poor into the welfare system."

Second, would Family Security help or hurt the President? Would it be a political plus for Nixon? The bold move would enhance Nixon's image as a leader willing to confront a messy issue and demand the end of old ways. Nixon liked to think of himself as a modern-day Disraeli, a Tory bringing social progress, and Moynihan nurtured this image. FSS offered a dazzling opportunity to win a place in history. It was "a genuinely new, unmistakably Nixon program" that, in the hyperbole of Moynihan, was "likely to reverberate through the society for generations." Although Lyndon Johnson had proclaimed war against poverty, Richard Nixon would be the first president to carry the fight into the home of every poor child.

However Congress reacted, Nixon would gain. If Congress approved his plan, Nixon would be credited with reforming a despised institution; if Congress balked, Nixon would get a political issue. Democrats who controlled Congress would be responsible for perpetuating the welfare mess. Months after his welfare bill went to Congress the President told intimates that the Democrats *must* enact it. "Some people get barely a line in history," he said. "We will get more than that. We are going to get Family Assistance and we don't know whether it will work but we are . . . sure that the present system doesn't work. We will get postal reform. We will get draft reform. We will get something on the environment. Up there on the Hill they are going to try to stick us for all the rest of this year, but they are going to have to give us Family Assistance. If they don't we will kill them with it." (Interview notes, July 6, 1971, with a member of the White House domestic policy staff).

Numerous policy questions faced the bill draftsmen. Ehrlichman's guidelines required a "work package" and day care. Which welfare mothers should be subject to the work-or-train rule? Burns wanted to exempt only mothers with children younger than three. Ehrlichman, to whom Morgan turned for an answer, took the question to Nixon, who accepted Ehrlichman's recommendation to exempt mothers with preschoolers.

Should states that paid AFDC benefits higher than FSS be required to maintain their benefits? The working group couldn't agree. In his second draft of the welfare message White House speechwriter William Safire (1969a) left the matter open with this tentative passage: "Since this proposal takes financial pressure off the states these states will be required to continue to supplement the increased federal contribution so as to maintain the current level of benefits (CHECK FOR POLICY ON 'REQUIRE')."

DISREGARDING SHULTZ

On Tuesday, July 22, 1969, two days after Neil Armstrong's first steps on the moon, President Nixon set out to greet the Apollo crew at their Pacific splashdown. After his hour of celebration with the astronauts Nixon would circle the globe, visiting Communist Rumania and seven other countries. Although Ehrlichman had received medical shots for the twelve-day trip, he changed plans after the date for the welfare speech was fixed and stayed behind "to pull things together."

On Friday, August 1, Ehrlichman would enplane for a rendezvous with Nixon in Bucharest, carrying a welfare plan on which Nixon's speech could be based. In preparation, Ehrlichman summoned the working group to brief him on Thursday at Camp David, the presidential retreat nestled high in the Catoctin Mountain National Park near Thurmont, Maryland, 60 miles north of Washington.

Aware that there could be no turning back from a major welfare declaration on August 8, foes of the family income floor hoped yet to persuade Nixon to confine it to national payment standards for existing welfare recipients. At Camp David, Burns' chief aide, Martin Anderson, the lone FSS foe on the working group, tried to sway Ehrlichman, and through him Nixon, with an impassioned two-hour assault against FSS, illustrated by handmade charts. Anderson's charts, foreshadowing some used with deadly effect by Senate opponents more than a year later, indicated that New York City's AFDC mothers would have no incentive to work if one took into account the effect of earnings on federal and state welfare benefits and on tax liability.

On the other hand, Finch's man, Patricelli, argued that FSS's income guarantees ($1,500 for a destitute family of four) were too low. He urged that the floor be raised to at least $1,750 for a family of four and suggested that the extra cost be offset by lowering Shultz's disregard. What about that kind of straight trade-off, a higher guarantee for a lower disregard, Ehrlichman wanted to know.

"No!" Rosow was emphatic. "Shultz would have a hemorrhage!"

This was an old argument for Morgan's working group, which had joked: Should we approve the "Shultz disregard" or should we "disregard Shultz?" Rosow had preserved this $1 billion feature by warning that Shultz would protest to the president if it were slashed. "It was like pushing a button with Jerry," Patricelli said later. "We used to tease him about the disregard."

That last weekend Burns pressed his attack against FSS in Washington; Rockefeller sought to change it in Albany; and, strolling with Ehrlichman in a garden in Bucharest, capital of Communist Rumania, Nixon made his final decision.

To his rendezvous with the president in Bucharest, Ehrlichman carried a message from Burns, co-signed by Mayo, Kennedy, and McCracken, urging rejection of FSS. But Ehrlichman advised the president to proceed with the bold reform.

"The first thing I said when we met was that the problems were not insurmountable," Ehrlichman recalled. "I told the president that we'd already worked out some of them and I felt the others would be resolved."

The president wondered how FSS would go in the marketplace and how Congress would react. Who's going to be for this? he asked Ehrlichman, as he had often asked himself.

"We sat for a while on a bench and then strolled down to the water as we talked," said Ehrlichman. (Months later Nixon confided to an American audience that in a police state even gardens might be electronically bugged; and four years later, during the Watergate hearings, it was revealed that Nixon himself had secret recording devices, including microphone "bugs," at various places in the White House.) Ehrlichman relayed the argument that the $1,500 floor was

too meager for a family of four with no other income and that the
$1,040 earnings exclusion, accordingly, was too high for families with
wages. Suppose the floor were raised to $1,600, Nixon asked. How
much would the disregard have to be cut to balance the cost? Ehrlichman didn't know, but he would find out. "I was trying to close the
deal right there," Ehrlichman said later. "I went back to my room
and telephoned Morgan."

ROCKEFELLER'S CONTRIBUTION

Ehrlichman's transatlantic phone call found Morgan in the offices of
Governor Nelson Rockefeller at Albany. Morgan couldn't answer
Ehrlichman's question; nor could any of the other Nixon aides in the
room—John Price, Dick Nathan, or Daniel P. Moynihan. Nathan
agreed to get the answer from the Washington computer and relay it
to Ehrlichman the next day.

Rockefeller had invited the Nixon team to hear his complaint that
FSS offered negligible fiscal relief to New York. They met in the
same room where Moynihan, as secretary to Democratic Governor
W. Averell Harriman, had wooed and won Elizabeth Brennan, another Harriman aide, to be his bride. Rockefeller protested that most
of FSS's new federal funds would flow to the South. "It's a southern
strategy," Rockefeller grumbled.

Among liberals this phrase meant appeasement of influential whites
to make them the base of Nixon's southern support. Turning the
phrase upside down, Rockefeller applied it to massive help for
politically impotent southern families, white and black. This was a
"southern strategy" so repellent to the South's power structure that
Dixie congressmen of both parties seven months later voted overwhelmingly against it, even though it would have brought their region
many millions of dollars.

When Nathan observed that New York's state and local governments might save $100 million a year from Family Security, Rocke-
feller pointed to T. Norman Hurd, his budget director, and replied
scornfully, "Why, he *spills* that much on his way to the bank every
morning!"

To give New York more money the governor's secretary suggested that FSS incorporate the principle so often used by the state

legislature to assure each county a sufficient share of a statewide allocation. Why not guarantee every state some minimum savings? Accepting this idea, the Nixon men added to FSS a guarantee that no state would save less than 10 percent nor more than 50 percent. Thus, all states would get dollar relief and none would be absolved from all welfare costs, not even the handful of southern states whose low benefits would be superseded by the FSS floor.

TEACHER LOBBIES PROTÉGÉ

Since the president still was overseas, Burns pushed his anti-FSS campaign with Finch and Shultz, stressing political hazards to Finch and economic dangers to Shultz. Nixon had put Shultz in his Cabinet on the recommendation of Burns, who as chairman of Eisenhower's Council of Economic Advisers, had been impressed by Shultz's performance as one of CEA's senior staff economists. Now in the first big policy dispute of the Nixon administration the tables were turned and teacher lobbied protégé.

Unable to refute Burns' attack on FSS's work incentive, Shultz telephoned Rosow. "I've been talking with Burns all day," Shultz told him. "He's got questions about the work incentive, particularly in New York City. How do we answer him?"

"It's not easy to answer him on New York," Rosow conceded.

"Well, we've got to do it."

Enroute to the United States on Sunday, during a brief stop of Air Force One at Mildenhall Air Force Base, England, Ehrlichman telephoned Nathan and obtained the computer's reply to Nixon's question.

The next morning Ehrlichman summoned the FSS working group to his office in the White House to receive instructions for completing FSS. He told them they would brief the Cabinet on Family Security at Camp David Wednesday before the president unveiled it in his television address Friday.

THE COMPROMISE

Many who attended the meeting with Ehrlichman that Monday were vague later about the details, but Rosow said he never would forget. When he arrived, Rosow was startled to hear the group talking about an FSS floor of $1,600 with an earnings disregard of $500. This was not a cost trade-off! Cutting the disregard more than 50 percent would reduce the total FSS price tag! What was up?

"What?" Rosow almost shouted. "Who said $500?"

"The president," he was told.

"It'll never work!" Rosow was emphatic. "Shultz will never stand for it!"

Five hundred dollars a year wouldn't even cover the cost of going to work, Rosow thought.

"How about $600?" someone suggested.

"No!" said Rosow.

"What about $60 a month, $720 a year?" (The working group earlier had decided that a monthly rather than a weekly figure was needed for administrative ease.)

"That's a nice round figure," Anderson joked.

"Okay," said Rosow.

"Okay," said Ehrlichman.

So it was settled: $1,600 floor, $720 disregard.

Armed with authority from Nixon to work out a compromise acceptable to Shultz, Ehrlichman had used $500 as his initial offer. (Later, administration witnesses would assure Congress that the $720 figure had been carefully calculated on the basis of surveys of work expenses.)

ENTER: AGNEW

That afternoon Vice-President Agnew charged upon the scene with an extraordinary memo for Nixon. Proclaiming himself the president's "principal political representative," the vice-president rejected FSS and asked Nixon to give him the task of working out a better welfare policy, but his memo betrayed that he had not been listening to the welfare debate.

Agnew (1969) inveighed against FSS's help for the "working poor," but gave conditional endorsement to using FSS principles to help poor intact families headed by working fathers. Obviously he failed to realize that the latter families, by agreed-upon definition, were what the welfare debaters meant by "working poor."

Agnew's welfare advice defied ideological classification. He stood to the left of Nixon on compulsory work for welfare mothers but to the right of Burns on minimum welfare standards. Agnew said welfare mothers shouldn't be forced to work because they are "better left with the children," but he wanted to give low-benefit states like Mississippi a five-year no-penalty period for reaching the minimum standard of the Burns plan.

A bit pompously, Agnew said he was distressed by easy acceptance of "fallacious premises" about social problems; yet he neglected to examine his own assumption that "the entire idea" for FSS arose from the violent objections of the working poor to welfare for those slightly poorer. Asserting that FSS aimed to appease these working poor, Agnew reasoned that it was doomed to fail, inasmuch as a new class of disgruntled working poor would be created "just outside the boundaries of federal help," wherever they were drawn.

As we have seen, the idea of FSS came from economists seeking a more rational welfare system. Even after the president proposed it, the working poor never pressed for wage supplements for themselves, perhaps because they were ignorant of the proposal, perhaps because they shunned the stigma of "welfare." Among dozens of congressmen during the first year of debate on the proposal none was found who received a single letter from a potential beneficiary.

"BUT, DAD . . . "

Having assured the president that they shared an "adverse reaction to the professional social-worker philosophy," Agnew, who was to resign the vice-presidency in October 1973, when he was charged with income tax evasion and fined for the offense, argued that welfare clients required more, not less, scrutiny. In contrast, Nixon, attracted by FSS's plan for automated payments, welcomed Moynihan's assurance that FSS would "wipe out" social workers.

To illustrate the social-worker philosophy that he opposed, the vice-president cited the attitude of his oldest daughter, a social worker. When confronted with the finding that rehabilitation was not promoted by greatly increasing the size of welfare payments, Agnew told Nixon, his daughter replied, "But, Dad, they are *happier* with more money."

The vice-president protested simple affidavit applications for welfare: ". . . the liberal community has for years been drumming into every ear the idea that it is mean and wrong to keep a close eye on people who receive assistance. We have fallen into the trap of nodding our heads when this is said. I for one do not believe it."

Agnew predicted that Senate Democratic liberals (none of whom had proposed help for the working poor) would sneer at Nixon's program as stingy and then produce rival plans costing many times as much. "The six billion dollars estimated for the program [the working group estimated the cost at $4 billion] will be greeted on the Hill with shouts of derision, and then liberal Democrats will propose that three or four times that amount be spent. After months of heated oratory, suitably whipped to a froth by the liberal press, the issue will be Nixon's niggardly ideas against the progressive proposals of the Kennedy-Muskie Democrats."*

Agnew concluded by warning: "Finally, Mr. President, as your principal political representative, I cannot overemphasize the danger in the Family Security System as proposed. It will not be a political winner and will not attract low income groups to the Republican philosophy. . . .

"Finally, I would strongly suggest that I be empowered to bring about a conference with key governors and top administration staff people on the subject of welfare before anything goes to the Hill with the imprimatur of the Administration on it."

AVOIDING A DONNYBROOK

Agnew's memo alarmed FSS supporters on the working group. "If Agnew can be that strong, maybe he feels the president hasn't made up his mind," said one.

"Maybe he hasn't."

"We'd better go in there and 'sell.' We'd better go in and fight [at Camp David]."

Ehrlichman had told the working group that the purpose of the meeting was to explain to the Cabinet the president's FSS decision.

* The first Democratic countermeasure, introduced in the Senate in February 1970, four months after Nixon submitted his bill, carried a price tag of more than $20 billion a year. Its sponsor was Sen. Fred Harris, Oklahoma Democrat. Neither Muskie nor Kennedy nor any serious Democratic presidential aspirant was among the bill's six co-sponsors.

"But we weren't sure," Patricelli said later. "If there was overwhelming opposition, the decision could come unstuck."

As the Camp David meeting approached, FSS supporters were apprehensive, but Burns, their leading foe, was disconsolate, for in a long meeting Monday he failed to dissuade the president from proceeding with Family Security.

Late that afternoon a helicopter carried the president from the White House to the seclusion of Camp David, where he would rest from the pomp and strain of foreign travel. Cabinet officers would join him for dinner Tuesday night, stay overnight in guest cabins, and assemble Wednesday morning for the welfare session.

FSS had divided Nixon men into warring camps. Feelings were strong. Seeking to avoid a donnybrook that would leave scars in his Cabinet, the president ordered Finch and Shultz to stay on the sidelines.

"The president asked me, 'You really think this will work?' Finch recounted later. "He said he was going to come on real strong for FSS and that we should stay out of it."

Tuesday night as the Cabinet assembled for predinner drinks in "Aspen," the president's cabin, Commerce Secretary Stans took Finch aside.

"Sorry, Bob," Stans confided, "but I'm going to have to bomb your plan tomorrow."

"Be careful," Finch advised. "It's not *my* plan. It's the president's."

Young Poker Player

At 7:30 the next morning Moynihan, Morgan's briefing team, and other White House staff members gathered at the Pentagon's heliport for the flight to Camp David. Strapped in adjoining seats, Moynihan and Rosow talked over the sound of the rotor blades.

"What's it going to be like?" Rosow asked.

"Well . . . I don't know," said Moynihan, "whether or not it's accepted, it's going to be social history."

Moynihan's seeming detachment annoyed Rosow, who had not worked for weeks on FSS just to provide social history for a chapter

in a Moynihan book. Could Moynihan care so little? Or was he trying
to prepare himself for the worst? Probably, Rosow thought, he's just
as worried as I am.

Rosow reached into his briefcase for tables and charts to show
Moynihan. He had prepared them, Rosow said, to answer the criticisms of Burns.

"You're going to *argue* with Burns?"

"Sure. Why do you think I did all this work?"

"Good," said Moynihan.

Ten weeks earlier Ehrlichman had told Moynihan that the president had tentatively decided in favor of FSS with a work requirement.
A month ago Ehrlichman said the decision was final. Two days ago
the terms of the plan were made final. But for weeks Moynihan could
not be sure.

"For weeks I lived . . . as a person not that certain about his position," Moynihan said later. "I felt like a very young poker player who
has the winning hand, but nobody knows it. But he doesn't know
enough about poker to know for sure that he has the winning hand.
So many persons were acting like I didn't have the winning hand! It
could be because I didn't—and it could be because they didn't know
I had it.

"I had to be nice to everybody, not get anybody mad, be extremely
interested in everybody's alternate proposal. But . . . nobody was
acting like I had the winning hand! I stopped thinking. I froze.
I thought to myself, I'll just hold these cards."

As the helicopter carried him to Camp David," Moynihan said later,
"I *knew* I had the winning hand."

If so, he didn't act like it.

"Moynihan was really uptight," Finch recalled. "Three or four times
he came to me at Camp David and said, 'You really think he's going
to go through with it?' I just kept smiling."

SHANGRI-LA REVISITED

Camp David was once a summer camp for underprivileged girls
from Baltimore. In 1942 President Roosevelt converted the mountain
camp into his "Shangri-la," a secret haven from war worries. In its
peaceful setting, which provided an antidote to Washington's tension,

FDR received war bulletins, wrote speeches, and often mixed drinks for his guests as he regaled them with funny stories.

"Life was very informal," Sam Rosenman (1952, pp. 350–51), FDR aide, wrote of Shangri-la. "There never was any attempt at formal dressing; sports shirts and slacks were the custom. Certainly that was the president's habit—and old slacks his were."

Years afterward President Eisenhower christened it Camp David for his young grandson, who later married President-elect Nixon's daughter, Julie.* On this August morning in 1969, Camp David was no Shangri-la. Posing for the White House camera as the Cabinet session began in "Laurel" cabin, the group looked like a corporate board of directors. All wore business suits and observed their customary seating positions around an oblong table almost too large for the room. Before them were pads of paper, pencils, ashtrays, water carafes, and coffee cups filled from an urn at the end of the room.

Present were secretaries of 11 departments and the undersecretary of the twelfth,† plus Agnew, Burns, Mayo, Moynihan, Rumsfeld, Ehrlichman, Haldeman, the welfare working group, Representative Rogers C. B. Morton, Md., Republican National Committee chairman; and White House staffers.

Martin Anderson, who had attacked FSS in the same cabin six days earlier, chose a back seat so far from Burns that he couldn't pass notes to his chief. Was that an omen? Rosow wondered. Did Anderson think his battle was lost?

Opening the meeting, the president said its purpose was to brief the Cabinet on a proposal; he did not identify it as a presidential decision.

Alloted a total of 45 minutes, the four speakers had to be concise. Morgan cited general advantages of FSS and then called on Patricelli to explain its principles. The president soon interrupted.

"Just a minute," Nixon said. "You're going to tell us what's wrong with current welfare?"

* Nixon's other daughter, Tricia, used Camp David as her honeymoon hideaway after her June 1971 wedding to Edward Cox.

† Secretary of State William P. Rogers was in Indonesia and his stand-in was Undersecretary Elliot L. Richardson, who 10 months later was to replace Finch as HEW Secretary and thereupon assume the role of chief administration lobbyist for welfare reform.

"Yes, Mr. President," said Patricelli, "as I go through the charts [on FSS] I will explain how the present system works."

"Fine."

Patricelli told how Family Security would extend welfare eligibility to intact families headed by fathers working full time at low wages.

"Aren't we doing that because present welfare really breaks up the family?" Nixon asked.

"Yes, Mr. President."

"Tell us," Nixon asked, "how the present system works."

Now it was a presidential command. Drawing upon memory and some notes scribbled in the helicopter, and discarding his tight time limit, Patricelli, 29, for twenty minutes discussed, analyzed, illustrated the irrational hodgepodge of federal-state welfare. Midway through Patricelli's extemporaneous presentation the president turned toward Defense Secretary Laird and asked: "How do you get to be that smart?"

A CLEVER FINESSE

When someone asked the troubling question of how the program would function in New York City, Rosow was ready with a clever finesse. "This is a national program, and we can't base it on New York City," he said.

"Thank God!" exclaimed Nixon.

Ending the briefing, Nathan told of the plans for administration and gave the working group's cost estimates.

Now the president drew out his Cabinet, asking, "What do you think?"

All but a few were opposed, or skeptical, shocked, or silent. The most passionate foes were Mayo, who protested the dollar cost, and Agnew, who protested the political cost.

"You shouldn't just hand people things," said Romney. "The least effective way to help people is just to give them something . . . Once you get these people on the rolls, you'll never get them off."

Family Security would add to inflationary pressures that already had thwarted his housing goals by pushing up interest rates, Romney protested. The president insisted that wasn't so, arguing that the cost of welfare would continue to rise without reform.

Discouraged by the knowledge that the president already had ruled against him, Burns puffed on his pipe and once more explained why the president should not embrace FSS.

"If I had thought there was *no* chance I wouldn't have argued at all," Burns said later. "I don't talk for the record or just to hear myself talk. I thought perhaps there was one chance in one hundred ... My frame of mind was not that I could fight with great energy."

CHALLENGING THE BOSS

What Burns lacked in fighting energy was oversupplied by Robert Mayo. Eight months earlier, when Nixon picked banker Mayo to be his budget director, Lee M. Cohn, reporter for the *Washington Evening Star*, quoted the appraisal of an unidentified fellow banker: "Without belittling his judgment, he [Mayo] is not the sort of guy who stands around and argues with the boss or tries to change his mind." The obedient Mayo known to the banker disappeared in the Budget Bureau. When charged with defending the United States Budget, Robert Mayo became an argumentative watchdog. Already he had vetoed costly projects of his Cabinet colleagues, and now at Camp David he tried to veto a presidential project. Mayo implored the president not to undertake Family Security. The president replied to each of his arguments. Mayo repeated his case. Again the president answered. It was getting embarrassing. Treasury Secretary Kennedy, Mayo's former superior at the Continental Illinois National Bank and Trust Co., Chicago, signaled Mayo to shut up. But Mayo, his knuckles whitened from strain, pressed on a third time. The new budget, he said, would be unbalanced despite cutbacks in Vietnam War spending.

"You don't know all I know about Vietnam," said Nixon.

Mayo fell silent, chastened at last. A moment earlier, H. R. (Bob) Haldeman, the president's chief of staff, had whispered to a colleague, "If he [Mayo] makes that speech once more, he ought to be fired!"

(Ten months later when Mayo's budget bureau was expanded into the Office of Management and Budget, the president, to Mayo's chagrin, selected Shultz, not Mayo, to direct it. Explaining his choice of Shultz, Nixon said simply, "We track well together." Mayo went back to banking.)

FSS would help poor blacks and poor whites, who weren't likely to vote for Nixon. Someone raised the problem: "Who are we going to get with this?"

"We're doing it because we can't go on with the present system," Nixon said. He added that the only alternatives offered were proposals to patch up the present system, and "I am not for improving the present system."

How could the president be sure FSS would work?

He couldn't, but the present system was a social disaster, and "I'm not going to take one more step down that road."

At first eager for the debate, Nixon had tired of the repetitive discussion, and so he had rendered his judgment. It was settled.

To general astonishment the vice-president chose this moment, when the president was clearly committed, to attack. Either he hadn't paid attention or his outburst was pure dramatics.

It would be a political tragedy to go forward with Family Security, Agnew said. Conservatives would assail it as a guaranteed income. Democrats would ridicule it as a pittance. Workers would be turned into loafers. The poor would give no thanks to Nixon. And no votes.

Pulling his chair up and putting his palms on the table, the president repeated: "We don't know whether this will work, but we can't go on with the present system."

"IF THERE'S A TIE . . ."

Laird broke the tension. "This name, Family Security System, sounds New Dealish to me," he said, "I think we should get a new name."

The president nodded agreement. To this indictment all could consent. The name was bad. Four weeks earlier Ehrlichman had asked the working group to develop a name that "connoted" work. Speechwriter Safire, who later became a syndicated columnist, liked "workfare," but the working group unanimously had voted against it.

Now pencils came out, and Nixon men jotted down alternatives.

But the group broke for lunch without agreeing on a title for the welfare reform.

Looking for a souvenir, Moynihan asked speechwriter James Keogh for the paper on which Nixon had written his idea. "I thought it would be nice to have, but Keogh wouldn't give it to me," he said later.

Because he had to preside that afternoon over Senate votes on ABM, Agnew was first to leave the luncheon table. If there were a tie, he would cast his first vote in the U.S. Senate. On a tie vote anti-ABM forces would lose, but Nixon wanted the psychological value of a numerical victory.

"I guess we can count on your vote," said the president to his vice-president.

"Mr. President," said Agnew, "if there's a tie I may call you to see if you've changed your mind about FSS!" There was laughter at Agnew's parting shot.

(One of the anti-ABM amendments received a tie vote, which Agnew broke so that Nixon's ABM scored a clear victory.)

Not only had Budget Director Mayo failed to stop FSS from invading the budget, but he feared that supporters of the SST supersonic airliner also would raid the Treasury for huge funds.

Despairing and frustrated, spurned by the president, Mayo muttered to a luncheon companion: "I'd like to take the FSS and the SST and put them together and FSSSST! Send them both to the moon!"

6.

COVERUP OF AN INCOME GUARANTEE

"It sounds sort of blah"
—R. NIXON

UNLIKE A ROSE, which by any other name would smell as sweet, Nixon's welfare plan by some other name might smell less sour. Its New Dealish fragrance had aroused Nixon men to kill the title, "Family Security System," on Wednesday at Camp David; now the president groped for a more appealing name.

Martin Anderson, who believed in calling a spade a spade, had properly identified the plan as a "negative income tax," but assistant HEW secretary Lewis Butler had promptly banished that "red flag."

Nixon's welfare reform remained nameless on Thursday, August 7, 1969, forcing speech writer Bill Safire to refer indecisively to it as "Family/Work/Security" in a fresh draft of the next night's presidential speech.

During a slide presentation of the welfare plan on Friday afternoon to a score of high-level Negro government officials, Mr. Nixon unexpectedly entered the darkened office of Edward Morgan. Because the slides still were labeled "Family Security System," Morgan was embarrassed; but the president observed that the name didn't really matter. He appealed to the black officials to support his reform and told them that he hadn't put it to a Cabinet vote because a majority opposed it.

"I don't like to take a vote unless I know I'm going to win," he joked, quickly adding, to avoid misunderstanding, that his no-vote policy applied only to the Cabinet, not to the general electorate.

Although several references to "family assistance" appeared in the text of Nixon's speech, distributed to newsmen on Friday afternoon, officials cautioned that the plan was yet to be named. "Guys all over the government were trying to come up with a name," Butler said later.

Several hours before the president's 10 P.M. televised speech, Finch sat in his office brainstorming with two aides, Butler and Chuck Lichenstein. Several times Finch picked up his white phone, linked directly to the White House, to offer a suggestion: How about this? What do you think of that?

What about Family Assistance System?

"Shay," Lichenstein told Finch, mocking the sibilants in the phrase, "that's a great name—Family Ashshish-tansh Shish-tem!"

Satire had enlivened John Brandl's "Christian Working Man's Anti-Communist National Defense Rivers and Harbors Act of 1969." Social vision had elevated Bill Robinson's "Family Security System." The work ethic was honored in Sargent Shriver's 1968 expedient title, "Graduated Work Incentive Program."

But neither satire nor social vision nor work ethic enriched "Family Assistance Plan," which by default became the title of Nixon's revolutionary plan to guarantee an income to all families with children. This was a rare instance of undernaming a legislative proposal. The sterile phrase denoted mere "assistance," not daring the promise of "security." Further, the acronym, FAP, invited ridicule from critics like Senator Russell Long, who snorted: "FAP is a Flop!" and from the National Welfare Rights Organization, a welfare client group which was to urge "Zap FAP!" after turning against the plan.

Weeks later, after "family assistance" had been committed to draft legislation, the president confided to White House aides that he didn't like the name.

"It sounds sort of blah," Nixon said.

Two Speeches

On the night of August 8, 1968, Richard Nixon grinned and lifted his arms above his head to acknowledge the applause that swept Convention Hall at Miami Beach. Defeated for the presidency in 1960, defeated for governor of California in 1962 and pronounced politically dead by pundits, Nixon had fought back to win again his party's presidential nomination.

In an acceptance speech that touched on many topics, the nominee spoke compassionately of those American children living in a " . . . nightmare—poverty, neglect, despair." But he also said:

> I say it's time to quit pouring billions of dollars into programs that have failed . . . Let us increase the wealth of America so that we can provide more generously for the aged, for the needy and for all those who cannot help themselves.
>
> But for those who are able to help themselves, *what we need are not more millions on welfare rolls, but more millions on payrolls.* (italics added).

The convention delegates roared approval. Candidate Nixon liked that line; it was a real applause-grabber!

Now one year later to the very night President Nixon sat before television cameras in a quiet room of the White House to announce his blueprint for welfare reform to his countrymen.

How would he tell the voters that his plan would more than double the number of families eligible for welfare? How could he tell them it would make 12.4 million additional persons, parents and children, eligible for cash benefits?

The answer is he didn't.

Aware that the vast scope of the plan could anger and repel tax-payers already resentful of welfare's size and cost, and determined that his idea should at least get a fair hearing, the president tried to sell his concept of a family-income floor as a moral abstraction, without dimension.

Soon enough, in the morning newspaper, the voters would learn the vast numbers of poor persons to be offered cash help. It was not a secret. In response to a question at a press briefing, White House officials had given the estimates.

But Nixon knew that first impressions can be crucial. For its first exposure to the American public, Nixon cloaked the family-income guarantee in conservative rhetoric. He told his audience that he had devised a proposal to reinforce America's work ethic.

Fashioning a variant of Candidate Nixon's favorite welfare line,

President Nixon told the nation (1969a, p. 12): "What America needs is not more welfare but more workfare."

This clever sentence, applauded in living rooms that night and in newspaper editorials that weekend, made it appear that "welfare" and "workfare" were mutually exclusive. The sentence implied that a family got its living either from welfare or from work. The truth, of course, was that FAP's workfare was a blend of work plus welfare, of pay check plus a reduced relief check. So by definition, more "workfare" meant more "welfare."

Nixon wrote "workfare" three times into the seventh draft of the speech, but used it only once in the televised broadcast. Even so, the idea of workfare triumphed as the theme of his reform. Sixty times in the 35-minute speech he spoke the words "work," "jobs," or words rooted in "work."

One of the most widely quoted sentences (Safire b, p. 7) of the speech was inserted by Nixon himself, in his handwriting, to summarize its moral theme: "To put it bluntly and simply any system which makes it more profitable for a man not to work than to work, and which encourages a man to desert his family, is wrong and indefensible."

Wrong. Indefensible. Unfair. To working poor, to taxpayer, to recipient. In Nixon's speech this moral idea was subordinate only to that of workfare, which, in turn, was presented as the way to make things right for working poor, for taxpayer, for recipient.

The president led the audience to his conclusion that AFDC must be "done away with completely" by cataloging its sins: "It breaks up homes. It often penalizes work. It robs recipients of dignity. And it grows."

Then, one-third of the way through his speech, in a 31-word declaration of a new right for American children, he proposed his alternative:

> I propose that the federal government build a foundation under the income of every American family with dependent children that cannot care for itself—wherever in America that family may live.

He elaborated:

> For a family of four now on welfare, with no outside income, the basic Federal payment would be $1,600 a year. States could add to that amount

and most would do so. In no case would anyone's present level of benefits be lowered. At the same time, this foundation would be one on which the family itself could build. Outside earnings would be encouraged, not discouraged. The new worker could keep the first $60 a month of outside earnings with no reduction in his benefits, and beyond that his benefits would be reduced by only 50 cents for each dollar earned.

By the same token, a family head already employed at low wages could get a family assistance payment; those who work would no longer be discriminated against. A family of five in which the father earns $2,000 a year—which is the hard fact of life for many families—would get family assistance payments of $1,260 for a total income of $3,260. A family of seven earning $3,000 a year would have its income raised to $4,360.

Thus, for the first time, government would recognize that it has no less of an obligation to the working poor than to the non-working poor; and for the first time, benefits would be scaled in such a way that it would always pay to work.

Because all able-bodied heads of recipient families, except mothers of preschool children, would be required to "accept work or training," Nixon insisted that this plan was not a "guaranteed income."

He exaggerated the force of the work rule, failing to concede what the eventual draft of legislation made clear: that if an able-bodied parent refused to accept work or training, only the parent's payment would be withheld. Thus, for all children the federal floor of FAP would be an unconditional guaranteed income, standard across the nation.

AFDC then was providing no help to 65 percent of the nation's poor children; Nixon's plan would almost triple the number aided, covering all poor children. AFDC's income guarantees went only to broken families (and, in about half the states, to intact families with unemployed fathers) at payment levels and eligibility terms that fluctuated widely among states.

However, for the needy aged, blind, and disabled, Nixon proposed only a federally prescribed income floor, paid in part with state funds. His August 8, 1969, television speech on welfare reform, which proposed also a comprehensive manpower program, a revamping of the Office of Economic Opportunity, and "a start" on sharing federal tax revenue with the states, gave but one sentence to these beneficiaries of state welfare programs: "Under this plan, the so-called 'adult categories' of aid—aid to the aged, the blind and disabled—would be continued, and a national minimum standard for benefits would be set, with the Federal Government contributing to its cost and also sharing the cost of additional State payments * above that amount" (Nixon 1969a, p. 3).

Thus, Nixon proposed to leave these welfare programs under state rules of eligibility and state administration. (However, the initial draft legislation to implement the welfare reform message prohibited states from imposing a lien against the property of adult welfare recipients and from requiring adult children to contribute to the financial support of their needy parents—provisions inserted by Tom Joe.)

DOING "AWAY" WITH AFDC!

The president told the nationwide TV audience that AFDC would be "done away with completely." However, three paragraphs later (1969a, p. 3) he made a contrary pledge (which had been added to the speech at the eleventh hour): "In no case would anyone's present level of benefits be lowered."

As explained at the press briefing and as the congressional welfare message three days later made explicit, those eleven words meant that the states that paid AFDC benefits higher than those of FAP would be required to supplement FAP to maintain the higher payments for AFDC families. Nixon erroneously said there were thirty such states, but actually there were forty-two. His error occurred because his staff aides were comparing apples with oranges—FAP's income *guarantees* with AFDC's *average* payments. (For a discussion of the irrelevancy of these averages, see chapter 2.)

Thus, Nixon decreed the abolition of AFDC but pledged to require states to preserve its benefits in forty-two states! This contradiction mirrored the dilemma that lay at the heart of FAP, the conflict of

* Bernard F. Hillenbrand (1969, p. 698), executive director, National Association of Counties, complained in writing to the House Ways and Means Committee that the president's message failed to recognize the "county crisis" in welfare. More than half the nation's welfare recipients were enrolled in county-operated programs, and local funds paid about one-eighth of total cash welfare costs, including administration. "We were, in the President's message, the Invisible County," said Hillenbrand.

work incentives and adequacy. In the ensuing congressional fight it became a key issue of debate.

The issue was first debated briefly but intensely during FAP's birth in late February at the Department of Health, Education, and Welfare. Negative income tax advocates Worth Bateman and James Lyday argued on grounds of equity for giving welfare to the working poor on terms to preserve work incentives (i.e., guarantee 50 percent below "need" and a 50 percent marginal tax on earnings); but welfare expert Tom Joe, concerned for adequacy, protested that Bateman-Lyday's low-level negative income tax plan jeopardized higher benefits already received by most AFDC families.

"Extending help to the working poor was in theory a good thing to do," Tom Joe said later. "But it didn't confront the issues of AFDC. We were dealing with an established group, growing out of control, a messy program. An overwhelming number of AFDC mothers were not working, and couldn't respond to work incentives and, as a matter of policy, we probably wouldn't want them to respond."

From February until Nixon's speech on August 8, 1969, while the Nixon team debated the main issue of whether or not to advocate a federal income floor for families, the conflict of work incentives for the employable versus adequacy for the nonemployable lurked, unresolved, beneath the surface, a conflict inherent in any single program to aid *all* needy families.

Proponents of supplemental help for working poor families, proponents of "adequate" help for AFDC families, and proponents of food stamps for all needy families and individuals all pursued separate yet successful strategies, the combined result of which was vastly to enlarge the ultimate proposal for a federal income guarantee to families with children.

In their quest for money to finance a new low-benefit system with work incentives covering all families with children, Bateman and Lyday achieved a conceptual breakthrough; their proposal to cut AFDC loose from federal financing. This idea held political allure: Nixon could reform welfare by abolishing the detested AFDC.

Tom Joe, who wanted to protect the basic state guarantees of poor AFDC families, not the unlimited expense disregard that enabled a few to remain on welfare with high earnings, nevertheless countered with a simple strategy to protect existing AFDC benefits: just to get a commitment that nobody would be hurt, that states would have to maintain their benefits.

Later he explained: "Nobody would be hurt. Just that line. No technical matters. No elaborate theory. Once you put that line in, they were locked in. HEW drafted that line and gave it to Finch to be added to the president's speech. It added a dramatic punch. The guys who cleared it at the White House didn't know what it meant."

As a result, in his nationwide August 8, 1969, address, Nixon made irreconcilable promises—that FAP would reduce no one's benefit, yet would abolish AFDC.

However, when Nixon's FAP legislation finally was sent to Congress in October, it explicitly provided for preservation of AFDC, but financed wholly by states. The bill specified that states whose AFDC programs paid higher benefits than FAP to female-headed families (families without able-bodied fathers at home) must maintain those benefits and also extend the same higher benefits to families headed by unemployed fathers. Only twenty-three states then paid any benefits to families of unemployed fathers. Nixon's original FAP bill envisioned:

—50 states. FAP benefits but no state supplements for families headed by fathers working full time (working poor).
—8 states. FAP benefits but no state supplements for families headed by women and by unemployed fathers.
—42 states. FAP benefits plus state supplements to maintain AFDC levels for families headed by women and by unemployed fathers.

The bill created an incentive in some states for low-paid fathers to quit full-time jobs (eligible for FAP benefit only) and take a part-time job (up to 35 hours so as to remain "unemployed" by definition), thus qualifying for FAP plus state supplementary benefit. This feature, the work of HEW technicians who helped draft the bill, dismayed the analysts who had envisioned a more rational FAP. The bill's preferential treatment of "unemployed" fathers maintained welfare reform's tradition of creating a new inequity in the process of removing an old one. And the original FAP bill somewhat reduced the work incentive for welfare mothers by limiting their allowance for expenses.*

Another Nixon Income Guarantee

Nixon's advocacy of a vastly expanded cash welfare program was radical and unexpected, but his advocacy of an enlarged food stamp program could have been forecast the night of his election. Partisan competition between the Republican White House and the Democratic Congress assured, at last, a major expansion in food stamps, a move that Lyndon Johnson had refused to recommend, despite pleas of his own secretary of Agriculture, Orville Freeman.

No one, however, could have anticipated the bold and innovative form taken by Nixon's food stamp proposal. Instead of proposing simply to give the states and counties more food stamps for distribution to those whom they ruled eligible, in the old fashion of cash welfare, Nixon wound up proposing that food stamps become a form of *national income guarantee*.

Historically the food stamp program had been devised, and primarily operated, for the benefit of the farmer and food industries. Feeding the hungry was incidental to selling surpluses. Indeed, under

* Prevailing law gave AFDC working mothers (and "unemployed" fathers with part-time jobs who managed to get on AFDC-UF, available only in about half the states) full welfare plus the first $30 earned monthly, plus ⅓ of remaining earnings, plus full expenses. The original FAP legislation on mandatory state supplements killed the unlimited expense disregard. It allowed recipients to keep welfare plus the first $60 earned monthly, plus ½ of remaining earnings, up to the FAP eligibility limit; and above it, only 20 cents per earned dollar. So in the 42 FAP-supplementing states, earnings would be subject to the equivalent of a marginal tax rate of 66.7% up to the FAP eligibility limit (50% deducted from FAP benefit and 16.7% from state supplement), and to a tax rate of 80% above the FAP limit.

Herbert Stein, Council of Economic Advisers, complained in a September 2, 1969 memo to Ed Morgan about the pending draft bill. Stein objected to the tax rate, to the large number of matters left for determination by the HEW secretary, to the assets test, and several other provisions. Complaints also were made by McCracken and Rumsfeld. Steve Hess, aide to Moynihan, in a memo to Price, said that Herb Stein has a general worry: "that the bill is being drafted by representatives of the Federal welfare bureaucracy in HEW and amounts to a tacking on to the existing legislation . . . this should have your first priority."

the Roosevelt administration's program (1939–43) free stamps could be used only for foods declared surplus by the Agriculture Department. To make sure that no needy person obtained free any food for which there was consumer demand, free and full-price stamps were printed in different colors, blue and orange. In order to get free blue stamps, good for surplus foods, needy recipients had first to buy regular orange stamps, valid for purchase of nonsurpluses. John F. Kennedy revived food stamps as a small pilot program in eight areas in early 1961; and in August 1964, at the request of Lyndon Johnson, Congress passed the Food Stamp Act. Retaining the FDR aim of expanded food sales, Congress stipulated that the recipient family must pay for its allotment of food stamps the entire sum that it had been spending monthly for food without a subsidy.*

Hunger became a national moral issue one night in May 1968, when a powerful television show by the Columbia Broadcasting System brought into the living rooms of the nation many ill-fed American children, including an infant said to be dying of malnutrition. At the end of "Hunger in America" the images of hungry little faces faded mercifully from television tubes, but their after-images lingered long in the nation's mind.

"I have just put two well-fed children to bed," one distraught mother wrote, ". . . for God's sake, do something about those children!"

By the thousands the letters arrived in Washington, but Lyndon Johnson, a lame duck president, refused to recommend food stamps for new millions. Later that summer the Senate created a select Committee on Nutrition and Human Needs. Chaired by Senator George S. McGovern, South Dakota Democrat who was to oppose Nixon for the presidency in 1972, the committee started public hearings after Nixon's 1968 presidential election. The committee provided a

---

* The Food Stamp Act of 1964 expressly said that for any purpose under federal or state law the bonus value of food stamps was not to be considered income. The bonus value is the redemption value of stamps received in excess of the purchase price paid. In other words, bonus stamps are free. Congress thought of itself as giving *food*, not *money*, to the needy. So it did not integrate this form of aid with cash welfare, but made it an addition. The congressional agriculture committees had jurisdiction over food aid, the tax-writing committees over cash aid.

forum, and a government-paid staff, to promote the antihunger issue. When Nixon was inaugurated, 2.5 million Americans were receiving food stamps, and nationally known Democratic senators, all pressing for a vast food program, seemed to put the Democratic party itself on record against hunger. Nixon was compelled to answer the challenge.

The new Nixon administration quickly drafted a secret plan to offer food stamps to vastly more persons on cheaper terms. The plan was the work of the nutrition subcommittee (a counterpart to the Finch welfare subcommittee) of the President's Council for Urban Affairs. Secretary of Agriculture Hardin, who would have to justify food aid programs to Congress and the public, headed the subcommittee.

In March, Hardin's subcommittee presented its plan to an Urban Affairs Council meeting at the White House, but the group failed to reach a decision. With Finch's support, Hardin pressed for the Family Security System combined with food stamps, but when controversy ensnarled FSS, Hardin argued that the President could not afford to delay action on food stamps.

Arthur Burns opposed both food stamps and FSS. Moynihan wanted to delay the food stamp plan for fear that it might derail FSS. Nixon assured the fretful Hardin that he would propose a large food stamp program. But this would require a new addition to the budget, which, freshly revised, had been submitted to Congress in mid-April. Not wanting to face that, Nixon advised Hardin to wait a while.

McGovern, whose hunger-fighting allies had infiltrated the Nixon camp and knew about the Hardin plan, laid a trap for Nixon. McGovern introduced his own food stamp bill and invited Hardin and Finch to testify. As the date for their appearance neared, a McGovern aide handed a copy of the secret Hardin plan to a newspaper reporter. Disclosure of the Hardin food plan in the Saturday, May 3, 1969, *Washington Post* panicked the administration. Hardin and Finch would be asked why Nixon had failed to approve the plan. What could they say? Did Nixon have less compassion for the hungry than officers of his Cabinet?

On Tuesday, May 6, the day before the scheduled administration testimony, Nixon rushed to Congress a proposal for a huge new food stamp program, saying, "millions of Americans are simply too poor to feed their families properly. . . . Something like the very honor of American democracy is at issue. . . . The moment is at hand to put an end to hunger in America itself for all time."

As usual, the rhetoric of the proposition was extravagant, but this time the substance matched the rhetoric. The president was proposing that the U.S. Treasury offer to help pay the grocery bills of *all* the poor, wherever they lived, subject only to one condition. The offer would not be valid where county governments refused to administer, at their own cost, the all-federally-financed benefit of food stamps. With this exception,* the plan would enable every American individual or family to buy a minimum adequate diet by spending no more than 30 percent of income on food. The cost of the adequate diet was defined as the price of the Agriculture Department's economy diet (then $100 a month for a family of four).

To understand the plan, consider its application to four families of four with varying income if the economy diet cost $1,200:

1. Income of $4,000 annually—family would not qualify for a food subsidy, since 30 percent of $4,000 equals $1,200.

2. Income of $2,000 annually—family would have to pay only $600 (30 percent of income) for $1,200 worth of food. Each month it would receive $100 worth of food stamps for $50.

3. Income of $1,000 annually—family would receive $100 worth of food stamps each month for $25.

4. Income of zero—family would receive $100 worth of food stamps each month free.†

In public affairs the content of a proposal can be less important than the way it is perceived. Sometimes the label is the most important ingredient. The previous summer, at hearings on income maintenance before the Subcommittee on Fiscal Policy of the Joint Economic Committee of Congress, economist James Tobin said that

---

* But before passage the Democratic Congress in December 1970 added another condition—a work requirement for all able-bodied recipients of food stamps (except mothers of dependent children, students, the aged).

† At that time (summer 1969) poorest families in the North (zero income to $19.99 a month) had to pay $2.00 to receive $60 in food stamps; in the South those with monthly income below $30 had to pay $2.00 to receive $58 in stamps. Northern families with income between $420 and $450 could buy $124 worth of stamps for $100.

more than 1,200 economists had signed a statement about income maintenance that he had helped to sponsor, in sympathy with the Poor People's Campaign. The mass statement urged Congress to enact a system of income guarantees and supplements of the sort roughly described as a negative income tax.

"I think you need a new name," Senator William Proxmire, (1968, p. 297) Wisconsin Democrat, told Tobin. "It [negative income tax] has a nice, pure, clean arithmetic appeal—I can understand how 1,200 economists are for it, but it would be hard to find 1,200 other people for it. . . . I don't say this in a trivial or facetious way. I mean it very seriously. These programs depend very greatly on the label that is attached to them."

Now a better name had been found: Abolish hunger! For what the Nixon hunger fighters were urging, although they didn't think of it that way, was nothing less than a guaranteed income of the negative income tax variety.

President Nixon's antihunger plan of May 6, 1969, contained the three basic elements of the negative income tax. For a family of four the elements were: an *income guarantee* (the cost of the economy diet) of $1,200 a year; a 30 percent *"tax"* applied to income; and, thus, a *benefit cut-off* of $4,000 in income. The guarantee, of course, would be paid in government food stamps, or "funny money," rather than in cash.

FOOD STAMPS AND FAP

As an optional feature food stamps had been included in the draft of the welfare reform submitted to Nixon at Key Biscayne on April 4 by Finch and Moynihan. When the president, on May 6, rushed his antihunger program to Congress, it appeared to commit the administration to a policy of giving welfare families some aid in the form of food stamps.

However, in a late surprise, Morgan's welfare working group decided otherwise. To cut FAP's cost and to preserve its work incentive, the group eliminated food stamps from FAP. (If food stamps were continued, a working-poor family would lose about 65 cents for every dollar earned—50 cents in cash and 15 cents in food benefits;

with food stamps eliminated, the family would keep one-half of earnings.) The verdict was reached in a political vacuum. Agriculture Secretary Hardin, who understood the political urgency of a generous food subsidy, wasn't represented on the welfare working group that drafted FAP.

The president's speech was silent on food aid, but at the press briefing Washington newsman Nick Kotz asked if families drawing cash under the new welfare system would remain eligible for food stamps. Dick Nathan said no. Kotz, who was writing a book about hunger, *Let Them Eat Promises,* then asked if some families might suffer a cut in aid under the President's plan. The answer obviously was yes, since most AFDC families would get no greater cash benefit and at least some of them, under the old system, were getting food stamps as well as cash.

Intervening to block that line of questioning, Moynihan assured the press briefing that it would be arranged that nobody would be hurt. Afterward Moynihan raised the problem with Ehrlichman, who accepted Moynihan's recommendation and wrote Morgan the next day: "The question has been asked as to whether the present welfare recipients who receive food stamps in addition to AFDC payments might not receive less total aid under the Family Assistance Program. (There being no food stamps under FAP). The answer is yes, they could. However, we will ensure that no such situations actually arise. Individuals will be 'held harmless,' as it were."

In a special message outlining his welfare reform to Congress three days later, on August 11, 1969, Mr. Nixon said that for needy persons ineligible for FAP (married couples without children and single adults neither handicapped nor aged) food stamps "would continue to be available up to $300 per year per person," according to his May message on food needs.

"For dependent families," Nixon said (1969b, p. 4), "there will be an orderly substitution of food stamps by the new direct monetary payments." Immediately Senator George McGovern and antihunger lobbyists accused him of having reneged on his own May 6 program to fight hunger.

Under attack, the administration soon changed its position and asserted that recipients of FAP cash would remain eligible for food stamps after all. At any rate, that was one way, the simplest way, of holding them "harmless."

Thus, within seven and one-half months after taking office, a Republican president had called for two new federal income-guarantee plans, whereas before the nation had none. If Congress enacted both, the food stamp and FAP cash guarantee program together would assure a minimum income of $2,320 for a family of four (provided it lived in a county that distributed the stamps): $1,600 in cash and $720 in food stamps. (A family with zero income of its own would have to pay 30 percent of its FAP cash benefit, $480, to receive food stamps worth $1,200.)

Both guaranteed-income proposals owed their existence to the politics of party competition. The Democratic Congress spurred the Republican president to do what the previous Democratic president had refused to do—advance a bold food plan. The Democratic Congress made it possible for the Republican president to advance a radical cash income-guarantee plan with impunity. If Congress spurned the Family Assistance Plan it would be responsible for perpetuating the discredited welfare system. If it accepted FAP, Nixon would be credited with a dramatic social reform.

(By administrative action President Nixon put into effect much of his food stamp program in December 1969. One year later the 91st Congress, which rejected FAP in its closing hours, at the same time enacted a compromise version of Nixon's food stamp reform. To the distress of Senate liberals, the House added a work requirement for food stamps, but conferees softened it to include a $1.30 hourly wage floor, 30 cents below the regular federal minimum wage. Conferees probably got the idea of the special food stamp minimum wage from abortive negotiations then under way for a special FAP minimum wage, 75 percent of the regular minimum, for jobs otherwise unprotected. Unlike the FAP proposal, the food stamp plan did not provide for payment of *prevailing* wages for jobs that normally paid more than the new special minimum. The new food stamp law required the secretary of Agriculture for the first time to set national eligibility rules. It specified that households should be charged a reasonable investment, but "in no event more than 30 per centum of the household's income," for an allotment of coupons equal to the "cost of a nutritionally adequate diet," adjusted annually * for changes in food prices.)

A Democratic Plan

Moments after the president finished his television and radio presentation of the welfare plan on the night of August 8, 1969, Wilbur J. Cohen, the last Democrat to serve as secretary of HEW, appeared on NBC television.

"Is President Nixon's plan heading in the right direction?" asked NBC newsman Douglas Kiker.

Yes, but . . . summarizes Cohen's reply. Although he used almost 120 words to explain his "yes," none dealt with the goals or philosophy of the Family Assistance Plan. The former HEW secretary offered a supremely simple and unabashedly partisan defense of Nixon's proposal—that it really was a Democratic idea: "Yes, I think it's heading in the right direction because it's adopting most of the ideas that the Democrats have advocated for quite a number of years."

(One Democrat who sat listening in his living room was so infuriated by this response that he said later, "I almost threw my beer can at Cohen's face on the TV set!" The listener was an HEW crusader for the negative income tax, and he had been frustrated by Cohen's rebuffs.)

In an amiable, almost carefree way, Cohen proceeded to remember history the way he wished it had happened:

> Some thirty-five years ago President Roosevelt's committee recommended minimum federal standards in welfare. It was rejected by Congress.
> In 1949 President Truman's administration recommended that all the working poor be included. That was rejected by Congress.
> The matter of incentives was put into the law by Congress a couple of years ago and the day care; so all of the basic ideas that are in President Nixon's proposals are not new ones, and I hope the Republicans will now support what the Democrats have been advocating for quite a number of years.

* The 1973 Agriculture and Consumer Protection Act required *semiannual* adjustments in the food stamp allotment schedule to reflect price changes, starting January 1, 1974. On that date the food stamp guarantee for a family of four without any income rose from $1,392 to $1,704 per year.

Wilbur Cohen magnified the proposals of Franklin D. Roosevelt and Harry S. Truman. As we saw in chapter 2, FDR's original social security bill merely proposed that states be required to set benefits at "reasonable" levels, leaving the term undefined.

If Harry Truman, retired out in Independence, Missouri, were listening to Cohen that August night, he would have been astonished to hear that twenty years earlier he had proposed giving welfare to "all the working poor." At a news conference on February 18, 1949, when questioned about his welfare proposals, President Truman told reporters that he wasn't proposing to give welfare to the *unemployed*, much less the *employed*.

What Truman had proposed was that Congress make funds available to states for aid to any individual the states deemed "needy." In those days a person with a job generally was not considered needy.

Truman's proposal would have authorized the federal government to pay part of the cost of "general assistance," state and local aid provided needy persons who didn't fit federally aided categories. Social Security Commissioner Arthur J. Altmeyer (1949, p. 48) submitted to the House Ways and Means Committee data showing that more than 80 percent of the 400,000 persons then on general assistance were disabled, ill, too old to work but under 65, or needed at home to care for the handicapped. Altmeyer minimized the novelty of the proposal, explicitly denied that any "expansion" in relief was envisioned, and stressed that "positively under no circumstances" would the federal government try to define "need." States would continue to fix eligibility rules and payment levels, he said.

Congress rejected the proposal, but accepted another administration proposal to establish a fourth category for welfare grants, Aid to the Permanently and Totally Disabled,* thus authorizing federal help for state assistance to many needy persons then on general assistance.

Perhaps in 1949, perhaps by hindsight in 1969, Wilbur Cohen saw the potential for welfare expansion implicit in the Truman proposal.

Yes, Cohen approved the direction of the Nixon Family Assistance

---

* Truman also proposed in 1949 the prohibition of residency rules and citizenship requirements for welfare; but Congress rejected these ideas, which, in 1969 and 1971, respectively, were made obligatory by United States Supreme Court decisions.

Plan, but "of course" it did not go far enough: "My major criticism of the plan," Cohen said, "is that the president should have indicated what the future steps ought to be to make it a truly good plan."

Daniel P. Moynihan, who also appeared on the TV program, could not resist a gentle rebuke to Cohen. Nixon that night had moved far beyond any previous president, he said. "Finally a president of the United States has proposed it [national standards]," said Moynihan. "The President of the United States tonight proposed something that no president has ever proposed . . . which is a foundation under the family income of people, of families with dependent children who cannot take care of themselves."

Reaction

Over the years, whenever he made a very important speech, Nixon wanted an immediate sense of the public's reaction. Finch would arrange for some twenty persons, representative of the public—housewives, businessmen, students—to listen to the speech and report their response to it.

Such a group, selected by HEW Undersecretary Veneman, listened to Nixon that night.* When the president telephoned Finch after the speech, he received a very encouraging report: the private poll found "almost overwhelmingly favorable" reaction. These results were confirmed by the initial Gallup poll on FAP, taken on the weekend after the welfare speech, which found that by a margin greater than three to one, favorable opinions about FAP (65 percent) outweighed unfavorable ones (20 percent); and a minority of 15 percent had no opinion.

Finch recalled later that after the program Nixon himself "felt good" about the welfare speech.

At the White House telephone calls and telegrams poured in all weekend. Moynihan remembers: "The fellow who runs the tele-

* Gathered at Jim Lyday's house to watch Nixon's TV speech on August 8, 1969 was another group—most members of the "Thursday" NIT club, along with John Price of the White House, and other staffers of the Office of Economic Opportunity and of the President's Commission on Income Maintenance.

graph office said it was astonishing. On Saturday afternoon he said it was the greatest outpouring ever seen on a domestic statement—running 20 to 1 in favor."

Following up Nixon's August 8 speech, Herbert Klein, White House Director of Communications, arranged for two teams of "traveling salesmen" to campaign for FAP by briefing editorial writers and broadcasters across the nation. Because of the success of this initial sales campaign, Klein later was to model others upon it.

Named to the FAP sales teams were Morgan and Nathan, Rosow and John Price, all of whom had helped develop FAP. Price had written some of the earliest papers on the negative income tax, having edited the young Ripon Society's statements urging a negative income tax "to help the poor" in 1967.*

Saturday noon, before leaving for the western White House, his home at San Clemente, California, Nixon called the four men into his office.

"How does it feel, giving birth to it [FAP]?" he asked the men about to go on the road for Family Assistance.

"Mr. President," said Price, "you make a wonderful midwife!"

"You've done the impossible," Nixon told the group. "Now I want you to see that it passes and that it works."

The following week the two teams visited editorial offices in New York, Chicago, St. Louis, Dallas, Los Angeles, Cleveland, and Detroit; in mid-September they journeyed to other cities; and in late October to still others, in the meantime addressing numerous conventions and meetings.

The Sunday after Nixon's speech brought enthusiastic press comment.

The *Philadelphia Bulletin* said:

> . . . It is hard to challenge Mr. Nixon's finding that it is morally wrong for a family that is working and striving on its own to make ends meet to have to help support anyone who can but will not work.

* Attorney-General John Mitchell dismissed the Ripon Society as "just a bunch of juvenile delinquents" after it criticized the Justice Department's position on a voting rights bill. Later Mitchell greeted the White House aide with: "How is my favorite juvenile delinquent?"

The *Chicago Tribune* agreed:

Mr. Nixon's plan . . . rests on the sound and refreshing principle that no one should receive more for being idle than for working.

The *New York Times* found in Nixon's plan:

. . . elements of two advanced concepts, long pressed by reformers but pushed aside by the Johnson Administration out of concern over both their cost and practicality—namely, the negative income tax and children's allowance.

The *Memphis Commercial Appeal* commended Mr. Nixon:

He owes no political favors to those who would be helped most by his proposals. On the other hand, he risks alienation of some voters who supported him last fall.

Bold, courageous, innovative, said editorial writers in the early weeks following the Nixon speech on FAP. The White House, which compiled and analyzed comment, judged that 95 percent was favorable.

Said the *Suburban List*, Essex Junction, Vermont, on August 14:

Hubert has been out-Humphried and Richard Milhous Nixon did it. We could hardly believe our ears!

The *Detroit Free Press* called it "more radical than virtually anything done by the Johnson administration."

James Reston, *New York Times* columnist, who also saw a radical design beneath the conservative cover, observed on August 10:

A Republican President has condemned the word "welfare," emphasized "work" and "training" as conditions of public assistance . . . but still comes out in the end with a policy of spending more money for relief of more poor people than the welfare state Democrats ever dared to propose in the past. . . .

Now . . . he . . . proposes more welfare, more people on public assistance, which will take more federal funds than any other president in the history of the Republic. . . .

Mr. Nixon has taken a great step forward. He has cloaked a remarkably progressive welfare policy in conservative language . . . He has insisted that poverty in a prosperous country must be eliminated.

That Sunday afternoon, telephoning from San Clemente to talk with Moynihan, Nixon found his urban affairs adviser at the home of Stephen Hess, Moynihan's chief aide. There Moynihan, Hess, and John Price were sharing a feast of clams and beer.

"Do the people still like it?" asked Nixon.

"Like it!" exclaimed Moynihan. "Why, there are more telegrams coming in than at any time since Johnson announced he was quitting!"

Moynihan chatted a while with the exuberant president, then, cupping his hand over the phone, turned to Hess and Price and whispered a report that the president was sipping a martini, sitting in his living room with Mrs. Nixon: "They are euphoric!"

Turning back to the phone, Moynihan advised: "Enjoy it while you can, Mr. President. The criticism will soon start."

7.

RESPONSE: ME FIRST!

"Ech man for him-self"
—GEOFFREY CHAUCER, *The Knight's Tale*

"THE SENATOR hasn't studied it yet, but you can be sure he'll take the liberal position," an aide to Senator Gale W. McGee, Wyoming Democrat, assured the young woman from the League of Women Voters, who had come to the United States Capitol in September 1971 to lobby on behalf of the basic concepts of the embattled Family Assistance Plan.

If not deliberately evasive, the aide's remark betrayed naïveté. There was no "liberal position." Although two years had passed since President Nixon had startled America by urging it to provide a guaranteed income for families with children, and although the House had twice approved the proposal, the Senate never had. Both "liberal" and "conservative" positions were unresolved, and were passionately debated.

By his 35-minute television address on August 8, 1969, Richard Nixon had transformed the idea of federal income guarantees from a professor's daydream into a political possibility, throwing liberal Democrats into embarrassment and conservative Republicans into confusion.

The long fight over the Family Assistance Plan set conservative against conservative and liberal against liberal in an alignment both unusual and unstable. Especially vehement was the struggle among Democratic liberals, accustomed to the fraternal unity of their long march in support of ever greater government efforts to solve social problems. Nixon had proposed unprecedented federal intervention in welfare, advancing far ahead of the goals made explicit or those actually achieved by Franklin Roosevelt's New Deal, Harry Truman's Fair Deal, or Lyndon Johnson's Great Society. Yet some liberals came to denounce the plan and its supporters as immoral and racist.

Professing to speak for *the* poor of America, these liberals joined those conservatives who were demanding defeat of Nixon's welfare reform. Other liberals, stressing the plan's huge benefits for the *poorest* of the poor, while urging passage, also lobbied for more generous terms for *all* the poor, thus frightening both conservatives and "middle-of-the-roaders." This was the position taken by the League of Women Voters.

Between two crucial House votes on the Family Assistance Plan, on April 16, 1970 (H.R. 16311 of the 91st Congress), and on June 22, 1971 (H.R. 1 of the 92d Congress), representatives of one-sixth of the nation's congressional districts switched positions, aye or no, even though the intervening election scarcely altered party holdings of congressional seats.

Should Congress pass FAP? The replies revealed a state of ideological anarchy:

No, said the National Welfare Rights Organization: ". . . an act of political repression. Welfare for state and local governments and ill-fare for poor people." (NWRO's publication, *Welfare Fighter*, February 1971.)

Yes, said the League of Women Voters of the United States: ". . . a significant breakthrough towards . . . equitable and efficient welfare . . ." (Lucy Wilson Benson, president, June 22, 1971.)

No, said a Protestant church leader: ". . . a racist bill." (Cynthia Wedel, President, National Council of Churches, June 1971.)

Yes, said Jewish and Catholic groups: "If you kill it in the House it's the end of welfare reform." (David A. Brody, Washington representative, B'nai Brith, June 1971.) "Rather than . . . no step . . . we'd . . . have the first step taken." (Spokesman for U.S. Catholic Conference, June 1971.)

No, said an arch conservative from Iowa: ". . . this legislation will put a premium on production of more illegitimate children and encourage indolence." (Republican Rep. H. R. Gross, April 16, 1970.)

Yes, said a Republican conservative from Wisconsin: ". . . you now have a guaranteed annual income for idleness. If you pass [FAP] you will have a guaranteed annual income for work." (Rep. John W. Byrnes, April 1970.)

No, said a black congressman from Detroit: ". . . provisions of this bill insult the very people who are supposed to benefit from it." (Democratic Rep. John Conyers, June 22, 1971.)

Yes, said a liberal congresswoman from Detroit: "If I were a poor family in a state tonight that obtained $44 in welfare, I would consider this bill a reform and would curse the man who voted against it." (Democratic Rep. Martha W. Griffiths, June 22, 1971.) (In Mississippi the maximum welfare payment then was $48 a month for a mother and two children; $30 a month for a mother and one child.)

No, said the U.S. Chamber of Commerce: FAP would mean higher taxes and ". . . would triple our welfare rolls. Double our welfare costs." (Full-page newspaper advertisement against FAP, April 1970.)

Yes, said the National Association of Manufacturers: ". . . an opportunity to end the cycle of welfare dependency." (NAM letter to all members of the House, March 1970.)

No, said a black congressman from Baltimore: ". . . most reprehensible piece of social legislation . . . a giant step backward." (Democratic Rep. Parren J. Mitchell, June 18, 1971.)

Yes, said four of South Carolina's black political leaders, all Democrats: ". . . first step in the right direction." (James Felder, Herbert U. Fielding, and I. S. Leevey Johnson, members of the South Carolina state legislature; and James E. Clyburn, assistant to the governor for human resources, in a joint letter to the congressional Black Caucus, June 1971.)

No, said a conservative Pennsylvania Republican: ". . . gigantic giveaway which could further reward the indolent and malcontent." (Rep. Lawrence G. Williams, April 16, 1970.)

Yes, said a national group of educators and business leaders: ". . . a very important first step forward." (Committee for Economic Development, March 1970.)

No, said a liberal Democratic congresswoman from New York City: ". . . strikes out at poor people . . . a thrust backward." (Rep. Bella Abzug, June 22, 1971.)

Yes, said the Rev. Theodore M. Hesburgh, C.S.C., Chairman of the Civil Rights Commission: ". . . this legislation rests on deep moral principles and its enactment will advance this Nation toward the just and decent society for which we all strive." (Dec. 15, 1970, letter to the U.S. Senate.)

Frances Fox Piven and Richard A. Cloward (1971, pp. 344–45), of the Columbia University School of Social Work, who had urged campaigns to double and triple relief rolls to produce pressure for welfare reform, conceded that "at first blush" FAP seemed laudable because of its cash aid for the working poor. But they predicted that once FAP succeeded in "restoring order," the cash supplements would be withdrawn. This accorded with their theory that a capitalist society expands and contracts its welfare rolls "to regulate the poor."

Rarely, if ever, has a proposal met with such misinformed but energetic attack.

Since the debate reduced to near gibberish the terms "liberal" and "conservative," we shall adopt others, separating the protagonists into three groups: reformers, antireformers, and antiwelfarists.

The reformers were the *supporters* of Nixon's plan or of some legislatively viable version of it. Nominally led by the president, this group embraced some liberals, moderates, and conservatives. The group's strategic leadership was furnished by two conservative House members, Representative Wilbur Mills (Arkansas Democrat) and Representative John Byrnes (Wisconsin Republican), and by one liberal senator, Abraham Ribicoff (Connecticut Democrat), a former secretary of the Department of Health, Education, and Welfare; plus a small ad hoc coalition of organizations and individuals who were determined to seize the visionary goal of *federal* help for *all* poor children that Nixon had miraculously brought within reach.

The antiwelfarists were the *conservative foes* of the Family Assistance Plan. They included the U.S. Chamber of Commerce,* the

* To oppose FAP, the U.S. Chamber had to repudiate its own "grass roots poll" of a group of civic and business leaders that it had proudly delivered to the president in late October 1969. "That damn poll!" as it came to be known at the Chamber's offices, one block from the White House, was conducted in autumn 1969 at "urban action forums" sponsored by the Chamber in fifteen cities and attended by representatives of 445 communities from thirty-nine states. The poll

American Conservative Union, and *Human Events,* the weekly publication that by its own description was "biased in favor of limited constitutional government, local self-government, private enterprise and individual freedom."

The antireformers were the *liberal foes* of the Family Assistance Plan. These allies of the antiwelfarists included Americans for Democratic Action, American Friends Service Committee, the National Council of Churches, and black congressmen from the North.

Some conservative antiwelfarists were at first seduced by President Nixon's workfare rhetoric, but when they understood his proposal they recoiled in horror. Five months after Mr. Nixon advanced his plan, newspaper columnist James J. Kilpatrick publicly retracted his initial praise:

> President Nixon served up his welfare proposals last August, wrapped in a package of pretty rhetoric and tied with a bow of conservative blue. Sad to say some of us who should have known better were fairly swept off our feet. I hereby repent. . . .
>
> In his original presentation, which seemed so enchanting at the time, the President bore down heavily on the idea of "workfare" instead of "welfare." One of his conditions was that able-bodied recipients would have to accept suitable jobs, or undergo job training, in order to stay on the rolls.
>
> Well, forgive my disenchantment. Of the 9.6 million persons currently receiving welfare benefits, 4.8 million are children and another 1.5 million are mothers of pre-school children. Take away 2 million aged persons, 728,000 disabled persons, and 80,000 blind—all of them exempt from the Nixon work requirement—and only 500,000 prospects remain for the work-or-starve demand.
>
> Would the new system be effective, even as to them? Not likely. . . .

---

questionnaire stated that Nixon's plan would "help those working full time but who are still poor." The poll found 86.5 percent of the audience in favor of FAP, and one-fifth of these persons attributed their support primarily to its help for the working poor. After the Chamber renounced the poll, it was chided for the retreat by Representative Jackson Betts, Ohio Republican, who supported FAP, in a House floor speech. Milton Davis, general manager of the Chamber for legislative action, replied to Betts in a letter, saying that, at the time of the poll, "the administration's program was not recognized as something that would guarantee an income for many families with fully employed fathers." Don Kendall, president of Pepsi-Cola and a personal friend of Nixon, denounced the U.S. Chamber. In an address to the local chamber of commerce at Whittier, California, Nixon's boyhood home, Kendall declared that the national chamber, by its "shrill opposition" to FAP, had "isolated itself from the main body of business thought."

The professionally indolent already thumb their noses at hundreds of available jobs—behold the help-wanted ads in every major city! . . .

If the Nixon plan were adopted, the present $5 billion in annual federal payments would at least double. . . . Instead of 9.6 million persons on welfare, we would have nearly 22 million. . . . These would be the permanent poor feeding like parasites on the body politic unto the end of time.

Their philosophic bent, their conviction that broader government help would enlarge the ranks of the indolent, made the conservative antiwelfarists, such as columnist Kilpatrick and White House Counselor Arthur Burns, inevitable and logical foes of a family-income floor.

By the reverse token, the philosophic bent of liberals should have delivered them to Mr. Nixon as supporters of the Family Assistance Plan. No liberal could fault the three basic features of the design: 1) a minimum standard of welfare payments (not even attempted by the New Deal!) *; 2) extension of help to all poor families with children, including intact working families (a basic recommendation voiced in November 1969 by the presidential commission on income maintenance appointed by Lyndon Johnson and chaired by Chicago industrialist Ben W. Heineman); and 3) (in its final form) the federal take-over of welfare administration (answering the pleas of black leaders from the South!).

Initially, most liberals gave restrained approval to FAP, conceding it to be a "step in the right direction." But soon that phrase, which acknowledged the basic philosophic advance of FAP, faded from the discussion, along with mention of the working poor; and ultimately a large number of liberals renounced the reform, damning it as an attack on "the poor."

From the beginning many Democratic liberals found it uncomfortable to be associated with President Nixon on a social issue. They were loath to concede to their old enemy the qualities of good will, prudence, and virtue that his guaranteed-income proposal implied— the very qualities that Aristotle deemed essential to the political orator. Unable at first to disavow the sweeping reform itself (for

* John W. Gardner, Wilbur Cohen's predecessor as HEW secretary, praised FAP warmly. In endorsing FAP's help for the working poor, he wistfully said that he would have been "very proud" during his days in LBJ's Cabinet to have established the principle of a national welfare standard.

some of them instinctively felt, as LBJ's last secretary of health, education, and welfare, Wilbur Cohen, had said, that FAP was basically a "Democratic idea" even though no Democratic president had advanced it!), they tried to establish a motivational distance from the Republican who proposed it. Over cocktails, liberals assured one another: "But, of course, Nixon's not *sincere*. He doesn't really mean it!" This foolishness may have helped the liberals' sense of moral superiority, but it was irrelevant to the issue at hand. Would only "sincerely" motivated federal dollars buy shoes and toys for needy children?

In addition to questioning the president's sincerity, many liberals belittled the size of his income guarantee. For a family of four, $1,600 plus about $800 in food stamps was scored as "inadequate," "excessively low"; in the words of Socialist Michael Harrington, such aid would "officially institutionalize poverty."

Was it better to have no floor?

It was demonstrably absurd to allege, as antireformers eventually did, that Nixon's plan would hurt *the* poor. For the Family Assistance Plan would have affected in different ways three separate groups of the poor: 1) intact poor families headed by fathers with full-time jobs, barred from existing federally aided welfare throughout the country because they supported their families, even if their income were less than their families could obtain from welfare if they deserted; 2) the welfare poor of the South, where state-determined payments were low and eligibility rules strict; and 3) the welfare poor of major industrial states of the North and West, where benefits were highest. Primarily in the first category, the working poor, were FAP's millions of new "welfare" recipients so feared by the U.S. Chamber of Commerce; Nixon's FAP would supplement the earnings that confined their children to poverty. To the second group, the South's welfare families, chiefly broken families headed by mothers, would go vastly higher welfare payments; and these higher income thresholds, in turn, would qualify some additional similar families for aid. But to the third group, the welfare poor of the black ghettos of the industrial North, the visible and, in the view of some liberals, the most glamorous poor, would go *no* extra dollars. For this lack alone, they condemned FAP; they argued that a welfare "reform" should, first of all, improve conditions of all those on welfare.

In addition to the sin of omission against the North's welfare mothers, FAP was guilty of a sin of commission: it proposed to subject these mothers to a strict new requirement, enforced by the threat of a cut in their families' welfare check, that they accept work or training once their children were of school age, provided after-school day care were available without cost to them. Although the scarcity of day care assured most mothers immunity against the work rule, its rhetoric was so offensive to some liberals (like columnist Michael Harrington, who called it "demeaning"), that they deemed it grounds enough to oppose the bill to establish a minimum income for all American families.

Initially, Nixon's welfare reform offered AFDC families in the North and West a major concession—a federal guarantee against a reduction in the above-FAP welfare benefits that their states had granted them and could withdraw from them. But when Nixon began retreating from this early promise for maintenance of benefits, once the legislative process exposed its inequity and its difficulties, especially its hindrance to work, the ranks of the antireformers grew. Liberal opposition intensified against the second FAP bill, H.R. 1, which withdrew the original bill's proposed guarantee against cuts in the nation's highest welfare benefits.

Was it liberal to raise income for the poorest families on welfare and for the working poor, supplementing the latter group's wages up to the poverty line for their sized family? No, said the antireformers, not unless at the same time Congress acceded to the demands of leaders of the National Welfare Rights Organization on behalf of the North's black welfare mothers.

In this complex and often shifting situation liberals were tested on their commitment to pragmatic social progress, on their willingness to accept those victories over poverty that were possible. The antireform liberals failed the test.

Three months after President Nixon proposed the family income floor, Hyman Bookbinder, Washington representative of the American Jewish Committee, enthusiastically endorsed the measure and urged liberals not to let the best become "the enemy of the good," that is, not to oppose FAP for its lack of unattainable improvements. Having served for six years in Lyndon Johnson's poverty program and having been an adviser to Hubert H. Humphrey, Nixon's 1968 presidential opponent, Bookbinder (1969, p. 1634) said he was "not the cheerleader for the man who now sits in the White House," but that he felt obliged to say, and was happy to say, that he found Mr. Nixon's recommendations "very, very sound—the basis for the next important round in the development of social welfare legislation."

In the end the antireform liberals scorned the gains that were possible, sacrificing help for millions of America's poorest children in an effort to show that they were, to paraphrase George McGovern, rival to Nixon in the 1972 presidential election, 1,000 percent pure, more loyal than others to *the* poor. Their efforts furthered neither "the good" nor "the best" but instead helped entrench the status quo.

Exposure

Instead of judging the family income floor for its effect on poor families, on or off welfare, in North or South, special interest groups scrutinized the plan through the myopic lenses of self-interest. Labor unions (the AFL-CIO federation and the independent United Auto Workers), welfare workers, and the Southern power structure construed the original FAP bill as a threat to their economic or political status; governors objected that the measure would allocate more new funds to the working poor than to state treasuries assaulted by the rising flood of AFDC families.

At the outset the National Welfare Rights Organization supported passage of a more expansive version, urging Congress to "Up FAP!" But when hope for more generous guarantees dwindled and NWRO sensed that any welfare "reform" might worsen terms of welfare in the North and weaken its own organizing power, it campaigned for outright defeat. It recruited as allies civic and church leaders who were so guilt-stricken over the nation's history of injustice to poor blacks that they dared not question NWRO's judgment. NWRO's assertion that the bill was racist panicked them into automatic enlistment against FAP.

As time passed NWRO grew more vehement. It called FAP "Family Annihilation Plan"; it accused reformers Nixon, Wilbur Mills, and Abraham Ribicoff of conspiring to "starve children." Its monthly publication, *The Welfare Fighter*, in October 1971 printed a cartoon showing two poor charwomen, each in a patched dress. The black scrublady asked the white: "What's that FAP mean?" The white replied: "Fuck America's Poor!"

Presumably the cartoonist's charwomen shared NWRO's sentiments that husbandless mothers should have the right to an "adequate" income from welfare, an attitude that was not held by all charwomen, judging by the testimony of Representative Martha W. Griffiths, Michigan Democrat. Mrs. Griffiths (1968, p. 178) presented the complaints against welfare that had been made to her by some Michigan scrubwomen at a hearing on income maintenance, over which she presided as chairman of the Subcommittee on Fiscal Policy of the Joint Economic Committee.

The Democratic congresswoman said 26 women, black and white, who scrubbed floors for a living, had asked her: "Why should I pay taxes to support an 18-year-old rearing a family of illegitimate children?"

No matter how altruistic the rhetoric, political lobbying usually is motivated by much selfishness. Let us examine, one by one, the responses of organized labor, welfare workers, and the Southern Establishment to the Family Assistance Plan.

Organized Labor

As late as 1932 the American Federation of Labor went on record against enacting a law for unemployment compensation.

In 1937, when President Franklin D. Roosevelt called for a federal minimum wage law, the AFL fought against it.

Thirty-two years later, when another president proposed a different plan to help families of poor workers—government payments to supplement their wages—organized labor again said no. In all cases the same cause was at work: the desire to safeguard the bargaining power of unions.

Samuel Gompers, father of the AFL, had taught that every gain for the workingman should be won in collective bargaining, a doctrine that helped build craft unions. Gompers had warned against a statutory minimum wage on grounds that "the minimum tends to become the maximum."

Accordingly, AFL President William Green threw against FDR's wage-hour bill what Frances Perkins (1946, p. 260), Secretary of Labor, called "the whole weight of his organization," and thus inflicted on Roosevelt in December 1937 his first major legislative defeat in the House. After revisions to mollify the AFL, the measure finally became law the next spring. In her biography, *The Roosevelt I Knew*, Miss Perkins (pp. 265–66) recalled that then "everybody claimed credit for it"—including the AFL and its young rival, the CIO, which had given earlier support. She and the president, however, "always thought we had done it."

Earlier FDR's emergency program of government-made jobs also had encountered opposition from the AFL, which finally acquiesced only after a Wisconsin labor expert produced a faded newspaper clipping that could be interpreted as giving Gompers' blessing to the scheme; the 1898 clipping quoted Gompers as endorsing a "day labor plan" something like FDR's work relief program.

Now, decades later, the federal minimum wage, unemployment compensation, and "public sector" jobs all had long-established tenure as sacred cows of the labor movement.

"We are no Johnny-come-latelies when it comes to fighting poverty," Andrew J. Biemiller (1969, p. 1775), chief Washington lobbyist for the AFL-CIO, told the House Ways and Means Committee at early hearings on the Family Assistance Plan. But the AFL-CIO wanted poverty fought in ways that would increase labor's negotiating strength. Specifically, labor wanted a higher minimum wage so as to jack up the national wage structure; it wanted a government guarantee of jobs for all the unemployed, making the government the "employer of last resort," so as to tighten the job market.

Not only would Nixon's plan have undermined the rationale for both these measures to strengthen wages. Still worse, labor feared that FAP's cash supplements might weaken the existing structure of wages. Thus, opposition of organized labor to FAP was a foregone conclusion and, indeed, had been foreseen by Robert Lampman, professor of economics at the University of Wisconsin, on the basis of the "rivalry" between the minimum wage and income supplementation, even before there was a Family Assistance Plan at the White House.

Seven days after it was unveiled, AFL-CIO President George Meany (1969, p. 2) declared war on President Nixon's plan to reform welfare and help the poor. "The AFL-CIO vigorously opposes the use of federal funds to subsidize the employers of cheap labor," Meany said. In November 1969, United Auto Workers (Glasser, p. 1876) said it was "very unfortunate" that several million people worked all year long and "still didn't have enough income to support their families," but that it opposed FAP. UAW said it feared that the plan would "subsidize sweatshop employers."

As a device to help poor workers, particularly breadwinners with differing family obligations, most economists considered supplementation of low wages superior to the minimum wage, which could be expanded only at the cost of low-skilled jobs. A variety of such schemes for meshing welfare with work through wage supplementation had been advanced, and all of them, including Mr. Nixon's plan, were known to economists as the "negative income tax," a term that economist Milton Friedman had invented to illustrate that the payment of supplements to low-paid workers would be the opposite, or "negative," of extracting income taxes from persons with higher incomes.

One early proponent of the negative income tax, James Tobin, a member of the President's Council of Economic Advisers in the Kennedy administration, who in 1972 served as an economic adviser to the Democratic presidential candidate, Senator George S. McGovern, has described the futility of relying on the minimum wage to combat poverty. Tobin (1968, p. 99) wrote: "An increase in the legal minimum wage seems to many observers the obvious remedy for the inadequate incomes of the working poor. It is not. Employers can be required to pay higher wage rates but not to hire workers on whom they take a loss. The likely result of an increase in the minimum wage is to increase unemployment and involuntary part-time work among the very groups the measure seeks to help."

Almost a quarter-century before Nixon proposed a negative income tax for families, the concept had been endorsed specifically as an *alternative to the minimum wage* by George Stigler, economist then at the University of Minnesota. Stigler (1946, p. 365) wrote that "there is great attractiveness in the proposal to extend the personal income tax, with negative rates, to the lowest income brackets." * Such a measure, he said, could achieve equitable treatment of the poor with a minimum of administrative machinery and also could provide some incentive for a family to work, provided the negative rates were "appropriately graduated." Stigler said this would be a more direct attack on poverty than minimum wage legislation.

The possibility that the minimum wage might eventually be replaced by the wage supplements of a negative income tax—an unspeakable heresy to organized labor—was called to the attention of the White House during the Johnson administration in a secret memo submitted by Sargent Shriver, then chief of LBJ's antipoverty war.

Shriver, in 1966, recommended that President Johnson vastly expand the drive against poverty by embracing a negative income tax plan that would be staged to provide gradually rising minimum income guarantees so that by 1976 all Americans would be guaranteed against "poverty." Once poverty was thus wiped out, Shriver's memo suggested (U.S. OEO, 1966, p. 1), need for the minimum wage would vanish: "Labor will be able to respond to demand without a starvation income. Thus, the market will become more sensitive to the real productivity of the worker."

The story brims with irony. The negative income tax concept that Shriver tried in vain to sell to LBJ as a remedy for *poverty* was accepted as a means of reforming *welfare* by President Nixon, who

* This proposal had been the subject of verbal discussions held by Stigler with his friend, Milton Friedman. Stigler's article was the first published reference to the direct negative income tax. However, essentially the same idea was published by Lady Juliet Rhys-Williams in her 1943 book, *Something To Look Forward To.* Also, Milton Friedman told the authors in 1973 that some time earlier he had come across what was "essentially a negative income tax scale, though with a hundred percent marginal rate," in a footnote in the second edition of a book first published in 1914, *Lectures on the Relation between Law and Public Opinion in England during the Nineteenth Century,* by A. V. Dicey. The footnote (on page xxxiii of the introduction) referred to the Old Age Pensions Act of 1908. "No doubt there are still other precursors," said Friedman.

had no notion of its hidden Democratic origins. Three years later Democratic presidential nominee George McGovern chose as his vice presidential running mate Sargent Shriver, the man who had become the secret godfather to Nixon's FAP by permitting basic research at OEO. A final irony completed the circle on August 29, 1972, eleven weeks before the presidential election, when Candidate McGovern, who earlier had proposed massive help for all the poor, working and non-working, via a yearly grant of $1,000 per person, deleted help for the working poor from his new welfare blueprint.

After the Nixon administration took office, one of the two Democrats who were to draft the Family Assistance Plan challenged past reliance on the minimum wage to help poor workers. In a February 1969 review of welfare issues, Worth Bateman, soon to depart as deputy assistant secretary of health, education, and welfare, said that the minimum wage was an ineffective and counterproductive device against poverty and he suggested that incoming HEW Secretary Robert Finch consider, instead, supplementary payments for the poor who worked. To remove from poverty only those families whose breadwinners labored full time, year round, Bateman noted, the federal minimum wage would have to be raised so high and its coverage expanded so extensively that there would ensue "widespread unemployment and industrial and regional dislocation, with the most severe impact falling on the unskilled (especially Negro youth who can't even get jobs at current minimum wages) and low-wage earners, particularly in the South (occasioning an exodus of migrants to northern states)."

Five months later Paul McCracken (1969b, p. 2), chairman of President Nixon's Council of Economic Advisers, reported in a secret memo to the White House that CEA analysis "quite conclusively demonstrates that the minimum wage has contributed significantly to unemployment among groups about which we have become particularly concerned (i.e., non-white teenage members of the labor force)." Should Nixon go ahead with his proposed Family Assistance Plan, McCracken suggested that it might be "an unusually opportune time" to seek a relaxation of the minimum wage.

Just as FAP's wage supplements threatened the minimum wage, so its minimum income seemed to challenge another labor goal. Under FAP when he could find no work or only part-time work, a family head could turn to the government for a *check*. Organized labor wanted him to be able to turn to the government for a *job*.

Organized labor met the challenge of the Family Assistance Plan by compelling the Nixon administration to change it through amendments that would promote the union goals of a broader minimum wage and public-sector employment.

The story began in the House Ways and Means Committee, where welfare legislation begins its journey through Congress. Because committee hearings produced both liberal complaints that Nixon's Family Assistance Plan offered too little, and conservative attacks that its guaranteed income would erode the work ethic, Chairman Wilbur D. Mills, a seeker of consensus, had misgivings about sending the bill to the House floor. But when he finally realized that support from Mr. Nixon and the GOP leadership would assure House passage, Mills swiftly moved H.R. 16311 through his committee. It was Nixon's bill, and Mills did not want responsibility for blocking it and defending the status quo.

Caught by surprise, the AFL-CIO resigned itself to House passage and when the bill reached the Senate demanded two major changes as the price of its support. Labor bitterly opposed a provision of the House-passed bill that specified that the head of a family receiving FAP benefits could be required, under penalty of benefit reduction, to work at a job not covered by the minimum wage so long as it paid the prevailing wage for that type of work. Whether or not the job were covered by the minimum wage, and irrespective of its prevailing wage, the AFL-CIO insisted that mandated work pay at least the federal minimum (then $1.60 per hour). (At one point the AFL-CIO even insisted that no FAP recipient should be permitted to *volunteer* to work at less than the minimum wage.)

Because it realized that the bill could not pass the Senate over AFL-CIO opposition, the administration retreated from its position that a FAP recipient should fill any available job at its customary wage and agreed to an amendment that would require mandated FAP work to pay at least three-fourths of the federal minimum (making the FAP minimum $1.20 at the time). The administration gave private assurances to conservative Republicans that this was a small concession inasmuch as there were no more than one million jobs that paid less than $1.20 hourly.

In a second concession to labor, the administration dropped its opposition to public-sector jobs, agreeing at first to enlarge the bill to provide 30,000 government-financed jobs, and, finally, 200,000 jobs, for unemployed heads of FAP families. This not only helped placate organized labor, but also made more credible the assertion that FAP would put welfare mothers to work. Earlier this claim had floundered on the question: Where are the jobs?

Welfare Workers

For years it had been dogma in the liberal community that administration of welfare should be transferred from states and counties to the federal government so as to improve treatment of the poor, especially in the Deep South, where blacks often suffered from punitive and racist rulings.

When Nixon first announced the Family Assistance Plan, the White House said the federal income floor would be nationally administered, probably by the highly respected Social Security Administration. At the White House press briefing, Moynihan said flatly, "This system will no longer expose the poor to random, punitive administration of county, state, and local governments."

But in the ensuing struggle to convert Nixon's welfare declaration into a legislative draft, the promise of federal administration was broken. The administration bill that finally went to Congress merely allowed federal administration at the option of each state.

Robert Clark, Mississippi state representative and the only black in the state's legislature, came to Washington to urge Congress to require federal administration of FAP. Clark (1970, p. 1514) said that Mississippi officials denied welfare to anyone "able to walk or crawl" and that if FAP were entrusted to the state, it would do "the very least it can get away with." Clarence Mitchell (1969, p. 834), Washington representative and chief lobbyist for the National Association for the Advancement of Colored People, urged that the bill at least authorize the federal government to take over the administration of the Family Assistance Plan from states that were "unwilling or unable to put it into effect."

Lobbying behind the· scenes for federal administration, Mitchell Ginsberg, welfare chief of New York City, finally won a partial loaf. He persuaded the Ways and Means Committee to put a cash "carrot" in the bill as an inducement to choose federal administration: payment of all administrative costs by the U.S. Treasury.

However, the liberal goal of federal welfare administration was opposed by one predominantly liberal group. It consisted of unionized welfare workers on the payrolls of many northern counties and states and of New York City, who fought FAP because, at worst, it would abolish their jobs and, at best, it would transfer them to the federal payroll, eliminating premium benefits in their union contracts. For instance, as local employees in New York City and in Milwaukee County, Wisconsin, welfare workers had free pensions, free health insurance, and eleven paid holidays; as federal employees they would have to share the cost of their pensions and health insurance and would lose two paid holidays a year. In New York City they would also lose a mini workweek of thirty to thirty-five hours.

As international president of the American Federation of State, County and Municipal Employees (AFL-CIO), the nation's largest union of public employees, (numbering almost one-half million members), Jerry Wurf was spokesman for some 30,000 welfare workers. In July 1970 he sent a representative to a Washington meeting called by liberal groups interested in supporting the Family Assistance Plan.

Afterward one participant reported: "The big thing now is that Wurf's union is opposed to federal administration. Wurf's gal wants to protect the state and local jobs. This puts Jerry's union in the position of hoping that the bill will keep in power the Klan guys who run the program in Mississippi. The AFL-CIO guy put her down. He said the AFL-CIO Council made it clear that it's working for federal administration."

Wurf later protested to the Senate Finance Committee that their transfer to the federal payroll would cut the pay of welfare workers. In New York City, he said, the work week would "leap up" to forty hours. There the regular work week of welfare workers was thirty-five hours, but it annually diminished to thirty hours from mid-June to Labor Day, with the ironic result that the bureaucrats worked less in the summer than some of the "unemployed" fathers to whom they gave AFDC checks. This anomolous situation lasted from February 1969 to October 1971, when HEW Secretary Elliot Richardson reduced the maximum work that could be called unemployment.

Wurf (1970, p. 1684) asked the senators to protect what he frankly called the "vested interests of our union and its members" by revising FAP. Otherwise, he said, FAP should be killed.*

Dixiecrats

In the South, which had been scarred for decades by the nation's worst poverty, the Family Assistance Plan would have fueled an economic and political revolution. Its hundreds of millions of dollars for the welfare poor and the working poor, black and white, would have relieved poverty, forced up wages, and freed many poor blacks from dependence on "the Man." On a new base of economic security—a guaranteed cash income from Washington, paid as a matter of right—the poorest rural blacks could have built new political power. FAP would have accelerated the rise of black government in the hundreds of small towns and dozens of counties with minority white population.

James Jones, young black field coordinator for the Federation of Southern Cooperatives in Atlanta, told *Fortune* Magazine in 1970 (June) that if FAP brought to Dixie's black families its promised income floor, "I know a lot of white people who will get told to go to hell."

FAP was especially a southern measure because poverty so afflicted the region. Here lived one-half of the nation's poor families, fully two-thirds of its poor black families. Here families were larger than average and work opportunities smaller. The Labor Department had

* In a measure enacted on June 30, 1973, Congress directed HEW to give preference to former state welfare employees when recruiting for the new federal income-guarantee program, SSI, to start in 1974.

found that the proportion of Negro workers who had to settle for part-time jobs, low-paid and irregular, was twice as high in Dixie as elsewhere.

Southern conservatives fought to keep the federal government from invading their region with a guaranteed income. By giving cash to some six or seven million more Southerners, chiefly persons in poor working families, Washington would turn workers into welfare parasites, they protested, as Arthur Burns earlier had argued in trying to dissuade Mr. Nixon from the plan.

"There's not going to be anybody left to roll those wheelbarrows and press those shirts," said Representative Phil M. Landrum, Georgia Democrat.

Dixiecrats complained that the Family Assistance Plan, by official estimates of the Nixon administration, would make eligible for welfare cash more than one-third of the people of Mississippi and about one-fifth of the people in Alabama, Arkansas, Georgia, Louisiana, Tennessee, North Carolina, and South Carolina. They were appalled that already almost 6 percent of Southerners were receiving welfare. A welfare reform, they said, should first of all reduce the rolls. But FAP would triple the rolls in Dixie.

Kevin Phillips, conservative columnist, described the fears of many Southerners in July 1970: "Bluntly put, the program [FAP] would strike at the rural social-economic and political power base of Dixie's conservative Democrats." Phillips concluded that poor people "would be better off" under FAP, but that Dixie's middle class "could be badly hurt."

Many white Southerners feared that FAP's guaranteed income would shrink the supply of cheap labor, bankrupt marginal industry, boost the cost of locally produced goods and services, increase taxes, and put more blacks into political office. Like labor leaders and welfare workers, they viewed the Family Assistance Plan as a threat to their own position.

So it was not surprising that congressmen from the eleven states of the Old Confederacy in April 1970 voted against Mr. Nixon's welfare reform by a margin of 79 to 17 (Democrats opposed it 60 to 11 and Republicans 19 to 6). Mills was chagrined that he could persuade no more than 10 fellow Democrats from Dixie (including the easy votes from such liberal urban oases as Tampa, Miami, and New Orleans) to follow his leadership. He attributed this, in part, to an avalanche of anti-FAP literature sent into the region by the U.S. Chamber of Commerce. Had the disputed welfare proposal come from a Democratic president, the margin of southern rejection would have been greater. Party loyalty largely accounted for the six "yes" votes from Republicans, including Representative George Bush, Texas Republican, whose vote soon proved costly to his political ambitions. Later that year Bush was defeated in his campaign for a U.S. Senate seat after his Democratic foe, Lloyd M. Bentsen, just before the election unleashed a statewide publicity barrage aimed at establishing that a vote for Bentsen was a "vote against big welfare" and higher taxes. (After his election defeat Bush was named by President Nixon to be U.S. representative to the United Nations.)

One Bentsen ad, published in the Nacogdoches (Texas) *Daily Sentinel* on October 29 and again on November 2, 1970 declared:

14 Million More
On WELFARE

H.R. 16311, the "Family Assistance Act," which contains the Guaranteed Annual Income provisions, passed the U.S. House of Representatives on April 16, 1970. George Bush was a co-sponsor of this bill and voted YES on its passage. If this bill becomes law it will have the following effects:
—*Double the cost of federal welfare the first year.*
—*Increase the number of people eligible for welfare from 10 million to 24 million.*
—*Substantially increase the tax burden on all taxpayers.*
Lloyd Bentsen opposes this law.
Lloyd Bentsen believes we should take better care of the people who cannot help themselves, and not add millions more to the welfare rolls.

The bill for which Bush had voted called for a cash floor, for a family of four, of $1,600, plus about $800 in food stamps to those in counties offering them. The 1971 bill, H.R. 1, would have set a cash floor of $2,400 and no food stamps.

For those poor Southerners whose counties failed to offer Uncle Sam's food stamps—the number declined sharply during the FAP debate—FAP's income floor represented a huge gain. It was triple the maximum AFDC cash for four persons available in Mississippi and double that in North Carolina and Arkansas.

The work requirement of the Family Assistance Plan that was seen as draconic by liberal defenders of the North's welfare mothers was ridiculed as an ineffective fraud by FAP's conservative foes, particularly in the South.

Even if a job were available and the family breadwinner flatly refused to take it, FAP's guaranteed payments would continue for the family; only that fraction of the family payment alloted to the breadwinner would be subtracted.

Moreover, H.R. 1, the 1971 version of FAP, proposed to allow poor parents, without any penalty, to reject the kind of low-paying job that customarily would be available to them in the South. The initial FAP bill would have permitted assignment of FAP recipients to any job paying the "prevailing wage" and would have permitted states to administer the program. Translated for Mississippi welfare mothers, that would have meant, in the future as in the past, work assignment as maids at pay of $3 or $4 a day, or even less. But the second FAP bill, H.R. 1, mandated federal administration and specified that family heads had the right to decide whether or not to work at less than $1.20 an hour ($9.60 per eight-hour day). They could voluntarily accept, but could not be required to take, a job paying less than three-fourths of the federal minimum wage.

The $1.20 minimum would have become a powerful lever for lifting substandard wages of the South's rural black poor, most of whom had never known wage protection. Under H.R. 1, black fathers would have been guaranteed a federal income for their families whether they worked or not, unless "the Man" chose to pay sharply higher wages for domestics, farm hands, dishwashers, service station helpers, and a host of other jobs not covered by the federal minimum wage.

A father of four working full time at the minimum wage ($1.60 per hour) would get a supplement of $747 to bring his income to the equivalent of $1.97 an hour. Working at $1.20 an hour ($2,400 a year), he would get a supplement of $1,280 to boost his income to the equivalent of $1.84 an hour. And if he were laid off, his income could drop no lower than $2,400, the equivalent of $1.20 an hour.

Thus, FAP would have provided federal insurance to make good part of any losses from economic reprisals that might be inflicted by white employers seeking to discourage blacks from voting in the black-dominated rural areas.

One observer, Steve Van Evera, writing in the fall 1971 issue of *New South*, viewed this reprisal insurance as one of FAP's great promises. It could give black political power "the greatest boost . . . in the rural South since the Voting Rights Act of 1965," Van Evera wrote.

He quoted a white voter-registration worker in the Mississippi Delta as saying that, as matters then stood: "They give the black folks here a choice—a choice between having enough to eat and doing politics. If a black messes with politics around here, he's bound to be off his land with no place to go in a real hurry."

8.

THE KILLING OF
FAMILY ASSISTANCE

"You're a fink if you're for it. You're a fink if you're against it."

—HYMAN BOOKBINDER

SPEAKING for thirty minutes over a national radio hookup on February 23, 1934, U.S. Senator Huey Long, the colorful populist from Louisiana, called on Americans to join his new "Share Our Wealth Society."

Long proposed levying a 100 percent tax on all fortunes of more than $5 million per family and taxing away all family income in excess of $1 million a year. From this revenue (as long as it lasted) the government would provide every family with "enough for a home, an automobile, a radio, and the ordinary conveniences," plus an annual payment of $2,000 to $3,000. "Every Man a King" was the slogan for Long's new society, which soon boasted three million members throughout the nation. An assassin's bullet in September 1935, however, ended Long's life and dream.

By one of the strange ironies of history, it was Huey's son, Russell who, as chairman of the Senate Finance Committee, presided over the death in 1972 of President Nixon's proposal to assure every family of four a minimum income of $2,400 a year.

Russell Long fiercely opposed Mr. Nixon's plan. Chided for being less generous than his father, he grinned and told the authors: "My daddy told me before he died that he wasn't proposing to give anything to a family that didn't work."

Wilbur Mills' Miracle

In December 1969, Representative Wilbur Mills, chairman of the House Ways and Means Committee, which had been studying Mr. Nixon's Family Assistance Plan since it was sent to Congress in October, said that it could not pass. "The public isn't ready for this —and won't be for years," Mills told associates. "The liberals say it's not enough. The conservatives say it's a guaranteed income." *

Yet, with the help of the committee's senior Republican, Representative John Byrnes (Wis.), Mills shepherded FAP safely through the House on April 16, 1970, by a vote of 243 to 155.

In the interim Mills had sweetened the measure, with the consent of Mr. Nixon's HEW undersecretary, John G. Veneman, to make it more alluring. The sweeteners were more cash for governors (the promise of some federal reimbursement for supplementary welfare payments that forty-two states were required to make to FAP's $1,600 cash floor under the 1970 bill) and more cash for welfare adults (increasing to $110 per person—up $20 from the draft bill's proposal—the national minimum payment that states were required to make, largely with federal funds, to needy aged, disabled, and blind persons on their welfare rolls under the bill).

Then, armed with a parliamentary rule against amendments, Mills and Byrnes presented the issue as Family Assistance versus Aid to Families with Dependent Children. Taking the offensive, they argued that those who voted against FAP were guilty of continuing the welfare mess.

Fatal Hearings

This powerful argument on behalf of FAP—that it would abolish AFDC—was muted in the United States Senate. Two public hearings

* Next to Mills in committee Democratic seniority was Representative Hale Boggs (La.), who perished in autumn 1972 on an Alaska plane trip. Boggs felt that the Democratic Congress could not ignore the challenge of FAP. When Mills observed to Boggs in late January 1970 that the committee would never approve anything like FAP, Boggs disagreed. "The votes are here," said Boggs. "If you won't take the bill to the House floor, I will!"

in the Senate in 1970 dealt punishing blows to Mr. Nixon's Family Assistance Plan. One was conducted in spring and summer by the Senate Finance Committee, a body dominated by conservatives and almost void in urban representation.* It called into question the extent to which FAP constituted a "reform" by dramatizing antiwork absurdities of existing social welfare programs that would not be corrected by FAP.

The other, months later, was conducted by the National Welfare Rights Organization, a group organized less than three years earlier to give welfare recipients a lobbying voice, in a Senate hearing room provided by Democrat Senator Eugene J. McCarthy (Minn.). This hearing aroused defense for the welfare status quo.

Having already decided to oppose Mr. Nixon's family income floor, McCarthy was willing to do anything within reason to help NWRO's welfare mothers discredit it in the liberal community. "With the welfare mothers opposing it, it makes it easy to vote against," McCarthy told the authors in November 1970 shortly before he joined conservatives in a vote that buried the bill in committee. (Ironically, McCarthy had been the first national politician to propose an income guarantee—in an April 1968 presidential primary campaign speech.)

NOTCHES

On April 30, 1970, second day of testimony before the Senate Finance Committee, several big charts were trundled into the hearing room. They had been prepared reluctantly by the Department of Health, Education, and Welfare to the specifications of Senator John J. Williams (Del.), senior Republican on the committee, who likewise was determined to discredit FAP.

Soon after the hearing began Williams zeroed in on revelations of the Chicago chart, which purported to show how Mr. Nixon's

* The committee's 7 Republicans all were conservatives (and 6 of them came from sparsely settled states west of the Mississippi). The 7 GOP states holding Finance Committee seats accounted for less than 4 percent of the U.S. population. Three of the committee's 10 Democrats were conservatives from the South whose voting records appealed to the American Conservative Union, an implacable foe of FAP. They were Chairman Long, Harry Byrd, Jr. (Va.), and H. Talmadge (Ga.).

The Chicago Chart

Cash			
Earnings	Zero	$ 720	$5,560
FAP payment	$1,600	1,600	0
State supplement	1,628	1,628	0
In-kind			
Food stamps	408	312	0
Medicaid			
(average vendor payments per family)	789	789	0
Public housing bonus	1,116	1,116	1,116
Taxes			
U.S. income tax	0	0	(–262)
State income tax	0	0	(– 16)
Social security tax	0	(– 37)	(–289)
Total cash and in-kind income	$5,541	$6,128	$6,109

"workfare" plan would affect a welfare mother and three children in that city if they occupied public housing and received food stamps and free medical care. The average "value" of Medicaid benefits for a family of four had been translated into dollars, and Williams insisted on describing all the benefits as "spendable income." He directed his questions (Senate Finance, 1970, p. 278) to Robert Patricelli, deputy assistant secretary of HEW.

WILLIAMS: "If they increase their earnings from $720 to $5,560 under this bill, they have a spendable income of $6,109, or $19 less than they would have if they sit in a rocking chair earning only $720. Is that not correct?"

PATRICELLI: "That is correct, Senator. They would have less if they earned $5,560 than if they earned $720, provided they get public housing, medical payments, and so forth." (In Chicago, he said, only 18 percent of AFDC families lived in public housing.)

WILLIAMS: "They are penalized $19 because they go out and earn $5,560?"

PATRICELLI: "That is correct."

Committee Chairman Russell Long: "How can anybody justify [such] a situation . . . What possible logic is there to it?"

PATRICELLI: "There is none, Senator."

WILLIAMS (pointing to the chart of maximum potential benefits for a Wilmington, Del., mother of three): "He [*sic*] would be better off just to spit in the boss' face to guard against a pay raise." (The correct pronoun was "she," since a Delaware father with a full-time job could get neither Medicaid nor state supplementary welfare cash for his family.)

The Williams charts exposed a crucial aspect of our programs for the poor that Congress had ignored—the notch! The notch is that place in a tax or benefit schedule at which the beneficiary would be ill-advised to earn another dollar because it would cause him a net loss. Treasury and congressional tax staff experts zealously guard against any change in the tax law that would create a notch, and so our income tax schedule has none.

Not so the schedule of benefit programs for the poor. The last $1.50 a month in wages that disqualified a mother from the last $1 in cash welfare would also cost her much more in food stamps ($24 in the fall of 1972) and free medical care for her family (valued conservatively at $40 a month).

Even before the Senate received FAP in summer 1970 Williams asked HEW for charts showing how FAP would mesh with other benefits in four cities (the other two were Phoenix and New York). The former Delaware chicken-feed dealer, who was retiring from the Senate at the end of the session, so little understood the situation that he specified that he wanted "all the notches, the *good* ones as well as the bad."

Pointing out that FAP was innocent of notches, having been drafted so that work always increased income, HEW officials suggested that the senator gather the data about other programs elsewhere (food stamp rules from the Agriculture Department, housing benefit schedules from the Department of Housing and Urban Development).

"No," said the senator. "I want all of it from you, and I want it with the official signature of HEW."

"I was terrified that the charts Williams requested would show horrible things," said Alair Townsend, HEW analyst who helped prepare the charts. (Alair Townsend, who previously served on the staff of the Heineman Commission, later became technical director of the staff of the Subcommittee on Fiscal Policy of the Joint

Economic Committee of Congress, which initiated a study of income transfer programs.)

Drawn to Williams' specifications,* the charts laid bare FAP's contradictory promises. A welfare mother with a job could get a pay raise, yet be worse off because of the sudden end of an in-kind benefit. An intact family could actually be worse off if a father with low earnings worked full time than if he worked only part time' for less income.

Jerome Rosow, assistant labor secretary who had helped to devise FAP, complained later that "it was stupid to give Williams the charts." Rosow said the format demanded by Williams misrepresented the situation and exaggerated benefits. Even though no welfare family in the United States received one dollar in cash from Medicaid or public housing,† the charts assigned dollar values to these benefits, which Williams then triumphantly exhibited as "spendable income."

By his devastating attack, Williams stripped FAP of its legislative rationale. Before noon of the next day the AFDC-expansive version of the Family Assistance Plan was dead. Recessing the hearings indefinitely, Chairman Long declared that his committee would not consider FAP until it was revised so that, in combination with other benefits, increased work would actually produce increased income, as the president had advertised. Stunned by this setback, disheartened

---

* Williams did not understand how welfare was financed. This exchange occurred between him and HEW Undersecretary Veneman at hearings on April 30, 1970 (Senate Finance, p. 285):

Williams: "You pay 50% of the state supplement now?"

Veneman: "Yes."

Williams: "And if the state of New York wanted to give them $10,000 you are obligated to pay half? . . . I just wonder if we should not have the Secretary from the State of New York sitting here. I did not know the State of New York was telling you what you had to do."

Veneman: "They do."

Williams: "That you had to pay 50%?"

Veneman: "In essence that is what happens now under the present law. The State sets grant levels and we match the grants."

† Medicaid payments were made to doctors, pharmacists and hospitals. The Medicaid benefit listed on the charts was the average cost per family of these payments. The public housing bonus also was a bookkeeping figure, the difference between what the family paid the housing authority ($80 for a 3-bedroom apartment on the Chicago chart) and its "market value" (estimated at $173 on the Chicago chart).

Nixon men were compelled to return to the drawing boards.* After the miracle of getting the income guarantee through the conservative Ways and Means Committee (and then the full House), they had expected smooth passage in the more generous Senate. They had forgotten that the bill had to clear the Senate Finance Committee in order to reach the "liberal" Senate, and they neglected relations with that vital group of seventeen men. A committee staff member complained later that HEW was not even returning his phone calls. "We're having trouble getting material from the HEW legislative people," he said.

Hearings resumed July 21, 1970. HEW's new plan, presented by Elliot Richardson, successor to Robert Finch as department secretary, abolished the notches exposed in the April hearings. In doing so, however, the plan eliminated some AFDC benefits (especially for "unemployed" fathers) and so repudiated Nixon's pledge that FAP would harm no AFDC beneficiary.

HEW's new sets of charts showed no sudden deaths of in-kind benefits. Benefits all tapered off with income. (Medicaid was replaced with a proposed family health insurance plan, for which premiums rose gradually with income above the FAP floor.)

No longer did the Chicago mother lose $19 by working her way off welfare. The corollary, however, was that she received *less* from being on welfare. At earnings of $720, for instance, her wages plus welfare benefits totaled $5,340, almost $800 less than on the old charts. Tapering benefits inversely to income had reduced net medical benefits by almost $600 and food stamps by almost $200.

Nimbly shifting their attack to new ground, Senators Long and Williams disparaged the more shallow pitch of incentives in the new notchless design. They complained that HEW had reduced the dollar incentive for an unemployed welfare mother in the four cities to go to work at the minimum wage.

---

* The HEW charts originally supplied to Williams failed to incorporate revisions already planned by the administration to eradicate some benefit notches. Weeks earlier Housing Secretary George Romney had submitted to Congress a plan to abolish the sudden death of housing benefits by setting the rent paid by tenants in federally aided housing at 20% of net income under $3,500 (25% above $3,500). The charts also ignored the Agriculture Department's new notchless food stamp plan.

Like a teacher, Richardson, who in less than two months in his new job had mastered the details of Family Assistance, patiently outlined the dilemmas inherent in welfare—the mathematically incompatible goals of adequate help, strong work incentives, and limited cost. Solving notches had produced the new problem of weakened incentives at lower wage levels, Richardson explained. Drawing arrows on an imaginary blackboard, he showed that this problem could be avoided only by extending the zero-benefit point (the cutoff) to very high income levels, qualifying millions more for help.*

"It is inevitable . . . within the limitation of reasonable cost that there be some compromise between incentives and the number of families covered, and therefore costs," he said (Senate Finance, 1970, p. 502). "It is a question of judgment where you strike this balance."

Richardson hoped to make the Finance Committee confront reality. But his pupils didn't want to learn facts or solve problems. What they said they wanted was magic: a reform measure that automatically increased incentives to work yet did not cost significantly more or make any people worse off than before. When Richardson explained why this couldn't be done, John Williams (Senate Finance, 1970, p. 503) complained that the lesson was "just flowery explanations." The erudite HEW secretary must have been shocked at the failure of the Senate's tax-writing committee to comprehend mathematics.†

Because the revised FAP reneged on the commitment to protect all AFDC recipients, it eased the way for some liberals, loath to be associated with a Nixon initiative, even on behalf of the working poor, to denounce FAP for hurting poor people.

---

* To permit the Chicago mother on the original Williams chart, whose cash and in-kind benefits at zero earnings were $5,541, to retain 50 cents in combined benefits out of each dollar earned, would push the cutoff income to $11,082 (twice the guarantee), *above the U.S. median family income*. Such a scheme would make well over half the nation eligible for full or partial welfare grants from the minority, probably cause massive withdrawals from work, spark an inflation that would erode some of the benefits intended to the poor.

† A Senate Finance Committee member told the authors that Richardson failed to establish a relationship with any senator. "Richardson is the Brahmin," he said. The senator said that Chairman Long had told him he was "disgusted" with Richardson and had said "I'll get that guy if it's the last thing I do."

ZAP FAP!

On the expectation that the Senate would vastly liberalize the measure, NWRO's Washington lobbyists in the spring of 1970 criticized Nixon's original bill, but did not fight against House passage in April. Later, after concluding that any welfare bill that could pass Congress would impose new constraints on AFDC benefits and might contravene some of the rights NWRO claimed for its welfare mothers, NWRO leaders, in the summer of 1970, changed their battle cry. They discarded "Up the Nixon Plan!" in favor of "Zap FAP!"

The poorest of poor American families, scattered over the nation but disproportionately numerous in the South, would be helped—vast numbers for the first time—by FAP's eligibility rules and benefit levels, but NWRO feared that the working poor would be helped at the expense of urban welfare mothers. For AFDC families already receiving benefits higher than FAP's floor, the president's program offered no additional benefits and some disadvantages. Many of these welfare mothers would lose their "right" to refuse to work, a right that had been confirmed by their designation as inappropriate persons for work assignment in New York and most other large northern cities. FAP would make it more difficult to gain benefit increases in the future and would reduce some working mothers' welfare supplements. "The working poor would get money but they'd take it from us," worried Mrs. Jeanette Washington, NWRO representative at an autumn 1970 meeting with liberal groups.

FAP would impede future benefit increases because it would increase their cost to state treasuries.* Under FAP, which proposed to end unlimited federal funding for state welfare, state legislatures would be less likely to grant cost-of-living increases in basic benefit levels, and it would be harder for NWRO to wrest from local wel-

* Whereas, under existing law, it cost no more than 50 cents in nonfederal funds to raise benefits, under the 1970 FAP bill it would have cost 70 cents per dollar up to the poverty line, 100 cents thereafter. The bill provided federal reimbursement of 30% of the cost of supplementary FAP payments so long as the family's total "counted" income did not exceed the poverty line, initially set at $3,720 for a family of four. New Jersey and New York, whose basic income guarantees exceeded the poverty line, would be obliged to maintain those benefits, but would receive *no* federal reimbursement.

fare departments special grants—in excess of regular benefits—for
school clothing, household items, furniture, winter coats, or for whatever special purpose NWRO might campaign. Many NWRO-orga-
nized demonstrations for special grants, like trade union strikes or
demonstrations, had been doubly productive, yielding millions of extra
dollars for needy AFDC families and simultaneously increasing
NWRO membership. Moreover, FAP would reduce welfare supplements for some working mothers, even eliminate them for some,
because it ended the unlimited disregard of income allocated to work
expenses.

The original FAP required maintenance of welfare supplements at
pre-FAP levels by "fill-the-gap" states, which paid AFDC benefits
smaller than full "needs" and allowed recipients to apply all or part
of any earnings to the needs gap (see chapter 2, page 00). But
this provision was scrapped in summer 1970 after it was recognized
that it would have required states *to raise* their supplementary welfare payment when a family's *earnings rose*. This was because
earnings that had caused no reduction in benefits under the state
program would diminish the FAP payment. To offset the FAP cut
the state supplement would have to rise. This paradoxical feature
became known as the bill's "galloping supplemental." NWRO protested that loss of the galloping supplemental would hurt working
welfare mothers in some states, such as Missouri.*

In its efforts to discredit FAP as an attack on the poor, NWRO
tried to convey the impression that every existing welfare benefit
was guaranteed against reduction, that it would be a "giant step
backward" if FAP failed to guarantee all regular and special AFDC
benefits. The truth was that each state controlled its welfare payment
levels and was at liberty to slash them to zero, obliterating AFDC
or federal-state aid to needy adults within its borders.

---

* In June 1970 the Nixon administration submitted a revision of FAP and in
October what the Senate Finance Committee scornfully labeled the "revised revision." The June version withdrew the requirement for galloping supplementals
and also for supplements to unemployed fathers. To protect current beneficiaries
of the higher income disregard in fill-the-gap states and of AFDC-UP, the October
version added grandfather clauses for maintenance of their benefits for 2 years after
the start of FAP.

WHOSE DUTY?

FAP brought to the surface a basic dispute over whose responsibility it was to support children—government or parents. Strongly held convictions of the welfare-paying public conflicted with claims of "welfare rights" asserted by NWRO's mothers. Reduced to fundamentals, NWRO's doctrine of welfare "rights" was that government was obligated to support children—and to support them "adequately"—*at the option* of their poor parents. FAP proposed to limit a father's right to desert,* a mother's right to refuse to work, a *step*father's right to refuse to support his stepchildren.† All these changes angered NWRO.

WANTED: A $10,000 JOB

The unofficial NWRO hearing was conducted November 18 and 19, 1970, by Senator McCarthy.

It was slavery and they would defy it, the welfare mothers testified. Accompanied by neatly dressed children, they jammed hearing room 1202 in the Senate's New Office Building to testify against the work requirement and other provisions of Mr. Nixon's Family Assistance Plan. Dressed in a colorful dashiki, George Wiley, NWRO's executive director, was the master of ceremonies. Senators assembled by McCarthy sat on the dais and listened as Wiley summoned witnesses from his list.

Among the witnesses was Mrs. Ethel Camp from suburban Arlington County, Virginia, who was separated from her husband

* The House Ways and Means Committee wrote a desertion penalty into the original FAP bill: placing a deserting parent in debt for any federal payments made to his family, less any amount he paid the family during his desertion. To collect the debt, the U.S. would take it out of sums otherwise due the deserter (such as old-age Social Security checks, farm subsidy payments, income tax refunds, etc.). The 1971 bill written by the Mills committee, H.R.1, prohibited crossing state lines to avoid parental support duties and decreed a jail sentence of up to 1 year, $1,000 fine, or both, for the new federal crime.

† The U.S. Supreme Court held on June 17, 1968, that unless state law obliged a man to support his stepchildren, welfare authorities could not halt AFDC payments to them on grounds of his income. Thus, in many states, no matter how rich the stepparent, AFDC aid must continue, but in all states, no matter how poor the natural father, AFDC aid must be denied if he works full time and remains at home.

and received about $5400 in cash and food stamps for herself and her five children. The room rang with cheers and clapping when Mrs. Camp declared: "We only want the kind of jobs that will pay $10,000 or $20,000 . . . we aren't going to do anybody's laundry or babysitting except for ourselves!"

"Yeah! Yeah!" shouted the audience, clapping agreement with the ultimatum of Mrs. Beulah Sanders, New York City, NRWO's vice-chairman:

"You can't force me to work! You'd better give me something better than I'm getting on welfare. I ain't takin' it. . . . I heard that Senator Long [Senate Finance Committee chairman] said as long as he can't get his laundry done he's going to put welfare recipients to work. . . . Those days are gone forever! . . . . We ain't gonna clean it!"

Senator Long should get his wife or his mother to do his shirts, Mrs. Sanders said. Taking note that Senator Abraham Ribicoff had observed at a recent committee hearing that welfare recipients should clean up city streets, Mrs. Sanders said Ribicoff should get his wife and mother to pick up trash, too.

"That's telling 'em! Hear that!" With a delighted gasp, the audience caught its breath. Applause erupted. It was as though after decades of treatment as "house slaves," the black women had turned upon the plantation aristocrats in proud and open revolt.

At the end of morning testimony a young man stepped forward toward some of the departing women. "Sandwiches at the Dodge House, ladies!" he invited. (Well-wishers had prepared a lunch for the welfare mothers at the nearby Dodge Hotel, later torn down.) "What kind of sandwiches?" one mother replied.

NWRO mothers appealed to senators at the special hearings to preserve their "right to marry." FAP would jeopardize that right, they said, by imposing new obligations on the stepfather. Declaring that this would lead to "disintegration" of the family, Mrs. Sanders testified: "Our mothers need husbands." (Later HEW answered NWRO's complaint by saying that since FAP entitled families to welfare help on the basis of *need*, not on the basis of the absence or unemployment of an able-bodied father, stepfathers should be treated the same way as natural parents.)

NWRO know-how, legal skill, and group strength helped individual families obtain bonus payments for "special needs." Everything else being equal, such payments went more often to the aggressive and articulate, or to those with such spokesmen, than to the meek.

For example, the basic income guarantee in 1970 for an urban AFDC family of four in Connecticut was about $3,515 a year, about $200 below the poverty line. But that year $4,821.80 went to the chairman of NWRO's national legislative committee, Mrs. Eliza Williams of Waterbury and her three children. Mrs. Williams' benefit, almost one-third above the poverty line, equalled the gross (and exceeded the take-home) pay of a man working year round at $2.40 an hour, 50 percent more than the federal minimum wage. And since they were on welfare, the Williams family was entitled to free medical care.

Mrs. Williams testified before Senator McCarthy in November 1970 that the House-passed FAP bill threatened her income: "My welfare benefits in Connecticut totaled $4,821.84 in the past year for myself and three children. Of this amount $3,513.60 was for the basic pre-added budget and rent, $497.25 was for medical transportation, laundry and telephone, which I receive regularly because of my special needs, and $811.00 was for special grants for clothing, furniture and household items. Under FAP only the $3,513.00 is guaranteed to me. The remaining $1,308.24 could be cut at the discretion of the state and many states have already cut out these funds."

Actually, in the absence of FAP, Mrs. Williams had no guarantee whatever. (In September 1971, within a year of Mrs. Williams' testimony, Connecticut reduced grants to 30 percent of its AFDC families by averaging into partial "flat grant" payments special needs like Mrs. Williams' phone.)

BEDPANS

Five months later, in April 1971, President Nixon replied to NWRO's complaints against the FAP work requirement. He told a conference of Republican governors:

"I advocate a system which will encourage people to take work. And that means whatever work is available. It does not mean the attitude expressed not so long ago at a hearing on welfare by a lady who got up and screamed: 'Don't talk to us about any of those menial jobs!' . . . Scrubbing floors or emptying bedpans is not enjoyable work, but a lot of people do it—and there is as much dignity in that as there is in any other work to be done in this country—including my own . . ."

A few hours later NWRO's Wiley issued a two-sentence press statement: "You don't promote family life by forcing women out of their homes to empty bedpans. When Richard Nixon is ready to give up his $200,000 salary to scrub floors and empty bedpans in the interest of his family, then we will take him seriously."

But U.S. senators were taking seriously complaints from working middle-class mothers who wanted to know, as one put it, "What gives the welfare mother the right to sit home while others work?"

Major change was coming. NWRO was helpless to preserve the AFDC status quo, for the states and counties no longer could afford it. Trapped by the internal politics of their organization and by their own fiery rhetoric, NWRO leaders could not even talk of a legislative compromise; so they pursued a strategy of legislative obstruction. They tried to block welfare reform. If time had been friendly to their philosophy, this could have been wise. But time frowned on NWRO's aims, bringing cuts in state benefits and more harsh terms.

Throughout 1971 many states reduced welfare grants, and late in the year California and New York began work-relief programs that required some recipients to work for their welfare grants.

In December 1971, when H.R. 1 still was languishing in the Senate Finance Committee, the U.S. Senate three times passed and finally enacted—without objection from a single senator—a new law requiring every welfare mother, upon penalty of loss of benefits, to register for work when her children reached school age, effective July 1, 1972. This unequivocal rule, which came to be known as the "Talmadge amendment" after its sponsor, the Georgia senator, replaced the "appropriate person" work rule of the 1967 law, from which HEW Secretary Wilbur Cohen had permitted states to excuse most unwilling mothers. The new law required the Labor Department to establish a program of "public service employment" in each state for welfare mothers not placed in private jobs. For public service work, welfare mothers would get no compensation beyond their welfare check. To goad the states into compliance with the new Work Incentive Program (WIN) rules, the Talmadge amendment provided that states would lose a portion of their federal welfare funds, effective July 1, 1974, unless they referred to WIN at least 15 percent of adult welfare recipients.

When he signed the bill on December 28, 1971, President Nixon praised its "workfare" provisions as reflecting the "national interest," but said that when Congress returned in January it should complete the work of reform by passing H.R. 1.

H.R. 1's Reform of FAP

The longer Congress debated welfare reform and tinkered with FAP's design, the more objectionable it grew to NWRO and its constituents. NWRO had cheered on November 20, 1970, when the Senate Finance Committee killed the 1970 FAP bill on a 10–6 vote in which three Democratic liberals (Eugene McCarthy, Minn.; Fred Harris, Okla., and Albert Gore, Tenn.) joined the conservative majority. The defection of Harris was a surprise, for he earlier had promised to support sending the bill to the Senate floor, where it could be liberalized. Rejection of FAP by the Senate Finance Committee was a victory not only for NWRO, but also for the United States Chamber of Commerce, which fought FAP because of its cost and philosophy.

Seven months later, on June 22, 1971, a resurrected Family Assistance Plan, more repugnant to NWRO, passed the House. The critical vote came not on final passage (288–132), but on keeping FAP in the bill (234–187). Thus, FAP in 1971 was opposed by 32 more House members than in 1970. To the dislike of NWRO, the new bill ended requirements for state supplementary payments, replaced "current need" as the basis for calculating benefits with an annual accounting period, and extended the work requirement to mothers of preschoolers. The bill also changed the work incentive bonus (although the change was more apparent than real for those who participated in the food stamp program).

In spring of 1971, responding to the impasse with the Senate

Finance Committee, the House Ways and Means Committee had redrafted FAP so as to divorce it from AFDC. Given the priority title of H.R. 1, the 1971 FAP bill called for abolition of federal aid for state welfare payments, and of food stamp eligibility for its cash recipients, as did the Heineman Commission plan. H.R. 1 proposed a federal income floor (for a family of four) of $2,400, up $800 from Nixon's original figure to offset loss of food stamps at the floor level.

There would be no requirement that states continue any benefits above the federal floor. The states would have to pay for any supplemental benefits and to account for their relationship to noncash benefits. This design, in addition to answering some of the embarrassing questions raised by the Senate Finance Committee,* helped make welfare reform an alternative to Nixon's proposal for general revenue sharing, which was opposed by Chairman Mills and by Representative John Byrnes, senior Republican committeeman. H.R. 1's 50 percent higher federal floor would wipe out all family welfare costs for twenty-two states and would save the other states huge sums.

Reflecting Mills' desire to combat general revenue sharing with welfare reform, the price of H.R. 1 climbed $6 billion above that of the administration's October 1969 FAP bill, and the administration consented to the extra cost.

H.R. 1 proposed to reverse historic federal and state roles. For example, if Connecticut wanted to provide a basic income guarantee of $3,000 for a mother and three children (lower than its 1971 guarantee to an AFDC family of four) the federal government would give the family $3,000 and bill Connecticut for the state supplement of $600 to the $2,400 floor.

---

* "I want answers to every question this committee [Senate Finance] has raised," said Mills in sending HEW Undersecretary Veneman a list of some 67 points after the 1970 attack on FAP. Mills, who prided himself on technical competence, had not scrutinized the original bill with his customary care, for he regarded it as *Nixon's* bill. H.R. 1 became *his* bill. Resentment of the Senate Finance Committee staff toward Ways and Means Committee Chairman Mills is revealed by the comment of a staff member: "If the senator [Long] works hard enough and diligently enough, his idea will show up as a 'Mills bill'!!"

In lieu of a *requirement* to maintain higher benefits, H.R. 1 contained a strong, probably irresistible, political and financial *inducement* for higher-benefit states to protect their AFDC families against loss. That is, if a state voluntarily *enlarged* cash income guarantees to offset loss of food stamps at supplemental income levels, the federal government would give the state a guarantee: whatever this supplementary benefit cost for expanded welfare rolls in the future, the state *never* would be billed in any year for more than the sum it spent in 1971 on cash benefits. Thus, there would be strong incentive for Connecticut and the other twenty-seven states whose AFDC guarantees than exceeded the FAP floor of $2,400 for a family of four to supplement FAP up to the existing guarantee level, plus cash value of food stamps. Such a move could be defended as putting a limit on taxpayers' costs while protecting welfare recipients.

When the House Ways and Means Committee redrafted the Family Assistance Plan in spring 1971, it also revised provisions for "adult" welfare. With approval of the Nixon administration, the committee decided to propose two separate programs for the needy aged, blind, or disabled (as it did for families with children)—a federal program to provide a uniform income floor, and optional state programs to supplement that floor (with fiscal rewards promised to states that opted for federal administration of state supplementary payments). Thus was born our first federal cash-income guarantee, conditioned on need only. Initially, H.R. 1 proposed a nationwide floor of $130 per person ($195 per couple) for the elderly, the blind, the disabled.

CURRENT NEED VS. YEARLY ACCOUNTING

It was because of an unsolicited letter from Worth Bateman (1971),* the man who had derailed the Nathan plan by his analysis, that the Ways and Means Committee changed the accounting period. Analyst Bateman warned that the original FAP plan to adjust monthly

---

* Bateman had drafted his warning in an article originally submitted to the *Washington Post*, but withdrawn before publication for fear of offending HEW Undersecretary Veneman, who had faithfully championed FAP from the start. When Mills received the article, attached to Bateman's letter, he interrupted a closed committee session to read it aloud. In the room was John Veneman! "Where did *that* come from?" demanded the HEW undersecretary.

benefits each quarter on the basis of *voluntary* reporting of income changes could result in average annual overpayments of about $1,000 to about 1.2 million families whose income fluctuated during the year.

In response the committee decided to base monthly benefits on estimates of income for a current calendar quarter, adjusted for carryovers from the three previous quarters of any "countable" income (above the $1,035 quarterly breakeven for a family of four).

When they saw H.R. 1 welfare bureaucrats protested the change, charging that it would injure some poor families, especially seasonal workers. Chairman Mills said it would assure equal benefits to families with equal annual income, no matter how it was spread over the year. NWRO, the congressional Black Caucus, Common Cause and numerous other groups denounced the new accounting period.

THE ORIGINAL FAP VS. H.R. 1—WORK

H.R. 1 divided needy families into those with and those without an employable person (and ruled, as Arthur Burns had insisted, that once her youngest child was three * and if day care facilities were available, a mother was employable). Employable families, including those of already fully employed fathers, were to be put into a program called "Opportunities for Families" (OFF), and given wage supplements by the Secretary of Labor. If no jobs were found for them and they had no other income, OFF families would receive the full FAP guarantee ($2,400 for four persons). When they worked, their FAP payment would be cut by a portion of earnings (the first $720 of earnings would be disregarded plus one-third of the rest). Nonemployable families, those headed by an incapacitated father or by a mother with a child below three, would get FAP payments from the secretary of health, education, and welfare.

Many critics since have charged that the work incentive formula of H.R. 1 was a basic retreat from the original FAP (H.R. 16311 of the 91st Congress).

This is an error.

On the surface it might appear that the original FAP had a lower marginal tax rate (rate at which benefits were reduced per extra

---

* Until July 1974 mothers would be exempt from the work rule if they had a child under six years old.

dollar of earnings). For every extra dollar in earnings (above the annual $720 disregard) the cash FAP payment was cut 50 cents, whereas H.R. 1 provided for a cut of 66.7 cents. Under the original FAP, however, a recipient also lost 15 cents in food stamp benefits for every extra dollar earned, raising the effective tax rate (on earnings up to $4,000, when the food stamp allowance fell to zero) to 65 percent (approximately the 66.7 percent rate of H.R. 1).

Milton Friedman (1969, pp. 1944–57), father of the negative income tax, had protested to the Ways and Means Committee in November 1969 that although the marginal tax rate of FAP was stated to be 50 percent, it actually was far higher because of social security and other taxes and the method of handling state supplements and food stamps. He told the committee that it would be a "tragic mistake" (p. 1948) to enact FAP as it was and urged the committee to insist that no combined marginal tax exceed 50 percent. But the committee ignored him.

After a twenty-two–month study, the Democratic-appointed Heineman Commission on Income Maintenance in November 1969 had proposed three features that were incorporated in H.R. 1: a $2,400 cash floor for a family of four, abolition of food stamps, and no requirement that states maintain benefits above the floor. The Commission urged states to supplement, but ruled against federal funds to help achieve this. The Commission plan had a lower tax rate than H.R. 1, 50 percent, but the rate applied to the first wage dollar (whereas H.R. 1, like the original FAP, had a zero tax on the first $720 in earnings).

Daniel P. Moynihan (1973, p. 249) writes that it was "not accidental that the Heineman Plan and FAP were so similar." He says both were constructed from the same data base (1967 Survey of Economic Opportunity conducted for OEO by the Census Bureau) and that "both sought to have the maximum impact on poverty with the minimum amount of money."

Also, Robert Harris points out that his Commission staff did "a lot of work" on costs for the Bateman-Lyday group that designed FAP and that Moynihan and Heineman conferred on the emerging proposals of their two welfare reform groups. About six weeks after Nixon unveiled his $1,600 Family Assistance Plan, Heineman told the full Commission that Moynihan had urged him not to escalate the commission plan's income guarantee level, saying "I hope you will not make us [the president] look mean."

Harris told the authors: "Although the Commission independently chose a $2,400 level, the fact that it was close to where Nixon came out [$1,600 plus almost $800 in food stamps] kept most members from strongly fussing to raise it.* Given that Nixon was doing good, we consciously desired to support him."

The Heineman plan's most significant differences from FAP were three: its lower tax rate, its lack of a work requirement, and its coverage of the total population, not merely families with children. H.R. 16311 provided that welfare benefits would cease when earnings (for a family of four) reached $3,920. The cutoff income for H.R. 1 was $4,140; † and for the Heineman plan, $4,800.

(President Nixon welcomed the Heineman Commission recommendations in November 1969 and invited Democrat Heineman to deliver the report to him at the White House, where it was publicized. But the House Ways and Means Committee, controlled by Democrats, failed to arrange a mutually agreeable time for Heineman to testify during hearings on FAP. The committee merely filed his

---

* Dissenting recommendations urging a higher guarantee were written by Commission members: Clifford L. Alexander, Jr., of the law firm of Arnold and Porter (with concurrence of David Sullivan, general president, Service Employees International Union, AFL-CIO, and A. Philip Randolph, president, A. Philip Randolph Institute); Julian Samora, University of Notre Dame sociology professor; and Asa T. Spaulding, Durham, North Carolina county commissioner. Remaining members, in addition to Heineman, were James W. Aston, board chairman, Republic National Bank of Dallas; Sherwood O. Berg, dean of the University of Minnesota Institute of Agriculture; Edmund G. Brown, former California governor; D. C. Burnham, Westinghouse Electric Corporation chairman; John M. Dalton, former Missouri governor; Otto Eckstein, Harvard University economics professor; Margaret S. Gordon, associate director, University of California Institute of Industrial Relations; Anna Rosenberg Hoffman, of Anna M. Rosenberg Associates; Barbara Jordan, Texas state senator (elected to the U.S. House of Representatives in 1972); Geri Joseph, president, National Mental Health Association; Maxwell Rabb, Strook, Strook, and Lavan; Henry S. Rowen, Rand Corporation president; J. Henry Smith, Equitable Life Assurance Society president; Robert M. Solow, M.I.T. professor of Economics, and Thomas J. Watson, Jr., IBM board chairman.

† H.R. 1's "breakeven" income should have been $4,320 ($720 plus 1.5 times $2,400; but to save money the Ways and Means Committee decided to disallow payments smaller than $10 monthly. At the expense of poor families, this reduced the cutoff point by $180 a year ($45 a quarter).

written comments in the back of the hearing record. Nor did the Senate Finance Committee hear Heineman.)

TOO LITTLE FOR WHOM?

Groping for an explanation of the anomaly of some otherwise "liberal" congressmen voting against a guaranteed income floor for poor children, some Washington newsmen offered the misleading answer that FAP offered "too much" for some conservatives and "too little" for some liberals. FAP would expand welfare. Hence, no matter how much or how little it gave to whom, it was "too much" for its conservative foes, who defined the welfare problem as too many beneficiaries. But to say that FAP offered "too little" to satisfy its "liberal" foes was to bypass the basic question: too little for whom? After all, the measure would have doubled the number of families getting welfare cash and would have roughly doubled the level of welfare guarantees in many counties of the South.

After voting in 1970 to provide a nationwide but *state-administered* minimum income of $1,600 a year for a family of four (H.R. 16311, which then died in the Senate), some of the North's big-city Democrats, in the next Congress fourteen months later, voted to kill H.R. 1, that would have provided the same size family with a *federally administered* income guarantee of $2,400 a year.

No one could doubt that the second bill, H.R. 1, would have transformed the lives of poor black families in the South, giving them undreamed of economic security and its corollary, political power. In June 1971, time of the H.R. 1 vote, an intact South Carolina family of four was denied welfare cash even if the father were unemployed and the family penniless. A deserted mother with three dependent children and no income, in South Carolina, could get a maximum of $1,236 a year ($103 a month) in welfare cash, provided she satisfied state eligibility rules (a matter decided by county officials, under pressure to protect local taxpayers from welfare levies).

If they had the luck to live in counties that offered federal food stamps, the unemployed father's family might be able to collect $1,296 in food benefits, its total income; and the deserted AFDC family $925 in food stamps.

In contrast, H.R. 1 proposed to give each of the two penniless families $2,400 in cash, all dispensed from the U.S. Treasury by federal office holders under federal rules. Moreover, every family of four with earnings of less than $4,140 (and no other income) would be eligible for some supplementary federal welfare. All told, H.R. 1 would extend eligibility for welfare cash to an additional 265,000 poor parents and children in South Carolina.

Hence it was that the four black political leaders of South Carolina, all Democrats, appealed to the twelve black congressmen of the North, all Democrats, to support the bill (see chapter 7, page 131).

H.R. 1 offered comparable economic gains for AFDC families in Louisiana, where cash benefits for a needy mother with three children exceeded the South Carolina level by just one dollar a month. Even more oppressive was the status quo in Arkansas, Alabama, and Mississippi, where an AFDC mother and three children were limited to welfare payments of $1,212, $972, and $720 a year respectively.

Altogether, 3.6 million poor parents and children in the eleven Confederate states and 3.4 million in the other thirty-nine states, barred from cash help in the status quo, would become eligible under H.R .1.

BLACK VS. BLACK

Why then did eleven of the twelve black members of the U.S. House of Representatives reject the pleas of South Carolina blacks and vote "no" on June 22, 1971, to help for the South's poor?

Bluntly put, they were obeying the first rule of political survival. They were voting their constituencies. They represented the blacks of northern urban ghettos, not the blacks of the South.

In February 1971, almost five million black children and adults, mostly mothers, were on AFDC rolls. About half of these AFDC recipients lived in black neighborhoods of seven northern urban centers (Chicago, New York City, Detroit, Cleveland, Philadelphia, Los Angeles, and Baltimore) that elected ten of the twelve Negro members of the House. The other two black members were from St. Louis, Missouri (where one of nine of all the city's residents was on AFDC) and from Oakland, California. All but the last represented districts that were predominantly black. In the ghetto constituencies of most of these members welfare was the major legitimate "business," the leading source of income.

NWRO, the welfare mothers' own organization and lobby, supplied political organization and political leadership in these ghettos to create a new small but vociferous voting bloc in Congress, a "welfare bloc," dedicated to promoting the economic interests of those AFDC recipients who already received benefits equal to, or higher than, the national average. Their aggressive vigor and intensity gave NWRO mothers political influence in their neighborhoods far beyond their numbers (claimed to have soared by August 1971 to 125,000 dues-paying members in 800 local groups from a beginning figure of 6,000 three years earlier).

In the spring of 1971 NWRO sent out the alarm, by word of mouth, by organizers, by pamphlets, by leaders, that H.R. 1, the 1971 FAP bill, threatened some welfare mothers' benefits and would curtail their welfare "rights."

The campaign reached the hysteria of claiming that FAP would "destroy" welfare mothers. At a rally against H.R. 1 at the U.S. Capitol in the summer, NWRO mothers demanded that the Senate "Kill FAP instead of me!" To the tune of "Battle Hymn of the Republic," they sang these lyrics by Neil Downey, Washington, D.C. volunteer supporter:

> Oh, they've got a bill in Congress
>   that they're calling H.R. 1;
> And it's coming to destroy us,
>   every single mother's son.
> F–A–P is what they call it,
>   and you'd better understand
> The letters stand for Family Annihilation Plan.
> Gory, gory, what a helluva way to die!
> Gory, gory, what a helluva way to die!
> Gory, gory, what a helluva way to die!
> Kill FAP instead of me!

When NWRO shifted its position to "Kill FAP!" the black congressmen followed. In April 1970 only one of the eight black members of the House, Mrs. Shirley Chisholm, New York City, voted against FAP (five voted yes, two failed to vote); but in the next Congress, in June 1971, eleven of twelve voted no (all but Representative Ralph H. Metcalfe, who voted with Mayor Daley's Chicago regulars).

It was a normal political phenomenon. If Congress were voting on a "farm reform" to extend subsidies to new crops but restrict terms of existing price guarantees for tobacco growers, congressmen from the "tobacco belt" would try to defeat the "reform." In a parallel way, congressmen from the "welfare belt" opposed the "reform" that would extend subsidies to the working poor, but would alter terms of existing benefits of their constituents.

The growing influence of black political power in big cities was demonstrated on April 5, 1971, when NWRO's "Adequate Income Act of 1971" was introduced in the House by all twelve black members and by nine white members (five from New York City, one each from East St. Louis, Los Angeles, Chicago, and a poor rural area of West Virginia). NWRO's welfare bill would make one-half of all Americans eligible for welfare benefits; it would guarantee a family of four $6,500 even if the able-bodied father refused to work —double the income earned by a father working full time year round at the minimum wage of $1.60 per hour.

NWRO leaders could not compromise with reality. Their constituents, mostly black, were downtrodden but militant, indignant over long decades of mistreatment. Once their resentment against society was converted into claims for their due, appeasement was out of the question. The welfare mothers demanded a guaranteed "adequate" income as their right, the birthright of all Americans; and they demanded jobs for their men. In 1968 they defined adequate as $4,400 for a family of four; in 1969 the cry became "$5,500 or Fight!"; in 1971 they demanded a guaranteed income of $6,500.*

Although it was anathema to the general public, NWRO could not retreat from its proclamation of the right to income without work. Any NWRO leader who surrendered on that issue would be condemned by the group's belief that only the selfishness of fellow Americans kept a decent income from the pockets of America's poor millions—black, white, brown, or red. Such a leader would be branded a sellout and deposed.

* NWRO said it based this demand on Bureau of Labor Statistics figures for a "minimum adequate" budget. BLS said its figures represented not minimum costs, but rather "lower-level" costs of a market basket of goods and services for an urban family.

THE POWER OF GUILT

Through skillful lobbying that exploited their guilt for being white and unpoor, George Wiley, NWRO's executive director, induced some representatives of church and liberal groups to support demands of his welfare mothers that Congress reject Nixon's plan for a national floor under the income of poor families. (In late 1972 Wiley left NWRO to form the Movement for Economic Justice, and in August 1973 he tragically drowned in Chesapeake Bay.)

Brandishing a dread epithet, Wiley warned that it would be "racist" to pass H.R. 1. Some of the liberals to whom he appealed "knew" all along that anything proposed by Nixon must be villainous, and it was reassuring to hear from Wiley that their instincts were sound. Wiley persuaded a bloc of religious, black, child development, and social work groups that formed an ad hoc "Campaign for Adequate Welfare Reform Now" that H.R. 1 was guilty of racial bias because it provided the same guarantee ($2,400) to a family of four as to a needy adult couple. His argument was that because the recipients of old-age relief were predominantly (80 percent) white, they received more favorable benefits than AFDC families, almost half black.

For NWRO it was easy to enlist welfare-social workers as allies, particularly since some already feared that FAP would abolish their jobs. For years organized social workers, preoccupied with status pretensions of being a "profession," had shunned the rough and tumble of political action to help the poor. As late as 1961 leaders of the social work profession had advised the government that unless an army of social workers were created to guide and counsel them, the poor could be harmed by welfare cash.* But now all was changed. The welfare poor had organized, and the welfare workers looked to them for guidance!

* An Ad Hoc Committee on Public Welfare, chaired by Sanford Solender, social worker and executive vice-president of the National Jewish Welfare Board, reported to HEW secretary Abraham Ribicoff in 1961 that "expenditures for assistance not accompanied by rehabilitative services may actually *increase dependency* and eventual cost to the community" (italics added). In response, President John F. Kennedy sent Congress in 1962 a special welfare message, the first since FDR's Social Security message, calling for more social services for the welfare poor. The 1962 Social Security amendments raised to 75 percent the federal government's share of the cost of rehabilitative and preventive social services (and eventually led to an explosion in such costs).

Social workers seemed to feel a compulsion to atone for past neglect by rallying behind demands of the welfare poor, no matter how absurd. When NWRO militants disrupted a meeting of the National Conference on Social Welfare in New York City in May 1969, the conference offered a grant of $35,000 to NWRO. In 1971 social workers rushed to endorse NWRO's demand that the U.S. Treasury guarantee an income of $6,500 a year to a family of four that didn't work and provide supplementary payments to those that did work—even though the result would be that more than one-half of all Americans would be collecting welfare payments from the remaining minority, at a cost conservatively estimated at $70 billion.

In the spring of 1971, shortly before he assumed the presidency of the National Association of Social Workers, Mitchell Ginsberg,* former chief of New York City welfare and then dean of the Columbia University School of Social Work, acknowledged:

"There is a guilt feeling in NASW, particularly among the young ones, and the older ones want to be 'with it.' It's funny. For so many years we [NASW] ignored them [welfare clients], and now they can do no wrong. We can't take a position against NWRO. We *can't discuss* it."

Among those who joined George Wiley's "Campaign" coalition against H.R. 1 in June 1971 was Joseph L. Rauh, Washington attorney and a nationally known indefatigable worker for civil rights causes. Rauh was "Mr. Liberal" himself, a former chairman of Americans for Democratic Action (ADA) and a member of its board of directors. In a telephone poll, Rauh persuaded ADA's board to retract its former support for FAP. But after H.R. 1 passed the House with support from most liberal Democrats, including ADA stalwarts, ADA decided not to count the critical vote on deleting FAP (Title IV) from H.R. 1 as an index of racism after all. Of the eight House members with "perfect" 100 percent ADA voting records in 1970, who still were members in 1971, six defied ADA's board to vote for FAP. In choosing key votes on which to judge performance of House members in 1971, ADA (1971) excluded the FAP vote.

* During the long battle for FAP, Ginsberg became the nearest thing to a full-time lobbyist for the reform. On near-weekly trips to Washington he planned strategy with Leonard Lesser, Center for Community Change, and, often, with Clint Fair, AFL-CIO.

Senator George S. McGovern, then campaigning for the 1972 Democratic presidential nomination, introduced NWRO's $6500 guaranteed income bill in the Senate on the afternoon of July 29, 1971, after promising the action to the group's national convention earlier that day. McGovern had told the cheering welfare mothers: ". . . the fight has just begun. . . . I intend to see that the question of human dignity your bill raises gets a fair hearing in the Senate of the United States." In August 1972, when attacked by Senator Hubert H. Humphrey, Minnesota Democrat whom he had defeated for the presidential nomination, for sponsoring a bill that would cost $72 billion and put half the nation on welfare, McGovern insisted that he had introduced the NWRO bill only as a courtesy. Humphrey countered by pointing out that McGovern had failed at the time to designate S. 2372 "by request."

H.R. 1 Goes to the Senate

When the House first passed FAP in April 1970, it was widely assumed that the Democratic Senate, traditionally more "liberal" than the House, would embrace and expand the income guarantee. Wilbur Mills warned sternly that he wouldn't consent to adding "one penny" to FAP.

Actually, the Family Assistance Plan probably was doomed from the outset by the implacable hostility of Chairman Russell Long and John Williams and by the conservative philosophy that ruled their committee.* No rhetoric, no presidential wooing could persuade this body that welfare expansion could be welfare reform or improvement.

Senator Long snarled that the FAP bill was a "welfare expansion and mess perpetuation bill." Scoffing at FAP's work rule as a sham, Long said FAP would pay "a guaranteed wage for not working." He

---

* At the end of December 1970, after the first FAP bill died in the closing days of the 91st Congress, Senator Abraham Ribicoff, Connecticut Democrat who had led an effort to save the bill, said: "FAP had no legislative basis. It's something you have to believe in. It goes against the philosophy and morals of most senators and House members."

recoiled from Pat Moynihan's praise for FAP as a guarantee for every family, united or not, derserving or not, working or not.

To bypass the blockade of the committee's conservative majority and win action on the Senate floor would have required strong public support for FAP. Time and exposure, however, brought not support for FAP, but instead widespread and varied opposition. In this atmosphere no senator risked battle for the reform save one, Abraham Ribicoff, Connecticut Democrat, a former HEW secretary who grasped the profound need for a national income guarantee for America's children.

When H.R. 1, the 1971 version of FAP, reached the Senate in late June, Finance Committee Chairman Long greeted it with suspicion. In opening hearings on July 27, the Louisiana Democrat said that "as bad as the system is, the mind of man still is capable of making it worse."

By this time the beleaguered band of ideological reformers knew the Finance Committee was, as Wilbur Mills later said, "hopeless." Their object became to attach a Family Assistance Plan more generous than H.R. 1's version, on the Senate floor, to some other measure that had originated in the House Ways and Means Committee. Ribicoff, who had tried such a maneuver in vain the last days of the previous Congress, agreed to lead another attempt.*

The support of most of these reformers was conditioned upon liberalizations in H.R. 1. They demanded that a good concept be made better. The basic question remained, however, whether or not to offer a federal cash-income floor to all families with children, plus wage supplements for fathers poor despite full-time work.

---

* In December 1970 Ribicoff had led an abortive attempt, with the aid of Senator Wallace Bennett, Utah Republican and fellow member of the Finance Committee, to get a floor vote on a compromise version of FAP that he had negotiated with HEW Secretary Richardson. To win liberal support for FAP the Nixon administration had consented to 7 of 10 liberal demands and made counterproposals on another 2. The Ribicoff-Bennett amendments included creation of public service jobs, federal administration, maintenance of full benefits for current recipients, and establishment of a special FAP minimum wage (three-fourths of the regular federal minimum) for jobs for which prevailing rates were lower. Daniel P. Moynihan hailed Ribicoff's efforts in a note written on White House stationery: "Dear Abe, When the history of this moment is written—even if I have to write it—one man is going to stand very tall indeed. Why are there so few like you? No matter. It is enough that you at least are there."

FISCAL RELIEF

The only strong and unqualified pressure for H.R. 1 came from those who wanted welfare change not for reasons of philosophy, but rather for the promise of fiscal relief. These were many of the nation's governors and county officials. To these men, frustrated by ever-rising welfare budgets, the structural reforms of H.R. 1 were relatively unimportant. What they wanted was money, and H.R. 1's federal floor for current welfare recipients would supply it.

Early in 1971, New York and New Jersey, the two states most liberal to AFDC families, had reduced some AFDC benefits in order to spread funds over the soaring number of welfare families. Their action confirmed a reversal of the national uptrend in welfare benefit levels. By mid-summer another seventeen states had reduced grants to at least some welfare recipients. Delaware's welfare director told a reporter, "We're just keeping our heads above water and praying for H.R. 1." Stephen Cole, a lawyer with the Center on Social Welfare Policy and Law at Columbia University in New York, said in mid-August that it was impossible to keep track of welfare cuts. "Calls come in every day about a law, proposal or executive order to reduce welfare spending," he said. National welfare costs then were running 27 percent higher than a year before. In Michigan and Rhode Island state welfare costs took one-fourth of the state budget. In Wayne County, Michigan, welfare consumed 54 percent of the county budget.

On August 15, 1971, two years and one week after he first proposed FAP, Richard Nixon weakened the fiscal relief argument on behalf of the reform. In announcing a tax-cutting and job-stimulation program to enliven the economy, the President recommended a year's delay in the effective date of the welfare reform, thus slashing his budget and pushing the hoped-for welfare funds off until mid-1973.*

---

* After the postponement the League of Women Voters asked its members to write the President requesting him to reaffirm his priority for welfare reform. "You did so well," a national board member reported to members later, "that we received a most amusing telephone call from OMB [Office of Management and Budget] asking us to turn off the avalanche and direct it to HEW. We declined to do so, feeling that the White House had the greater need."

In January 1971 the League had chosen welfare reform as its primary goal in the 92d Congress. President Lucy Benson, an old friend of HEW Secretary Richardson, and legislative action specialist Betty Vinson worked with others in the reform coalition.

Long promptly laid aside the "mis-named welfare reform bill" for the higher-priority items sought by Nixon, promising to resume work on H.R. 1 early in 1972. In early autumn Nixon appointed Richard Nathan, who had headed the preinaugural welfare task force, as deputy undersecretary of HEW for welfare reform, a new post. At the swearing-in ceremony HEW Secretary Richardson called Nathan's task the "Mount Everest of Public Administration." Nathan announced that administration of H.R. 1's welfare programs would require 80,000 employees (ending 61,000 state welfare jobs), boosting the HEW bureaucracy almost 75 percent.

RIBICOFF'S AMENDMENTS

To press for more and quicker fiscal relief, thirteen governors, including five Republicans, regrouped behind a larger reform bill developed by Senator Ribicoff. The Connecticut Democrat introduced his measure as an amendment to H.R. 1 on October 28, 1971, with eighteen co-sponsoring senators (including three Republicans). The bill was endorsed by the National Association of Counties and by a spokesman (John Lindsay of New York City) for the National League of Cities and the U.S. Conference of Mayors, as well as by thirteen civic, labor, and church groups.*

Ribicoff's bill proposed an initial guarantee of $3,000 for a family of four ($600 above H.R. 1) and graduated increases each year so that by 1976 all would be guaranteed an income above the poverty threshold. It proposed to let recipients keep the first $720 earned (like H.R. 1) plus 40 percent of the rest (compared with 33 percent in H.R. 1). As a result, Ribicoff's bill would have offered cash to all families of four with incomes below $5,720, whereas the benefit cutoff for H.R. 1 was $4,140. Ribicoff's measure extended help to singles and childless couples, incorporated demands for protection of current welfare recipients, and exempted mothers of children under six from the work rule.

* League of Women Voters, Common Cause, AFL-CIO, United Auto Workers, American Federation of State, County and Municipal Employees, National Association of Social Workers, American Public Welfare Association, American Jewish Committee, American Association of University Women, Council for Community Action, B'Nai Brith Women, Americans for Democratic Action, and National Conference of Catholic Charities.

Gentle ladies of the League of Women Voters who lobbied for the Ribicoff amendments were shocked at some of the vitriolic mail pouring into the Senate office buildings against welfare. The mood of the country has turned "uglier," said one. The League learned also that many senators felt the Ribicoff amendments went "too far" and would split the "liberal" vote.

Ribicoff said his measure would make 30 million persons eligible for benefits in the first year and cost $13 billion more than existing welfare. The Connecticut Democrat was stunned three months later when HEW estimates of his bill's cost were presented at Finance Committee hearings by a foe, fellow committeeman Senator Carl T. Curtis, Nebraska Republican. HEW said Ribicoff's proposal would entitle 40 million to benefits in 1973, one-fifth of the nation; and 72 million in 1976, one-third of the populace.*

In mid-November 1971, Senator Charles Percy of Illinois (where soaring welfare costs were consuming 84 percent of that fiscal year's increased state revenue) said that although he supported H.R. 1, poor people and states couldn't wait until July 1973 for help. The millionaire senator earlier had testified (Percy, 1970, pp. 1581–82) that his Chicago family during the Great Depression had experienced the despair of receiving "our food from a truck and an allowance to keep our electricity on." He said that work relief (which gave his mother $90 a month for playing the violin in the Chicago Symphony Orchestra) had been a godsend to his parents. Percy offered an amendment to the tax-cutting bill to require the federal government to pay up to one-fourth of new welfare costs incurred by states after July 1971. The next day, to meet this threat to H.R. 1, John Ehrlichman phoned Percy to pledge that the Nixon administration

* Apparently affronted by HEW's failure to give him their coverage estimates and weary of fighting for a proposal unpopular with most voters, Ribicoff a few days later (on January 28, 1972) suddenly announced that he was withdrawing support for the proposal to give cash to the working poor. He startled his aides and the reform coalition by saying that he would oppose income supplements until they were tested in a demonstration project that would take years. Ribicoff charged that the President "doesn't really believe in" the plan. Nixon responded by sending HEW Secretary Richardson and White House domestic affairs chief John Ehrlichman to Capitol Hill to woo Ribicoff. The result was a compromise: a provision to have the working poor program go automatically into effect on a firm date after pilot programs unless Congress objected at that time.

would support a similar amendment to H.R. 1 when it reached the Senate floor in spring 1972, and Percy withdrew his amendment. A jubilant Elliot Richardson told the press: "Welfare reform is in sight!"

It was not to be. Governors and mayors, despairing of help through welfare reform, which was mired in Long's committee, and mindful that Nixon's general revenue-sharing bill offered more money sooner, put such pressure for general revenue sharing upon Wilbur Mills, a new entry in the race for the presidential nomination, that he capitulated. In early April a revenue-sharing bill promising $5.3 billion the first year passed the House and was on its way to certain bipartisan Senate passage. This action robbed FAP of its solitary major political attraction.*

"YOU'RE A FINK . . ."

Liberal opposition to FAP had grown. Some of the arguments ignored facts and were instinctive. The impression was widespread that H.R. 1 would reduce wage standards. For example, the previous summer *New York Times* columnist Tom Wicker asserted that H.R. 1's workfare would force a mother to work at $1.20 an hour instead of the legal minimum. Actually, H.R. 1 extended wage protection to jobs that previously paid *less* than $1.20 per hour. No FAP parent could be required to accept $1.20 an hour for a job that by custom or law normally paid more.

Wicker also wrote that H.R. 1 provided no incentive to lure states into supplementing the federal income floor of $2,400 for a family of four. This was untrue. H.R. 1 provided such strong financial incentives for state supplementation that the Nixon administration's H.R. 1 cost estimates assumed it would result.

Ignoring the need to examine how FAP would affect whom, critics denounced the measure wholesale.

Common Cause President Jack Conway (1972, p. 1268) found FAP's "potential for hurting people" so great that he told the Senate Finance Committee his group would "actively oppose" H.R. 1 unless

---

* Until late June, H.R. 1 retained one other sweetener for welfare reform—a proposed rise in Social Security benefits. But the Senate removed this proposal, boosted it to 20%, and tacked it to a debt ceiling bill for quick passage so that voters would have enlarged benefit checks before the November presidential and congressional elections.

it offered some choice other than the House version of FAP. Common Cause demanded passage of the Ribicoff amendments. The *Washington Post* on March 6, 1972, deserted H.R. 1, moaning that it had become "something of a disaster . . . that should not be enacted into law in its present form." The *Post* mistakenly asserted that the work incentives of H.R. 1 were weaker than those of the original FAP.

On March 25, 1972, fighting against the Ribicoff measure as well as H.R. 1's FAP, the National Welfare Rights Organization conducted a passionate "Children's March for Survival" to the Washington Monument to protest FAP, which would have tripled the cash incomes of the nation's poorest families with children. Organizers gave the children posters to carry. Some depicted Abraham Ribicoff, Richard Nixon, Russell Long, and Wilbur Mills as "the D.C. Four Against the Poor." The placards shrieked that these four men had "conspired to starve children, destroy families, force women into slavery."

As the struggle intensified, Hyman Bookbinder, Washington representative of the American Jewish Committee, who at the outset had warned against holding out for perfection, said wearily, "We're clobbered from all sides. You're a fink if you're for it. You're a fink if you're against it. So why not be a fink for doing nothing?"

LONG'S PLAN

In April the Senate Finance Committee voted to kill Title IV of H.R. 1, the Family Assistance Plan, as NWRO had demanded, but went on to present its own substitute, which was anathema to NWRO.

By a 10–4 vote, Long's committee endorsed a plan to abolish welfare grants for 40 percent of AFDC families—those with children of school age—and to offer instead government jobs paying wages equal to $2,400 yearly (regardless of family size). The plan also provided federal wage subsidies to low-income workers in private employment (receiving between $1.50 and $2.00 per hour) and a special work bonus equal to 10 percent of wages covered under Social Security (up to a maximum bonus of $400 annually, with reductions in the bonus as wages rose above $4,000 and a bonus cutoff at $5,600 in earnings). Long's plan for residual welfare families was to set floor payments of $2,400 for four or more persons, $2,000 for three.

Now there were three major proposals: H.R. 1's Family Assistance

Plan, which not a single senator had been willing to sponsor; Ribicoff's amendments to H.R. 1, which by now had twenty-two co-sponsors; and Long's guaranteed job plan.

NIXON'S DESERTION

It had become clear that the Family Assistance Plan, which Mr. Nixon had hailed as his No. 1 legislative objective in the 1972 State of the Union Message, could not pass the Senate unless the administration agreed to compromise with a bipartisan group of senators headed by Abraham Ribicoff. Compromise provisions sought by Ribicoff's group included a guarantee that welfare payments in high benefit states not be cut, and a $200 boost in the plan's federal floor.

On June 16, 1972, two Cabinet officers, HEW Secretary Richardson and Labor Secretary James D. Hodgson pleaded with Richard Nixon to deal with Ribicoff. To reinforce their pleas, Senator Percy the night before sent a letter to Mr. Nixon signed by nineteen Republicans, urging "a humane and decent compromise reform measure" . . . without which "we firmly believe welfare reform is almost certain to die."

Earlier in June the White House had received an "option paper on welfare reform provisions, H.R. 1," developed jointly by the Office of Management and Budget, HEW, the Labor Department, and the Domestic Council staff. Three choices were analyzed: A—stand pat with H.R. 1; B—compromise with Long, and C—compromise with Ribicoff.

Option C, said the memo, (U.S. OMB 1972, p. 7) was "the only possible strategy which can get us a bill, and it would attract a majority of Republicans." Further, said the paper, a compromise could be reached without sacrifice of either principle or cost, since the terms essentially would restore some original FAP provisions and update payment levels.* Given the composition of the House-Senate con-

---

* The option paper detailed seven elements of the compromise sought by Ribicoff and said two were major: mandatory state supplementation of the federal floor, including value of the food stamp bonus; and a $2,600 benefit level, plus cost-of-living rises in the future. The paper endorsed both, stating that H.R. 1 provided strong financial incentives for state supplements, that all cost estimates assumed it, that all previous versions of FAP contained it. The option paper also said that the $2,600 Ribicoff compromise floor was more than justified by the rise in living costs since August 1969, when Nixon first advanced FAP, and that it would make fewer persons eligible in fiscal year 1975 than the 1969 bill would have qualified in fiscal 1973.

ference committee, the analysis continued, the final version to emerge from conference would be very close to H.R. 1.

"Even if we lose," said the paper, "we will be in the strongest possible position to exploit the issue: we will have done all we could to fight for real reform and the Democratic Congress killed the bill."

The analysis acknowledged political liabilities of Option C: that it would promote a coalition of interest groups and senators of both parties who had not supported the president; that enough far-left senators might desert Ribicoff to endanger the majority; and that "we will be open to increased criticism from the Chamber of Commerce and conservatives, particularly Republican members of the Senate Finanace Committee, whose votes we will need on other issues."

President Nixon announced his decision on June 22, 1972, five days after the Watergate break-in. Nixon told a news conference that he would stay by his "middle position" in support of the House-passed H.R. 1. (for which the option paper said only twenty Sentate votes could be won). "I think it is the right position and I believe it is a position that can get through this Congress," he said.

Previewing his 1972 presidential reelection campaign, Nixon had decided that he would be wiser politically to have an issue than an enacted plan. Nixon knew what the League of Women Voters had discovered, that welfare reform was a highly unpopular issue, that welfare expansion was hard to defend.

The victory went to Russell Long, whose conservative committee had kept its finger in the dike long enough for all the special interest groups to learn how FAP would affect them. In the conflict of values that came with full exposure, FAP was shot down.

MCGOVERN DESERTS THE WORKING POOR

On August 29, 1972, George S. McGovern, the newly nominated Democratic candidate for the presidency, retreated from his plan to give every American a $1,000 grant,* having discovered that it

---

* On Jan. 13, 1972, McGovern endorsed a position paper written by Gordon Weil, staff aide, entitled "Tax Reform and Redistribution of Income." The paper included this passage: "I [McGovern] propose that every man, woman and child receive from the federal government an annual payment. This payment would not vary in accordance with the wealth of the recipient . . ." The paper listed as one of several possibilities a payment of $1,000 per person, but did not commit McGovern to a specific figure. As he campaigned in the primaries, McGovern, seeking to be

would take money from the vast middle class with an income above the median ($10,300 was the median family income in 1971). McGovern (1972, p. 4) told the New York Society of Security Analysts that his new plan would not take "one penny more in federal taxes" from anyone whose income came from wages and salaries.

"The best answer to welfare," said McGovern, echoing Nixon and Long, "is work. And that is my answer."

Then, in a perfect non sequitur, McGovern proposed a welfare plan that omitted those who are poor despite work! Acknowledging that "even the unacceptable Nixon Family Assistance Plan recognizes the need to boost the incomes of those who earn too little," Candidate McGovern proposed a plan that ignored this need. He said merely that he hoped the "full employment" and other advances of a McGovern administration would relieve the working poor.

McGovern confined his welfare aid to those already on state-federal welfare. He said AFDC families unable to work should receive $4,000 a year (per family of four) in cash and food stamps from the federal government. For all aged, blind, and disabled persons, needy or not, with or without Social Security earning records, he proposed Social Security payments of at least $150 monthly. For those able to work he proposed guaranteed jobs at unspecified wages. It was the old popular and misleading formulation: Help for the helpless and work for the able-bodied. McGovern refused to face the inability of work to conquer poverty.

The End

On October 4, 1972, the Senate finally got its first chance to vote on a proposal containing key elements of the Family Assistance Plan that Mr. Nixon had sent to Capitol Hill three years earlier. The opportunity came when Ribicoff offered his compromise version of FAP as an amendment to the Social Security-welfare bill drafted by the Finance Committee (the committee's edition of H.R. 1). In making a

---

more specific than his competitors, began mentioning the figure of $1,000. Richard Dougherty, McGovern's press aide, recalled that when criticism of McGovern's $1,000 proposal arose, it began "in rather low key and George defended it, and by defending it, he got himself more and more tied to it."

motion to kill Ribicoff's amendment by tabling it, Senator Long said the concept of Family Assistance made him "tremble in fear for the fate of this Republic." Long repeated the argument that proved most powerful against Nixon's plan—that wage supplements to working poor families "would increase welfare rolls."

By a vote of 52 to 34 the Senate rejected Ribicoff's compromise version of the Family Assistance Plan, which Nixon had refused to support.

On October 15 Senate-House conference committee stripped H.R. 1 of both Nixon's FAP (earlier voted by the House) and new restraints on the existing AFDC program voted by the Senate,* but retained the little-noticed plan to guarantee a minimum cash income to all the aged, the blind, and the disabled. Two days later Congress passed H.R. 1, minus the income guarantee for children.

The dream was over.

* Conferees deleted a Senate plan to establish a national apparatus for tracking down runaway fathers of welfare families and forcing them to support their families. This rejected plan envisioned the establishment of regional blood-testing laboratories to determine paternity of welfare children, as well as a "parent locator center" in the Justice Department.

9.

SAVED: INCOME GUARANTEES FOR THE AGED

"It's not even controversial!"
—WILBUR COHEN

THAT DARING DREAM of radicals, the right to a minimum income from the United States Treasury, has come true for all but one group of those Americans who society feels should not be obliged to work.

For those who are elderly, blind, or disabled, income by right was enacted into law on October 17, 1972, to take effect at the start of 1974. Since January 1, 1974, persons in these three groups, if judged needy under federal rules, have been eligible for special new Treasury checks each month from the Social Security Administration, even though they may never have paid Social Security payroll taxes. These Supplemental Security Income checks, however, come from general revenue, not from the Social Security trust fund.

Excluded from our first federal income guarantee were the nation's children, the only other group that is not expected to work. Ironically, these were the very persons for whom Richard Nixon originally had proposed this historic birthright (although he later abandoned the fight for a children's income guarantee). The 92nd Congress left poor children to the mercy of states, many of which were slashing welfare payment levels despite the rise in living costs.

In advancing welfare reform in August 1969, President Nixon asked much from Congress for poor children and their parents, but little for those without dependent children. Nixon's Family Assistance Plan offered cash income guarantees, conditioned only upon need, for all children and for mothers of preschoolers. In addition, FAP offered bonuses for those heads of poor families—mothers or fathers—who worked. FAP would have doubled "welfare" rolls and would, for the first time, have offered cash to intact families of fathers with full-time jobs, a significant fraction of the nation's poverty-stricken families.

Although Nixon initially proposed to leave welfare for the aged, blind, and disabled under state management, he asked Congress to require that states, who then were free to set benefits wherever they chose, assure recipients a federally prescribed minimum income. (Nixon's first draft proposal said $65 a month, but by the time the bill went to Congress this figure was raised to $90 because the drafters learned that the change would cost very little. They discovered that thirty-eight states already assured the needy aged who had no other income as much as $90, but had to pay the full guarantee to only the minority who lacked Social Security income. Earlier the bill drafters had mistaken states' *average* payments for their maximums.)*

Congress welcomed this modest plan, liberalized it, and transformed it into our nation's first minimum cash-income guarantee. The only other national program offering cash on the *basis of need* (veterans' pensions) was limited to veterans.

Since January 1, 1974, the federal government has guaranteed to those over 65 years of age, and to the blind and disabled of any age, a minimum income. (H.R. 1 set the initial guarantee at $130 per person monthly, and $195 per couple; but before the program even began, Congress voted to boost the initial levels to $140 and $210, respectively, and to raise payments again in July 1974 to $146 and $219.)

Supplemental Security Income is a matter of right. The Social Security Administration requires no work record of recipients, makes no claims against their estates (two-thirds of the elderly, even some of

---

* In October 1969 state relief checks to the aged averaged $73, but the median state guarantee to a penniless old person was $118.50. (In some states, because the figure included "rent as paid," these "guarantees," overstated the case. A lower rent reduced the cash guarantee.)

the poorest, own their own homes), and makes no demands that grown children, if well-to-do, contribute to support of needy parents.

For more than 70 percent of aged poor beneficiaries, the Supplemental Security Income check is a supplement to a Social Security check. The extra payment confined to the poor is alleviating much of the poverty among America's aged. Each recipient (or couple) is allowed to add to the basic SSI payment $240 from any source. Thus, since January 1, 1974, SSI has assured every needy recipient of Social Security a total minimum yearly income of $1,920 ($2,760 per couple).

SSI recipients are also allowed to add a sizable proportion of earnings to their SSI check.* Ironically, Congress gave to the aged, blind, and disabled the wage supplement it denied to working fathers.

Federalization

Enactment of guaranteed income for the aged signified a revolution in the philosophy and financing of public charity in the United States. The new income guarantee shifted from states to the federal government the responsibility for the basic welfare decisions of who gets how much. Except for an emergency program that operated briefly in half a dozen states during the Depression of the 1930s, the federal government previously gave no relief money directly to the poor, but instead helped states and counties operate their programs of public assistance. (In the fall of 1973 more than half the total number of relief recipients were enrolled in county-operated programs.) Prior to 1974 Uncle Sam helped pay the costs of welfare for four categories of the needy: blind, aged, and disabled adults; and broken or unemployed families with dependent children.

In the field of welfare federal dollars failed to bring federal control,

* Not subtracted from the SSI check of the aged is the first $20 monthly of any income, plus the first $65 in earnings and one-half the remainder. Hence, in January 1974 an individual with no unearned income was eligible for an SSI supplement until earnings reached $365 (a couple until $505). Rules are even more generous for the blind and disabled.

for the states decided which groups to help, who among them was needy, and how much to pay them. This nonsystem produced a bizarre and unfair assortment of benefit levels and eligibility rules. Half the states refused to aid families of unemployed fathers, and Nevada never established a program to aid the disabled, despite the offer of federal funds to help finance such welfare.

Supplemental Security Income has removed from state rolls all of these welfare groups except families with children. Because SSI's rules were much more liberal, almost twice as many persons were thought to be eligible to join its new rolls as departed from state welfare rolls. An estimated 6.2 million Americans were eligible in mid-1974 for Supplemental Security Income—4.6 million aged (more than one of every five Americans over 65!) and 1.6 million blind or disabled persons (SSI covers disabled children, who were excluded from the old state-federal welfare disability programs).

THE FIFTH COMMANDMENT

By adopting Social Security in 1935, America began to collectivize the duty to "honor thy father and thy mother" that was commanded to Moses at Mt. Sinai. At bottom, Social Security is just a mechanism that, by use of the taxing power of the federal government, takes money from sons and daughters and gives it to their elderly parents and grandparents (and to younger disabled workers, their families, and families of deceased workers). When the program was young, payments into the Social Security trust fund greatly exceeded benefits paid out. In 1974, however, there were twice as many aged parents, compared to the number of sons and daughters of conventional working age (twenty to sixty-four years) as in the 1930s,* and nine of every ten aged persons received a monthly Social Security check. Today's recipients are getting back more than they paid into the fund. In fact, the amount of money in the Social Security trust fund would not pay the bills for a full year. All Social Security payroll taxes currently collected are currently spent on benefits for those on the

* In 1970 there were only five persons of conventional working age per aged person; in 1930 there had been ten. Moreover, the trend toward early retirement meant that the actual increase in the proportion of retirees to persons of working age was greater than measured by the conventional ratio.

rolls. By enacting a guaranteed income for its aged America has completed the collectivization of the filial commandment.

BEFORE AND AFTER

The dramatic impact of the SSI guarantee is seen by comparing the treatment of the needy aged before and after 1974.

The setting is a Social Security office. The place is Charleston, South Carolina. Enter John Smith, 75, retired farm worker, and Jane Jones, 65, widow of a night watchman. (Both are relatively young for old-age relief recipients; in 1970 half were more than 77 years old.)

Because Mr. Jones paid payroll taxes for many years, Mrs. Jones is entitled to benefits. Smith, however, has no "quarters" of Social Security coverage, for he worked only for small farmers and never paid payroll taxes. But he has used up his small savings and needs help. Neither Smith nor Mrs. Jones has a job; neither has any regular source of income.

It is January 1973. The Social Security clerk shakes her head and tells Mr. Smith that he has come to the wrong office. "You must go to the welfare office," says the clerk, "I'm sorry, but Social Security cannot help you. You have no benefit rights." (Reluctantly, Mr. Smith goes to the welfare office. There he learns that the maximum help available to him is $80 monthly, plus $22 in bonus food stamps.)

The Social Security clerk tells Mrs. Jones that she is entitled to $108 a month in Social Security. She frowns, disappointed. She had hoped for more. How will she manage?

A year passes. It is January 1974. Now the clerk tells Mr. Smith that although he never paid Social Security taxes, he will begin receiving a monthly check ($140 at first) from the Social Security Administration.

The clerk tells Mrs. Jones that she may be eligible for some payment in addition to her monthly $108 Social Security benefit. "Let's talk about it," says the clerk. Although Mrs. Jones owns her own house and a 1971 automobile and has $1,500 in the bank, it is determined that she qualifies for a second check from the Social Security Administration to raise her total monthly income to $160. Mrs. Jones will receive two checks, a $108 regular Social Security check (called "retirement income") and a $52 Supplemental Security Income check.

The SSI check will be golden yellow, to distinguish it from the regular green Social Security check.*

Mrs. Jones' guarantee is $20 higher than Mr. Smith's because under the SSI law the first $20 in Social Security benefits or other income is not "counted." Thus, Mrs. Jones' $108 Social Security check is treated as an $88 check, entitling her to a $52 supplement. The clerk does not ask Mrs. Jones whether she has any children who could contribute to her support (she has a physician son who earns $45,000 a year).

Only if Mrs. Jones got $160 per month from other sources would she get no SSI. If her son had been giving her this much monthly, he would have been motivated to stop when she reached the SSI age of sixty-five (or to conceal his aid to her), because anything he gave her *regularly* would then be fully subtracted from her SSI check. However, if he gave her *infrequent* and *irregular* small gifts, her SSI check would be unaffected.

Guarantee Terms

Benefit levels—A recipient's SSI payment equals the deficit between his countable income and his guarantee. There is a uniform federal floor, but guarantees vary among states, reflecting state supplements to the floor. At the start of Supplemental Security Income in 1974, the twenty-four states that had been paying an old-age relief check larger than the basic SSI federal floor to the penniless were required to preserve pre-SSI benefits of previous recipients by paying state supplements.† Should a state refuse to comply, it would lose federal reimbursement for Medicaid (medical assistance to the needy).

* Social Security Administration officials said it was decided to adopt a separate color for the SSI check so as to speed up reissuance of lost checks and general processing and to avoid confusion of aged recipients, most of whom also get a green Social Security check. "If one check is missing, we can say which one is it, green or yellow?" said Sumner Whittier, director of the new SSI bureau. Some welfare recipients protested the policy as stigmatizing. The House Ways and Means Committee had stressed that it did not want SSI to be considered another Social Security check.

† Alaska in July 1973 paid a maximum of $250 per person in old-age relief, Michigan $224, and Massachusetts $204. These were the nation's top guarantees.

These higher-benefit states are rewarded if they also supplement the SSI floor for new recipients and if they agree to federal administration of all supplements—reversing the traditional order by turning over state funds to the Social Security Administration for payment to the needy. Their reward is the promise that no matter how much a state's SSI population expands in the future, it never will have to pay for SSI supplements more dollars than its calendar 1972 welfare outlays for the aged, blind, and disabled. Uncle Sam will pay any excess.

One immediate effect of SSI was to help the poorest of the aged poor, those living in the twenty-six states whose previous welfare checks to the penniless aged were below the SSI federal floor. Such states included Mississippi, where the maximum state payment had been $75; Missouri, $85; South Carolina, $90; Maryland, $96; Tennessee, $97; Georgia, $99; Indiana, $100; Louisiana, $107; and Kentucky, $111.

Not only has SSI increased the cash incomes of many who formerly were on state relief rolls. It also has qualified an estimated 2.8 million elderly persons for cash help who were ineligible under state rules.

Resource limits—A needy aged, blind, or disabled person is entitled to an SSI payment to boost his total income up to a specified minimum if his resources do not exceed $1,500 (not counting a house, car, household goods, or personal effects of value determined by the HEW Secretary to be reasonable). The resource limit per couple is $2,250.

Under the old system, however, one state required an aged person to use up his last dollar before receiving relief; another allowed a cash reserve equal to one month's cost of living; six limited cash reserves to $300 or $350. Even "liberal" New York denied relief to an old person with liquid resources greater than $500 and specified that this counted the face value of life insurance "for burial." One state barred relief to anyone whose house had a value more than $750 above that of "modest homes in the community," and the rules of some states required applicants to sell their car before obtaining help.

Estates—The new federal program forgoes efforts to recover SSI funds posthumously. To receive SSI, the applicant does not have to encumber his house. In contrast, twenty-five states required the old-age relief applicant to give the welfare department a lien against his house or a claim against his estate, practices that curbed applications.

Relatives' financial responsibility—Supplemental Security Income also benefits thousands of middle-income families. These families live in the seventeen states that used to require grown children, if they had the means, to help support needy aged parents, a burden that sometimes coincided with that of paying college tuition. In the new federal program, there is no "means" test for an applicant's relatives. (In 1972 a California family of four with earnings of $20,000 could be required to pay as much as $165 per month—$1,980 per year—to the county welfare department as partial reimbursement for public assistance given to one or more parents. When foes challenged this law, the California appellate court stated that the practice of requiring financially able children to support their needy parents was hallowed by "four centuries of Anglo-American history.")

Under SSI neither the basic federal benefit nor the federally financed portion of any state supplemental payment is subject to state liens or state rules about relatives' financial responsibility. According to SSI regulations, states may apply such rules to the portion of the supplement paid with their own funds, but the federal government will not administer such rules nor vary the state supplemental payment to comply with them.

UNSEEN REVOLUTION

Only later are some revolutions seen. Some are not detected in the making because they occur in steps so small that they appear continuous. However, the revolutionary right to cash income was won for the aged, the blind, and the disabled in a single section of an Act of Congress, not by incremental steps.

Nevertheless, when the historic law was enacted, politicians ignored it and most newspapers failed to report it. It is probable that many members of Congress who voted for it did not realize what they had accomplished.

When this revolutionary guarantee was established by enactment of the omnibus measure, H.R. 1, it was noted by only five members of Congress other than the two committee chairmen responsible for describing the bill! Other provisions of the law captured attention—those dealing with the rules of the Social Security insurance system (a benefit increase for all widows, extension of Medicare to the disabled under 65 years of age, and a more generous work bonus for Social Security annuitants). Several members deplored the lack of a provision to protect recipients of the June 1972 20 percent increase in Social Security benefits from full offsetting cuts in welfare benefits —cash from public assistance, veterans' pensions, food benefits, housing subsidies.

Representative Phillip Burton, California Democrat * who had come to be regarded as an "ex-officio member" of the House Ways and Means Committee and the Senate Finance Committee because of his mastery and manipulation of the welfare bill, was the one House member to point out that Congress was making history in establishing SSI. "When the history of this particular legislation is written," said Burton (*Congressional Record,* Oct. 17, 1972, p. H 10299), "It will be noted that this new supplemental security income porgram . . . with a federally stated minimum will prove to be the one most remarkable achievement that this particular conference committee report contains."

Unimpressed by Burton's speech, Representative James A. Burke, Massachusetts Democrat, complained minutes later that Congress hadn't analyzed "the needs of the elderly who are totally dependent upon Social Security." Burke ignored the new program to guarantee all needy Social Security recipients $150 in monthly income!

On the Senate floor Abe Ribicoff praised Russell Long for "what was achieved with the aged category," and then defined SSI as taking people "off welfare!" † Senator Frank Church, Idaho Democrat, chairman of a Select Committee on Aging, called attention to the replace-

---

* Burton had become a welfare expert in the California legislature, where he had served with Jack Veneman on a welfare committee. Having read Nixon's original FAP sentence by sentence ("No, comma by comma!" he later insisted), he was surprised at its generosity. The bill forbade state liens against homes of the needy aged—a provision inserted by Tom Joe at HEW. A rising power in the Democratic Study Group, Burton aroused support for FAP.

† In June 1973, when the House was debating changes in SSI rules about food stamp eligibility, one member challenged Rep. Martha Griffiths, Michigan Democrat, for referring to Supplemental Security Income as "welfare."

ment of adult welfare programs by SSI's "new income supplement plan." This, Church said, was "one of the most significant changes in H.R. 1." (Senate discussion: *Congressional Record*, Oct. 17, 1972, pp. S18488–18497).

Chairman Mills said SSI would "assure that virtually no aged person will have to live below the poverty level." Chairman Long said H.R. 1 contained "a lot of meaningful welfare reform for the adults."

That was all. It is perhaps no wonder that one wire service reporter writing about H.R. 1's passage asked the *Los Angeles Times* correspondent, in amazement, "Guaranteed income! What do you mean? *What* guaranteed income?"

Outlined in fourteen pages of H.R. 1, the 165-page Social Security Amendments of 1972, the right to income in old age was as much underadvertised as Lyndon Johnson's War on Poverty had been overadvertised.

The welfare revolution embodied in SSI escaped detection because few read the plan, because few understood the welfare status quo well enough to appreciate the plan; because man interpreted the triple endorsement of Richard Nixon, Wilbur Mills, and Russell Long as a guarantee that the plan was modest.

Except for the few persons who engineered it and for governors, who anticipated savings from its federally paid floor for the aged, blind, and disabled, few knew what was in Title III of H.R. 1. Most persons never even read the antiseptic title, "Assistance for the Aged, Blind, and Disabled." This title was replaced in the closing months of the debate, thanks to HEW Undersecretary John Veneman, by the protective but bland phrase, "Supplemental Security Income." (A staff member said the Senate Finance Committee accepted this name because it didn't want SSI called welfare.)*

Neglect probably helped passage of the nation's first guaranteed cash income. Politicians and the public focused attention on the other welfare section of H.R. 1, Title IV, the highly controversial Family Assistance Plan to guarantee a minimum income to families with dependent children. But FAP was killed in the Senate.

---

* In February 1973 approximately one-third of the aged population in Louisiana, Chairman Long's state, were on old-age relief (a proportion exceeded only by Mississippi). Long favored more generous treatment of the aged.

For many reasons SSI survived the death of FAP. Unlike the Family Assistance Plan, Supplemental Security Income concerned persons who were deemed worthy of help and who enjoyed some political power. Also, since it was couched in technical phrases that understated its impact, SSI received little scrutiny. Most important, SSI solved a problem for key politicians—how to defend the Social Security wage-related "insurance" system against growing assaults by "welfare."

WINNING THE GUARANTEE

Although the Senate Finance Committee, in November 1970, rejected Family Assistance, it ratified the FAP bill's provision for needy adults. The committee accepted the concept of requiring the states to pay a federally prescribed minimum income. By this time the amount was $110 per person, up from the October 1969 draft bill's $90, having been boosted by the Ways and Means Committee with the approval of the Nixon administration.

Standing among newsmen in a second-floor corridor of the New Senate Office Building, former HEW Secretary Wilbur Cohen waited while the Senate Finance Committee voted on the adult minimum floor. He almost bounced in jubilation and said: "Do you realize what they're doing there! It's not even controversial! It's not even controversial!"

By his welfare reform proposals of August 1969 Nixon had transformed the climate and accelerated changes not ventured when Cohen was in Johnson's Cabinet.

In spring of 1971, when the Ways and Means Committee redrafted FAP as H.R. 1, they voted to go another big step. The committee dropped the idea of state administration of a federally determined minimum (funded by states and the federal government) in favor of federal administration of a federally paid minimum—a true national cash guarantee.

This revolutionary plan was born under circumstances deplored by such civic groups as Common Cause, which frowns on all closed Congressional hearings. The incubator was a committee room closed to the public and press. Proceedings were dominated by two fiscal conservatives, Wilbur Mills and John W. Byrnes. In the secret negotiations that produced SSI, the Nixon administration was represented by HEW Undersecretary Veneman and Robert Ball, Commissioner of Social Security.

The primary motivation for the radical income guarantee was the preservation of Social Security. In addition, Mills and Byrnes welcomed the federal income floor for needy adults as a means of combating general revenue sharing. The 100 percent federally paid floor of $130 increased state savings over those promised by the 1970 FAP bill. Under terms of H.R. 16311 the U.S. would have paid only $76.25 of the federally required minimum floor of $110.

Over the years the relationship between Social Security benefits received and payroll taxes paid had been eroded by provisions intended to give income support to the retired low-wage worker, to the surviving dependents of workers who died, and to those who had worked only a short time at jobs covered by Social Security.

Milton Friedman (Cohen and Friedman, 1972, p. 32) calculated that by 1972 the minimum benefit paid was about one-third the size of the maximum, but the maximum "average monthly wage" on which benefits were based could be more than 80 times the minimum sufficient to qualify.

Every year politicians complained that Social Security was failing to pay the elderly a decent *minimum*, and in four years they nearly doubled the minimum payment, made to those with minimal payment of payroll taxes. It went from $44 to $55 in 1968, to $64 in 1970, to $70.40 in 1971, and to $84.50 in 1972. Like all Social Security benefits, the minimum was paid without regard to need, and so it went to the rich as well as the poor. In fact, analysts found that whenever the minimum was raised, most of the extra money went to the nonpoor, including retired Congressmen and others on government or private pensions.

Furthermore, because most states cut old-age relief checks one dollar for each dollar of Social Security benefits, increases in Social Security did not help those so poor that they also received welfare. Instead, the effect of higher Social Security benefits was to reduce welfare costs—moving some persons off relief rolls, reducing payments to others. This shifted more of the burden of fighting poverty and of caring for the aged from the income tax to the payroll tax, which falls most heavily on low- and moderate-income workers and on multi-earner families. (The higher a worker's earnings, above the maximum wage base taxed by Social Security, the lower his tax rate. For instance, in 1972, when the wage base was $9,000, a man earning that sum paid payroll taxes of $468—5.2 percent of wages. At earnings of $15,000 the tax still was $468, but only 3.1 percent of wages; at earnings of $20,000 the tax amounted to only 2.4 percent of wages.)

Congress periodically raised the Social Security tax rate and, almost as often, the taxable wage base. By 1973, Social Security taxes had overtaken federal income taxes in the budget of more than half the nation's taxpayers (Weinberger, 1973, p. 84).

Social Security Commissioner Ball told the congressional tax writers that there were limits as to how far they "could go in making the Social Security system itself a complete replacement for an income-determined or means-tested welfare benefit" without imperiling the wage-related and contributory nature of the system. Ball said the regular contributor to Social Security "would have a right to feel aggrieved if people with only slight attachment to the work force and low social security contributions received benefits as high or nearly as high as those who had worked and contributed regularly and substantially under the program."

Clearly, Congress could not raise the Social Security minimum high enough to provide a decent income for the minority totally dependent on it without giving a vast windfall to those not in need. And such a move would have cost the worker huge sums in the regressive payroll tax. In the name of the poor, however, some liberals pushed for a general boost—even a doubling—of all Social Security benefits. Although this proposal was economic nonsense, it was politically seductive.

A few other liberals recognized an outright federal income guarantee as the way to help the aged poor without further weakening the link between wages and Social Security benefits. Together with Ball, they pointed out to the conservative leadership of the Ways and Means Committee that the guarantee should put an end to the perennial question, "But how can anyone live on $55 a month? On $64? On $70.40?" That question would no longer make sense. No longer would anyone be expected to live on the Social Security minimum. All who needed more would receive a second Social Security check, a frank welfare supplement, and it would be financed not by payroll taxes but by the more progressive U.S. income tax.

To initiate the guarantee the Ways and Means Committee selected $130 per person because $130 then was the size of the median Social Security check. In June 1972, however, Congress boosted all Social Security benefits 20 percent, and the median climbed above $155.

To assure long-time workers at low-paid jobs a higher total retirement income than the needy aged who never paid payroll taxes could have under SSI ($150 a month), Congress voted a special Social Security minimum ($170) for those with thirty years of covered earnings.

THE NEW DEAL AND SSI

It is no accident that Title I of the Social Security Act concerns old-age relief for the needy rather than the old-age "insurance" system that has come to be synonymous with "Social Security." When Franklin D. Roosevelt's "economic security" bill went before Congress in 1935, the popular cause was immediate help for the aged. The Townsend movement, which demanded monthly pensions of $200 to all over sixty on condition that the sum be spent within the month, claimed 1200 clubs and was vociferous. The popularity of old-age welfare (Title I) helped carry to enactment the more controversial plan for compulsory payroll taxes to finance a modest wage-related pension (Title II).

Franklin D. Roosevelt had assumed that the old-age insurance of Social Security eventually would eliminate need for public relief of the elderly. Although it has failed to end welfare for the aged, Social Security has kept many of the aged from poverty and limited the poverty of many others. Thus it has made fiscally possible a national income guarantee for all the aged, whatever their work history. In 1972 a total of $33 billion in old-age checks went from Social Security to persons sixty-five and over (to 13.5 million retired workers and 5.1 million spouses and survivors). Because *most* of the aged also received Social Security checks, *all* could be guaranteed a minimum income at feasible cost. By 1972 two-thirds of persons receiving state old-age relief also received Social Security.

(From 1955 to 1974 only 7 or 8 percent of Social Security recipients over 65 also received old-age state relief. The expanded SSI program, however, has qualified one of five Social Security beneficiaries for needs-tested benefits.)

Social Security and SSI in the Future

As the proportion of the aged eligible for Social Security rises from its 1973 level of 91 percent, reflecting expanded coverage of jobs by the system, Supplemental Security Income will be increasingly a supplement to Social Security.

SSI has exposed attempts to turn Social Security into a non-needs-tested welfare system. Under SSI rules, it should become clear that to raise the Social Security minimum is to increase incomes only for those whose incomes already disqualify them for SSI (or who so dislike the idea of welfare that they do not apply for SSI). Had SSI not passed, the trend for increases in the Social Security minimum, at the expense of steeper payroll taxes, would have made Social Security a poorer and poorer "buy," eventually, perhaps, a very bad buy. SSI should protect the contributory and wage-related nature of Social Security from pressures for higher minimums.

However, SSI may threaten Social Security in another way. For dual recipients of Social Security and SSI, the monthly value of Social Security payments is limited to $20. Workers with small savings who are eligible for SSI may question the value of payroll taxes that bring them a premium of only $20 a month.

When a low-wage worker reaches 62, if he anticipates eligibility for SSI at 65, he will be tempted to retire. The fixed relationship—a $20 premium—negates the effect of reduced Social Security pensions for those who retire before 65. The man can retire at 62, collect three years of reduced Social Security benefits and, then, at 65, have exactly the same total retirement income that he would have had by waiting until then to retire. Thus, SSI will promote early retirement and further increase the ratio of aged retirees to workers. In the last half of 1969 almost 85 percent of those who retired were under 65.

When Social Security benefits rise, if provision is made for corresponding rises in SSI (and state supplements to SSI) the results will be to retain Social Security recipients on SSI welfare rolls. The SSI program then would cease to be an income-tested program for the Social Security recipient, and dual recipients would never go off welfare.

If Supplemental Security attains the dignity and sense of entitlement of Social Security, recipients of the latter will not hesitate to resort to it.

FATHERS FIRST

America rejected a federal income guarantee for its children on October 17, 1972, but enacted one for its aged. Better treatment of the needy aged than of needy children is customary in American welfare. At the outset states were slower to establish programs of state-federal aid for children than for the aged and, once adopted, the children's programs were relatively less generous. The median state guarantee for a needy child without other income ($58 in July 1973) has generally been less than one-half that for an aged woman living alone ($135). Alabama and Mississippi in July 1973 gave a destitute family of four less welfare cash ($104 and $60, respectively) than a single aged woman ($115 and $75).

Poor children and their mothers have suffered discrimination in welfare for several reasons. First, they lack political appeal and support. They have less voting strength themselves than the needy aged and their relatives, and the cause of their need—the lack of an able-bodied father in the home—often arouses condemnation rather than compassion. Second, economic forces act against them. In many states family welfare payments have been depressed in order to goad welfare mothers into the domestic or farm labor market at low wages. Also, it generally has cost states more to guarantee a given payment to a poor child than to a needy adult. Most of the poor adults have needed only a supplementary welfare check to reach an income goal, in contrast to penniless children. In addition, until 1966 federal law required states to pay a larger share of relief checks given to families than of those given to the aged.

Because of Supplemental Security Income the cash income of millions of Americans—even those who failed to work in their able-bodied years—now is a legal obligation of the U.S. government. For an unfair and confusing maze of state rules to decide who among the aged, blind, and disabled is poor enough to be helped, SSI substitutes objective and national standards of income and resources. SSI has transformed adult welfare in philosophy, procedures, and financing. The new law has begun a quiet revolution.

10.

THE COSTS OF EVASION

"You trade in a man for the man."
—JOHNNIE TILLMON

CONGRESS has legislated antifamily and antiwork rules for the poor that have encouraged the rise of broken and dependent families. Although Americans profess to esteem the values of family and work, our welfare policies have rendered them a sort of class privilege beyond the reach of some.

America's poor families are divided into two groups: unbroken families, eligible for free food but no cash; and broken families, eligible for cash, food, and free medical care. Piecemeal, through cash, medical care, public housing, daycare, food stamps, Congress has enacted a bigger welfare program than it is willing to offer to *all* its poor.

Not only is this arrangement unfair—it is costly. It has damaged the work ethic, weakened the family—and thereby contributed to juvenile delinquency and other social pathology. It has consumed billions of dollars without ending poverty.

Economic Emasculation

Our welfare policy has penalized the work of low-paid fathers. In mid-1973 a father who worked full-time at the minimum wage did not earn as much as the welfare benefits paid to a nonworking welfare mother in more than half the states.*

* From gross wages of $277, the father would have netted $233 after paying $16 in Social Security taxes and $28 in estimated work expenses. If he stayed home, his

By living with his wife and three children, a poor working man penalized them. The penalty exceeded $1,000 a year in five states, ranged between $500 and $1,000 in fourteen states, and between $250 and $500 in nine states.

Moreover, if the AFDC mother, whose welfare benefits already exceeded the wages that the father could earn, went to work, she could increase family income, further widening her economic advantage over the working father. Even though an estimated 60 percent of welfare mothers had children under six years old, a sizable fraction worked at least part of the time. A congressional study (Storey, Townsend and Cox, 1973, p. 100) indicated that almost half (47 percent) of sample households receiving AFDC had adult earnings at some time during the year. In *half the states* the AFDC mother who worked in 1973 retained eligibility for a partial welfare check until her earnings exceeded $5,500 ($2.75 an hour for a full-time job). And so long as she received a penny in AFDC aid, her family remained eligible for the minimum food stamp bonus ($288 per year) and for Medicaid (valued conservatively at $500).

To compete with her $6,288 "workfare" return from wages and welfare (cash, food, and Medicaid), the father would have had to earn about $8,000 gross ($4.00 per hour). Unlike the welfare mother he would not be reimbursed for taxes or other "work expenses"; and if he stayed home, no matter how low his full-time wages nor how needy his children, his family would be barred from federal cash. Also, in most states not even his children could receive Medicaid.

In high-benefit states the welfare and workfare rewards were even higher and, thus, except in those few states that used their own funds to supplement wages of poor fathers, the discrimination against the intact poor family was greater. A Minnesota AFDC mother of three, for example, could receive an AFDC cash supplement (plus Medicaid and the minimum food stamp bonus of $288 per year) until

---

family of five would have qualified for $72 in free food stamps (that is, he could have received $138 worth of food stamps for a payment of $66). Also, in fourteen states his children could have qualified for Medicaid, but in none could he or his wife. In thirty-one states the total available to the intact family of five persons was less than what the "deserted" family of four could have received in AFDC cash, food stamps, and Medicaid.

her earnings reached $7,000–$8,000; but a Minnesota father who remained with his family and worked full time disqualified them for federal cash aid, regardless of their need.

Of course, after ostensibly splitting so as to qualify for welfare, a poor family could pool income in underground "workfare." In 1974, the first national study of welfare's incentives for family splitting was undertaken. Based on July 1972 data for 100 counties representative of the nation as a whole, the study showed that, on an average, a hypothetical family of five would gain more than $3,000 in net income if the father "deserted" (Storey, 1974). That is, the family then could surreptitiously add to the father's wages (assumed to equal the median level for his area) more than $3,000 in cash welfare and food benefits.

Analysis showed that the family-splitting incentive varied a great deal, but generally was higher the larger the family, the greater the number of benefits, and the higher the father's earnings. For many low-income families the financial gain from splitting up outweighed the costs of setting up a second household.

Fiscal "Abandonment"

Indulging in what Daniel P. Moynihan has called "invincible prejudice on behalf of the poor," some social welfarists take offense at the suggestion that a poor father would respond to incentives to increase his family's income. They reject as a racial and class slur the theory that a poor father would "desert" to qualify his wife and children for welfare (after which they could secretly pool income).

Alvin L. Schorr, formerly dean of New York University's Graduate School of Social Work, for instance, has stated that fiscal desertion is just a "random anecdote." "The poor are not less sentimental about marriage and parenthood than you and I . . ." Schorr wrote (1970). The professor said that those who charge the poor with fiscal desertion are expressing "stereotypes based on fear or anger."

Schorr would have been startled to hear the National Welfare Rights Organization itself state that welfare policies induce "desertion" for the sake of family income. This theory was expounded by Johnnie

Tillmon, NWRO executive director, in testimony before the Joint Economic Committee of Congress in July, 1973, at hearings on the economic problems of women. Ms. Tillmon (1973, p. 391) complained that most states deny welfare if the able-bodied father is at home.* "Consequently, if a father is not bringing in any income and is not incapacitated by existing guidelines," said the NWRO official, "his family is ineligible for assistance under any category. The mother is left with no alternative except to *dismantle the family unit*. The mother at that point proceeds to seek assistance. AFDC now takes the tone of a super-sexist marriage. You trade in *a* man for *the man* [welfare]." (Italics added.)

The perverse incentives against fathers, families, and full-time jobs have worked. By 1972 female-headed families comprised 12 percent of all American families with children under eighteen, and two-thirds of them were on welfare. Welfare claimed one of nine American children; in Boston and New York City, one of four. Their father's "absence" was responsible for eight of ten of these welfare cases. Among blacks, 31.2 percent of births were illegitimate, 30.1 percent of families lacked a father at home, and 33 percent of children were on welfare. Cash welfare had made the state a substitute for the work effort of the low-paid father.

Recent studies confirm the testimony of Johnnie Tillman. Welfare's discrimination against fathers has had profound impact. A study by Marjorie Honig (1973) concluded that "high" welfare payments helped to cause both family splitting and resort to welfare dependency. She found that, independent of other forces, a 10 percent rise in AFDC stipends was accompanied by a rise of 3 to 4 percent in the share of female-headed families, based on 1960 data for forty-four metropolitan areas (p. 38). For 1970 the statistical association was slightly weaker. Honig also found that where male wage rates were high in relation to AFDC there was a drop in the proportion of females who headed families. Social research about motivations is treacherous, but it is foolish for a society to establish financial roadblocks in the path of behavior that it desires.

* In April 1973 only twenty-three states offered federally aided cash welfare (AFDC-UF) to poor families whose able-bodied father was "unemployed" and living at home. By definition "unemployment" included part-time work up to 100 hours a month.

A study by Barbara Boland (1973), Urban Institute, found that the apparent pool of families eligible for AFDC increased by 24 percent from 1967 to 1970, chiefly because of "expansion of eligibility up the income scale," but that the caseload *doubled* due to a much larger increase in participation. Boland (p. 139) estimated that by 1970 all but 9 percent of mother-headed families eligible for AFDC under state rules were in the program, whereas in 1967 an estimated 27 percent of eligibles did not participate. Boland (p. 150) estimated that about 30 percent of the AFDC mothers in 1970 were "not poor" by the Census bureau definition.

In this period antipoverty lawyers expanded welfare eligibility by successfully challenging many restrictive state welfare practices in the courts. Invalidated were father-in-the-home rules, residency requirements, denial of welfare to college students by states that permitted it to vocational students, the assumption that a stepfather's income was available to the family, etc. In addition, these lawyers achieved procedural safeguards for welfare recipients' right to benefits.

Delinquency

Although denying cash supplements to working poor fathers "saves" welfare funds in the short run, it is a costly economy in the long run. By promoting the rise of fatherless families, dependent on welfare, and by failing to make a frontal assault on poverty, we encourage costly troubles—juvenile delinquency, educational failure, and social division incompatible with the American ideal of equal opportunity.

Welfare-dependent families in fatherless homes contribute substantially to juvenile delinquency rates. Numerous studies have demonstrated that delinquency is associated with poverty and with broken homes. Charles Willie (1967) found that 60 percent of the variation in juvenile delinquency rates among Washington, D.C. census tracts could be attributed to socio-economic status or to broken families, singly or in combination. In a study of youth referred to Florida courts, Ronald J. Chilton and Gerald E. Markle (1972) found that delinquents came disproportionately from incomplete families, and they urged a program of income maintenance as a remedy for delinquency. Chilton and Markle said that the pressures that cause low income often contribute also to family breakup. It is social folly to persist in penalizing poor families that stay together.

Class Division

Not only does our welfare policy fracture families; it also threatens to fracture society, freezing some persons in poverty. Poverty amid growing plenty, said President Lyndon Johnson's Commission on Income Maintenance, is the American paradox. The Commission, whose members included some Republicans and represented industry, banking, politics, labor, the academic and legal professions, concluded after two years' study: "Our economic and social structure virtually guarantees poverty for millions of Americans" (President's Commission, 1969, p. 23). The danger grows of a permanent underclass, excluded from the American dream, whose political impotence reflects its economic poverty. After taxes as before, the richest fifth has eight times the income of the poorest fifth, and in absolute dollars the gap is growing (Thurow and Lucas, 1972, p. 5).

Although the poor of America, by the official definition of poverty, declined from 22 percent of the population in 1959 to 12 percent in 1972, this was misleading. In 1959 a family was "poor" if its income was 46 percent below the median family income, but in 1972 a family was not counted poor even if its income sank 60 percent below the median! The poverty index ignored the rising standard of living of most Americans. If the index had kept pace with living standards—not simply with prices of a static market basket of goods—a four-person non-farm family would not have been counted out of poverty in 1972 with less than $6,000 * (54 percent of median family income). Instead $4,275 was the official poverty threshold (38 percent of median family income).

Under the conventional definition, there is not enough "work" for all. Public employment can be expanded, but making government the employer of last resort would create serious new problems without solving the old. What would the jobs pay? At least $4,500 a year?

---

* But in 1972, one-sixth of American families had incomes below $5,000.

Then are we proposing to abolish all private jobs that pay less? Or do we expect an unskilled person to stay at a $3,500 job for a private employer when he can get $4,500 by working for the government? What about the worker with three children? Should the government pay him $5,000 for the same job that would pay a father of two $4,500? Shall we then abolish all private jobs paying less than $5,000 for men who have a wife and three dependent children?

We can raise the minimum wage, but we cannot compel employers to hire—or retain—workers on whom they lose money. And even if we could so coerce business and industry, a higher minimum would be insufficient for some large families.

A wage supplement geared to family size—payable to fathers, and mothers, working at both private and public jobs—would answer these problems. This was the remedy proposed by Lyndon Johnson's Commission. This was the remedy proposed by Richard M. Nixon.

Cash Supplements Work

The three-year New Jersey demonstration project on a negative income tax has given encouragement to advocates of cash supplements for low-paid fathers. Although they were guaranteed an income *without work,* and were not required to go to work or to stay at work, low-paid fathers remained in the labor force. On the average, they worked slightly less (two hours fewer per week) than the control group that received no supplements. However, the fathers who received guaranteed payments earned higher average wages than the others. With the support of an assured income base, some apparently were able to risk hunting for a better job—and found one. This is a desirable result, a good investment of tax funds. As such fathers continue to upgrade earnings, their wage supplements will decline, some ultimately to zero.

Here is one case where the economically cheaper policy is the better one. To provide partial "welfare" to an intact working family as a supplement to wages costs less than to provide full support for a broken and nonworking family. Yet it accomplishes more good. It strengthens the family, rewards work, and reduces poverty.

Party Competition and Social Change

"With Richard Nixon as president, the nation can expect few significant initiatives on the poverty front," wrote the professor in the January 1969 *Progressive*. "He will not junk the poverty program altogether, but he will have no appetite for innovations such as a guaranteed annual income."

At the time no one disputed this assessment by political scientist Reo M. Christenson, Miami University. It was not even a subject for discussion. Everyone knew that a Nixon White House would not venture radical social reforms.

The consensus could scarcely have been more wrong. The change of administration ushered in not just one, but *three* guaranteed income proposals. It unlocked the door of the White House to innovations. It enabled negative income tax advocates, whose schemes were dismissed as politically infeasible by the previous administration, finally to get a serious hearing at 1600 Pennsylvania Avenue.

The new man in the White House had a different constituency from his predecessor, Lyndon Johnson, and a new freedom. Welfare had been a subject shunned by Johnson. It was a subject tackled by Nixon. Nixon confronted the welfare mess because it had become an intolerable burden for many Republican governors. And since the Democrats controlled Congress, Nixon could propose a radical solution without risk. If the Democrats denied him the reform, *they* would be guilty of perpetuating the mess.

Within eight months of his inauguration, Richard Nixon, the only president to do so, proposed two federal minimum income guarantees —cash for all poor children (including those of working fathers and nonworking fathers) and free food stamps for *all* the poor. In 1971 he championed yet another federal income guarantee, cash for the needy aged, blind, and disabled—a sequel to his children's cash plan.

Nixon's food stamp proposal was due to competing pressure from congressional Democrats, especially from George S. McGovern. But the children's income plan was neither generated by the congressional political process nor fortified by it. In response to the Tory president:

—the Democratic Congress in December 1970 passed the food stamp guarantee, after inserting a work requirement.

—the Democratic House passed the children's income guarantee (Family Assistance Plan) in April 1970 and again in June 1971 (by a closer margin).

—the Democratic Congress adopted the income guarantee for the aged, blind, and disabled (Supplemental Security Income) in October 1972 and simultaneously killed FAP.

On behalf of poor children, a weak constituency, Congress failed to act. Nixon himself helped to doom FAP by refusing to support a coalition of Republicans and pro-reform liberal Democrats that would have tried to circumvent the Senate Finance Committee, graveyard of the plan. The single contribution made by Congress in 1969–1972 to cash welfare programs for families was a more stringent work rule for mothers whose children were of school age (the Talmadge amendment of December 1971). On the record the Democrats failed millions of poor children, but Nixon's last-minute desertion of his own plan blurred the issue.

Governors, the politically powerful group whose protests had led to Nixon's proposal of welfare reform, succeeded in obtaining fiscal relief—both through an explicit program of revenue sharing and through state welfare savings derived from SSI.

WELFARE SPENDING, 1969–1972

Cash welfare, medical care, and food stamps are the three most extensive programs to help the poor. When Nixon entered the White House in January 1969 these programs cost—in federal, state, and county funds—$11 billion a year, exclusive of administrative costs. By 1972 the total cost had doubled to $22.1 billion (cash welfare, $11.5 billion; Medicaid, $8.7 billion, and food stamps, $1.9 billion). AFDC costs ($7 billion) had more than doubled, reaching 11 million recipients. Food stamp spending had increased eight times, reaching almost 12 million persons.

In January 1974 the food stamp program guaranteed to most of the nation's needy population (those living in food stamp counties) $1,704 yearly for a family of four with no income. If a four-person family had gross income of $6,300, it could qualify for $288 in free food stamps.* By July 1974 the program was scheduled to cover all counties.

BASIC RESEARCH

For policy analysts who had tried and failed to sell it as their best antipoverty plan to Lyndon Johnson, adoption of the Family Assistance Plan concept by President Nixon was an exhilirating experience. These analysts stress that there could have been no FAP had they not been given the freedom to do "basic research" years earlier, when there seemed no possible payoff, at the Office of Economic Opportunity and the Department of Health, Education, and Welfare.

"The work at OEO on a negative income tax," said James Lyday (1972, p. 390) after he became an associate professor at the School of Public Affairs, University of Minnesota, "was viewed as a semicrackpot endeavor by most persons concerned with welfare . . . the leadership at OEO [Sargent Shriver was director] nevertheless permitted that work to continue."

Robert Harris (1973, p. 367), who had co-authored the seminal program analysis at HEW on income and benefit programs in 1966, said that ". . . the analysts proceeded against the judgment of most political seers. If the experts in welfare politics of the Johnson administration had been heeded by the analysts, the detailed work upon which the new president's staff was able to build in 1969 would not have been done. The analysts were clearly warned that they were wasting their time."

Prior to the 1960s all serious proposals for solutions to welfare focused on manipulating the existing programs of social insurance, manpower, and welfare itself. Because the analysts at OEO and HEW discovered that each "improvement" in existing welfare seemed to exacerbate inequities, putting poor families who were outside the program at a greater disadvantage relative to broken families on welfare, they turned to large-scale structural reform.

It took a break in political administration for this "semi-crackpot"

---

* The food stamp program tax rate (benefit-loss rate) was 30 percent. Thus the cutoff income for a family of 4 was $1,704 × 10/3, or $5,680 (after Social Security, federal and state income taxes, and certain extraordinary expenses were deducted). Because of widespread liberal protests against a schedule that would have tapered benefits to zero at the cutoff point, a $288 notch existed there.

work to gain a hearing at HEW and the White House, as Worth Bateman pointed out. (James Storey said that the change of administration opened up new ways of doing things at the Budget Bureau, too. "When Dick Nathan came, he was willing to listen to ideas that old-line bureaucrats rejected," Storey told the authors later.)

Reason vs. Politics

Its unorthodox origin, the drawing board of economists, plagued the Family Assistance Plan, for it denoted a rational plan aimed at directly reducing poverty, not a plan to attract other constituencies for their own self-interests. And when it reached Congress, the politicians and special-interest groups fell upon it.

Most major social proposals calculated to benefit a significant group are first articulated by that group and then so formulated as to gather support from others. For example, Medicare was proposed to aid the elderly, but also served to answer the worries of middle-aged America over heavy hospital bills of old parents. Medicaid, proposed to pay the medical bills of the poor, was drafted so as to free hospitals and doctors of nonpaying charity business. Housing programs, whose stated aim was to help the low-income population, gave mighty financial support to the construction industry.

Sometimes more elaborate coalitions of interest groups build. In the case of aid to elementary and secondary education, enacted in 1965 after a generation of bitter debate, success came only after three different groups were attracted: those seeing the act as a first step toward wider education aid, those wanting to establish a precedent for federal aid to church schools, and those concerned for the poor.

For a time FAP had support of three different groups, too: 1) governors who wanted fiscal relief, 2) those concerned for the poor, and 3) the economists who wanted a more rational and equitable way to fight poverty and dispense welfare. However, group number two was split by the contention of NWRO that the bill would hurt "the poor." Governors, whose pressure had helped put welfare on Nixon's agenda, pushed long for enlarged fiscal relief via FAP, but eventually concentrated their lobbying on a more fruitful bill, direct general revenue sharing. Some economists wavered because of the plan's legislative design.*

In December 1970, when he was leading a fight to save FAP at the end of the 91st Congress, Senator Ribicoff said he had received relatively "no mail" on behalf of FAP and *none* for beneficiaries. He said that Senator George Aiken, Maine Republican, had promised to vote for FAP even though he hadn't had a letter from anyone for it. In that year the authors found no member of Congress who remembered receiving a single letter on behalf of FAP from a potential beneficiary.

POWER OF RHETORIC

White House proposals for an alteration in the distribution of American income—that was the heart of Family Assistance—deserve examination on their substance, no matter who their author is, and no matter how much he himself *belittles their liberality*. FAP, however, was denied this courtesy.

To paraphrase Hans J. Morgenthau, in the political world ideas meet with facts, and the facts sometimes make mincemeat of ideas. However, the "facts" against which FAP ran aground were political realities: the unwillingness of politicians to make hard and unpopular choices; the reluctance of American voters to expand the "welfare" rolls.

Moynihan blames a lack of general analytic competence for the impunity with which FAP was misrepresented. "Seeking to get yet more than the President proposed, liberals misrepresented the substance of the measure, and ended by getting nothing," wrote Moynihan (1973, p. 533–54). "A measure intended to be generous, and which was gen-

* Even the original bill dismayed some analysts by such concessions to traditional welfare theory as the rule that states supplement the federal floor for "unemployed" fathers, giving them an advantage over the working poor; and the "current need" accounting period. Many protested the "weaker" incentives of H.R. 1, although its tax rate on cash and food stamps was almost identical to that of the first bill. And the analysts were annoyed in early 1970 when the administration surrendered a 50% tax rate on unearned income (such as child support payments) to the House Ways and Means Committee. The Committee voted to tax unearned income 100 percent and to use the $400 million saved for federal matching of state supplements to FAP.

erous, came widely to be perceived as punitive. Had there been more general analytic competence on hand, it is not likely that the measure could have been so utterly misrepresented—which was recurrently the case—with near total impunity."

Moynihan's faith in the power of analysis to rout distortion is somewhat naïve. Certainly in the FAP case at least, Moynihan is wrong. Those who spread misrepresentations—that FAP would compel welfare mothers to work for less than others received, that FAP would jeopardize benefits guaranteed by states (many states then were cutting benefits!), that H.R. 1 was racist because it offered less to a child than to an old person—aimed at a gullible and captive audience. FAP had put the "liberalism" of many on trial, and to prove themselves some had enlisted in the NWRO army against reform. Their ears were closed to any analysis of FAP but that of NWRO. Looking for simple moral issues of right and wrong, they welcomed NWRO's easy labels: racist, punitive, slavery!

The reformers knew otherwise. Their analysis persuaded them that a national income guarantee for *all* children was a breathtaking social reform. They knew that the measure could bring economic transformation to the South, our poorest region, and to backwaters across the nation, that it would triple incomes of thousands of Mississippi families. They knew that economic security brings a measure of political power. But the public debate pushed aside the sweeping substance of the measure to concentrate on the rhetoric, which in politics and government often is more important.

Like NWRO, the president misrepresented the matter. Nixon posed the issue as workfare versus welfare, although workfare, rather than being an alternative to welfare, was a *combination* of work and welfare. Because it was work-conditioned, Nixon insisted that FAP was not a guaranteed income, but actually FAP was an unconditioned guarantee for the *children*, even if their parents spurned work.

Nixon's liberal critics, who would have rejoiced if a Democrat had proposed Nixon's Family Assistance Plan, belittled the proposal. In their attempts to persuade the voters that FAP was liberal, they were able to exploit Nixon's own deceit. On August 26, 1971, the *Washington Post* lamented in an editorial entitled "The President Must Save the Welfare Bill":

The White House has yet to acknowledge that it is in fact proposing something in the way of a guaranteed annual income—much less has it troubled to try to explain the merits of such a scheme to the public. On the contrary, it has—with all its talk of bedpan emptying and floor scrubbing and crackdowns on chiselers—sought to picture the poor as willful and culpable dropouts from economic responsibility, and it has also sought to picture its own enlightened measure as something that would make the Elizabethan Poor Laws look munificent by comparison.

Mistaken plea! In both public opinion polls and new law (food stamp amendments, December 1970) the American public had demanded work from able-bodied recipients of public charity. A Nixon confession that FAP was a guaranteed income could be expected to drive *against* FAP virtually all voters except those already committed to the concept. Did *they* require Nixon's endorsement?

Nixon's failure to advertise the truth about his radical bill, which would have alienated his natural constituency, cannot excuse the liberals for failing to recognize and support it, for failing to educate *their* constituency. Concerned first for their political safety, however, most "liberal" politicians refused to defend the Family Assistance Plan. In order to champion FAP one had to defend vastly larger "welfare" rolls and brave the wrath of NWRO and its allies. This course of action could bring only political discredit, and so the politicians flinched from it.

WANTED: THE EXERCISE OF RESTRAINT

The FAP debate demonstrated that economic perils, as well as political troubles, afflict income guarantees.

As the devastating Senate Finance Committee hearings proved, focus on cash welfare alone is too narrow. A guarantee must be designed so that work is not discouraged by the fast rate at which earnings reduce combined benefits—from cash, Medicaid, food, housing. A congressional study (Storey, 1972) indicates that most recipients of cash welfare benefit from other benefit programs as well.

Milton Friedman has urged that the combined marginal tax rate (benefit reduction rate) not exceed 50 percent. But under a 50 percent negative income tax plan, a $500 increase in the guarantee brings a $1,000 increase in the cutoff income, qualifying new millions for partial supplements.

The logically inescapable conclusion, one resisted by the traditional liberal, is that the basic guarantee must be modest. Otherwise, the program will extend well into the middle class, cost many billions, yet give only a relatively small proportion of those billions to the poor.

Not only would a "liberal" guarantee give large aid to the non-needy but, ironically, some think it might impede lasting net gains for the poor.* Many politicians, whose premise was that "more" is always better, did not heed the arithmetic. After the initial shock of Nixon's radical proposal subsided, liberal politicians began outbidding him, just as Spiro Agnew had forecast.

Good vs. Good

Good will and exhortations will not solve poverty, nor will posturing for political credit. Painful choices must be made, for the issues cannot be reduced to good versus bad. In the frustrating field of work and welfare, unless we are willing to pay astronomical costs, we can have more of one good (such as generous help) only by accepting less of another (such as generous work incentive). A relatively modest guarantee facilitates a low and generous benefit-loss rate. A high guarantee requires a high marginal tax rate.

The old dichotomy of work versus welfare is a corrupting falsehood that evades reality. To escape poverty some workers require income supplements. We have granted cash wage supplements to welfare mothers and to the aged, the blind, the disabled. To continue to deny them to poor working fathers (and nonwelfare mothers) is to assault the work ethic and endanger the American family.

Although the Family Assistance Plan was lost, the struggle was useful. Nixon's proposal itself was a good deed. It put income guarantees

* Washington University economist Hyman P. Minsky (1969) has warned that any but a modest negative income tax might tend to induce inflation, reduce work, depress real incomes of workers and, in the end, erode the net benefits of intended beneficiaries. Christopher Green, McGill University economics professor, analyzed the impact of a negative income tax plan on aggregate output and the price level for the Heineman Commission. Green's summary (1969, pp. 118–19) was that the impact "depends importantly" on whether or not the economy initially is at a full employment level and on the method of financing the plan (by taxes or borrowing).

on the national political agenda. It led directly to our first national cash-income guarantee, Supplemental Security Income. It dramatized the antiwork, antifather, antifamily pressures of welfare policy. And it awakened America to the existence of millions of persons in working poor families, those whom Elliot Richardson has called "the casualties of the free enterprise system."

EPILOGUE

In his 1974 State of the Union address, Richard Nixon served notice that he would ask Congress to reopen the welfare debate that had collapsed fifteen months earlier upon the death of the Family Assistance Plan.

Nixon said he planned later in the year to make a "major new effort" to replace the maze of costly, uncoordinated, and inefficient programs that gave cash, food, housing subsidies, and other services to the poor. Observing that neither Congress nor the country had accepted his original plan, the president said he did not intend to resubmit a new version of the Family Assistance Plan.

However, the major guidelines that Nixon decreed for welfare reform pointed straight toward another negative income tax proposal, possibly more sweeping than FAP had been. He specified that a welfare reform should:

—provide strong work incentives for those able to help themselves.

—provide help in cash rather than in kind.

—be as simple as possible, with objective rules.

—focus help on those who need it most.

—provide equitable help nationwide.

These criteria could best be achieved by a classical variety of negative income tax—a program open to all on an objective test of income, and integrated with the positive income tax system, as Milton Friedman had proposed back in 1962. Aware of this, analysts in Caspar Weinberger's Department of Health, Education, and Welfare had been working for months to perfect such a plan and to sell it to the White House.

"Let us have as our goal," said Nixon, in an echo of the popular theme of his August 1969 workfare speech, "that there will be no government program which makes it more profitable to go on welfare than to go to work."

Urging Congress to join him in making 1974 a year of discussion and debate about welfare, Nixon said he hoped the debate would focus on the substance of the issues, "not on superficial labels."

It was an ironic plea to come from the president who had tried to camouflage the substance of his own good deed.

REFERENCES

Advisory Council on Public Welfare. 1966. *"Having the Power, We Have the Duty,"* Report to the Secretary of Health, Education, and Welfare. Washington: U.S. Government Printing Office.

Agnew, Spiro T. 1969. Memorandum for the President, "Welfare Reform" (August 4), 4 pages.

Altmeyer, Arthur J. 1949. Hearings, U.S. House Committee on Ways and Means, *Public Welfare Act of 1949,* H.R. 2892 (February-March). 81st Cong., 1st Sess. Washington: U.S. Government Printing Office.

Americans for Democratic Action. 1971. Legislative Newsletter (September 2), Washington, D.C.

Anderson, Martin. 1969a. "A Short History of a 'Family Security System'" (April 14), 6 pages. (Excerpts from Polanyi, Karl. 1957. *The Great Transformation.* Paperback edition. Boston: Beacon Press, copyright 1944.)

—————— 1969b. Memorandum for Arthur Burns concerning Polanyi's interpretation of Speenhamland (May 5), 4 pages.

Bateman, Worth. 1969. "Basic Issues in Income Maintenance and Welfare," 16-page analysis prepared for the new secretary of health, education, and welfare, in a loose-leaf book of HEW policy issues (February).

—————— 1971. "A Sleeper in H.R. 1?" (March 4), 5 pages.

Biemiller, Andrew J. 1969. Hearings, U.S. House Committee on Ways and Means, *Social Security and Welfare Proposals,* pt. 5 (November 6), 91st Cong., 1st Sess. Washington: U.S. Government Printing Office.

Boland, Barbara. 1973. "Participation in the Aid to Families with Dependent Children Program (AFDC)," *The Family, Poverty, and Welfare Programs: Factors Influencing Family Stability* (paper no. 12, part 1, in series "Studies in Public Welfare," prepared for use of the Subcommittee on Fiscal Policy, Joint Economic Committee of Congress). Washington: U.S. Government Printing Office.

Bookbinder, Hyman. 1969. Hearings, U.S. House Committee on Ways and Means, *Social Security and Welfare Proposals,* pt. 5 (November 4), 91st Cong., 1st Sess. Washington: U.S. Government Printing Office.

Burns, Arthur F. 1969a. Memorandum for the President, "Investing in Human Dignity, a Study of the Welfare Problem" (April 21), 33 pages (April 24, 13-page appendix).

———— 1969b. Memorandum for the President, "A Plan for Welfare Reform" (July 14), 13 pages.

Chilton, Ronald J. and Gerald E. Markle. 1972. "Family Disruption, Delinquent Conduct, and the Effect of Subclassification," *American Sociological Review*, 37 (February), 93–99.

Clark, Robert. 1970. Hearings, U.S. Senate Committee on Finance, *Family Assistance Act of 1970*, H.R. 16311, pt. 3 (August 25), 91st Cong., 2d Sess. Washington: U.S. Government Printing Office.

Cohen, Wilbur J. and Milton Friedman. 1972. *Social Security: Universal or Selective?* ("Rational debate" seminar). Washington: The American Enterprise Institute for Public Policy Research.

Conway, Jack. 1972. Hearings, U.S. Senate Committee on Finance, *Social Security Amendments of 1971*, H.R. 1, pt. 3 (January 26). 92d Congress, 1st and 2d Sess. Washington: U.S. Government Printing Office.

Council of Economic Advisers. January 1964. Annual Report, in *Economic Report of the President*. Washington: U.S. Government Printing Office.

———— January 1966. Annual Report, in *Economic Report of the President*. Washington: U.S. Government Printing Office.

Ehrlichman, John D. 1969. Memorandum to Ed Morgan re: FSS. (July 10), 2 pages.

Finch, Robert. 1969a. "A Nixon Alternative," Proposal for the President (April 1), 13 pages.

———— 1969b. Memorandum to the President, "Response to Arthur Burns' Welfare Proposal" (April 30), 16 pages.

———— 1969c. Memorandum to the President, "Scenario on Welfare Reform" (June 11).

Friedman, Milton. 1962. *Capitalism and Freedom*. Chicago: University of Chicago Press.

———— 1968. "The Case for a Negative Income Tax," in Melvin Laird, ed., *Republican Papers*. Paperback ed. Garden City, N.Y.: Anchor.

———— 1969. Hearings, U.S. House Committee on Ways and Means, *Social Security and Welfare Proposals*, pt. 6 (November 7), 91st Cong., 1st Sess. Washington: U.S. Government Printing Office.

Garfinkel, Irwin. 1974. "Income Transfer Programs and Work Effort: A Review," *Public Welfare Programs: How They Affect Recipients' Work Behavior*. (Paper No. 13 in series "Studies in Public Welfare," prepared for use of the Subcommittee on Fiscal Policy, Joint Economic Committee, U.S. Congress.) Washington: U.S. Government Printing Office.

Glasser, Melvin A. 1969. Hearings, U.S. House Committee on Ways and Means, *Social Security and Welfare Proposals*, pt. 6 (November 7), 91st Cong., 1st Sess. Washington: U.S. Government Printing Office.

Glazer, Nathan. 1969. "On Task Forcing," *The Public Interest*. 15 (Spring) 40–45.

Green, Christopher. 1969. "A Macroeconomic Analysis of the Economic Impact of Negative Income Taxes," *The President's Commission on Income Maintenance Programs: Technical Studies*. Washington: U.S. Government Printing Office.

Griffiths, Martha. 1968. Hearings, U.S. Congress Subcommittee on Fiscal Policy of the Joint Economic Committee, *Income Maintenance Programs*, pt. 1, proceedings (June 18), 90th Cong., 2d Sess. Washington: U.S. Government Printing Office.

Harris, Robert. 1973. "Policy Analysis and Policy Development," *Social Service Review* (September), pp. 260–72.

Heineman, Ben W. 1969. "Guaranteed Annual Income: A Placebo or a Cure?" Speech prepared for meeting of National Industrial Conference Board, New York City (March 21). Published in the *Conference Board Record*, 6 (May 1969), 28–31.

Hillenbrand, Bernard F. 1969. Hearings, U.S. House Committee on Ways and Means, *Social Security and Welfare Proposals* pt. 3 (October 22), 91st Cong., 1st Sess., Washington: U.S. Government Printing Office.

Honig, Marjorie. 1973. "The Impact of Welfare Payment Levels on Family Stability," in *The Family, Poverty, and Welfare Programs: Factors Influencing Family Stability* (paper No. 12, part 1, in series "Studies in Public Welfare," prepared for use of the Subcommittee on Fiscal Policy, Joint Economic Committee of Congress). Washington: U.S. Government Printing Office.

Laird, Melvin R. 1969. Memorandum for the President, "Family Security Plan" (May 7), 12 pages.

Lampman, Robert J. January 1970. "Transfer Approaches to Distribution Policy." (Paper prepared for meetings of American Economic Association, New York, during December 1969.) Madison: Institute for Research on Poverty, University of Wisconsin.

Levine, Robert A. 1965. Memo to Joseph Kershaw on September 7 meeting of White House Task Force on Income Maintenance (September 8).

—— 1970. *The Poor Ye Need Not Have with You: Lessons from the War on Poverty*. Cambridge, Mass.: M.I.T. Press.

Lyday, James. 1972. "An Advocate's Process Outline for Policy Analysis: The Case of Welfare Reform," *Urban Affairs Quarterly*, 7 (June), 385–402.

McCracken, Paul W. 1969a. Memorandum for the President, "Possible Resolution of the Welfare Reform Controversy" (May 24), 3 pages.

—— 1969b. Memorandum for Mr. Edward L. Morgan, "Comments on Second Draft—Family Security" (July 21), 2 pages.

McGovern, George S. 1972. "A Balanced Full Employment Economy," remarks before the New York Society of Security Analysts, New York City (August 29), 8 pages. Text from McGovern/Shriver 1972 headquarters, Washington.

Meany, George. 1969. News release from the AFL-CIO, for Friday, April 15, 5 pages.

Minsky, Hyman P. 1969. "The Macroeconomics of a Negative Income Tax," unpublished paper prepared for the American Academy of Arts and Sciences, Conference on Income and Poverty (May 16–17).

Mitchell, Clarence. 1969. Hearings, U.S. House Committee on Ways and Means, *Social Security and Welfare Proposals*, pt. 3 (October 24), 91st Cong., 1st Sess. Washington: U.S. Government Printing Office.

Moynihan, Daniel P. 1969a. Memorandum for the President on New York City welfare situation (January 31), 12 pages.

—— 1969b. Memorandum for the President, "Domestic Program Abstracts— Backup Memoranda" (April 1).

———— 1969c. Memorandum for the President recommending early announcement of welfare plan (April 11).

———— 1969d. Memorandum for the President, "Comment on Dr. Anderson's 'A Short History of a Family Security System'" (April 22), 2 pages.

———— 1969e. Memorandum for the President, "Comment on Paul W. McCracken's Memorandum, 'A Possible Resolution of the Welfare Reform Controversy'" (June 6), 5 pages.

———— 1969f. Memorandum for the President concerning timing for the welfare proposal (June 30), 2 pages.

———— 1973. *The Politics of a Guaranteed Income: The Nixon Administration and the Family Assistance Plan*. New York: Random House.

Nathan, Richard. 1968. *Report of President-Elect's Transitional Task Force on Public Welfare* (December 28), typewritten; 49 pages text, 14 pages appendix.

Nixon, Richard M. 1969a. Address of the President on Nationwide Radio and Television: Welfare reform. (August 8), 13 pages. Mimeographed ed. Washington: Office of the White House Press Secretary.

———— 1969b. Message to the Congress of the U.S. on Welfare reform. (August 11), 8 pages text and 1 page appendix. Mimeographed ed. Washington: Office of the White House Press Secretary.

Orshansky, Mollie. 1963. "Children of the Poor," *Social Security Bulletin* (July), pp. 3–13. Washington: Social Security Administration.

———— 1965. "Counting the Poor," *Social Security Bulletin* (January), pp. 3–29. Washington, Social Security Administration.

Percy, Charles H. 1970. Hearings, U.S. Senate Committee on Finance, *Family Assistance Act of 1970*, H.R. 1631, pt. 3 (August 26), 91st Cong., 2d Sess. Washington: U.S. Government Printing Office.

Perkins, Frances. 1946. *The Roosevelt I Knew*. New York: Viking.

Piven, Frances Fox and Richard A. Cloward. 1971. *Regulating the Poor: The Functions of Public Welfare*. New York: Pantheon.

President's Commission on Income Maintenance Programs. 1969. *Poverty Amid Plenty: The American Paradox*. Washington: U.S. Government Printing Office.

Proxmire, William. 1968. Hearings before the Subcommittee on Fiscal Policy of the Joint Economic Committee, *Income Maintenance Programs*. 90th Cong., 2d Sess. Washington: U.S. Government Printing Office.

Ripon Forum. 1967. "The Negative Income Tax," a Ripon research paper (April). Cambridge: Ripon Society.

Rosenman, Sam. 1952. *Working with Roosevelt*. New York: Harper.

Safire, William. 1969a. "Family Security," 2d draft (July 11), 13 pages.

———— 1969b. Friday Domestic Speech, 7th Draft (August 7), 22 pages.

Schorr, Alvin L. 1970. "Views on the Welfare Plan," *New York Times*. (December 1), p. C 47.

Schwartz, Edward. 1964. "A Way to End the Means Test," *Social Work* 9 (July) 3–12. Reprinted in Robert Theobald, ed., *The Guaranteed Income*, paperback edition. Garden City, N.Y.: Anchor, 1968.

Shriver, Sargent. October 20, 1965. Memorandum to Charles L. Schultze, Budget Bureau Director, "National Anti-Poverty Plan."

Shultz, George P. 1969. Memorandum for the President, "The Present Welfare

System and the Proposed Family Security System" (June 10), 28 pages of text, 6 pages of charts.

Stans, Maurice H. 1969. Memorandum for the President (May 8), 3 pages.

Steiner, Gilbert Y. 1966. *Social Insecurity: The Politics of Welfare*. Chicago: Rand McNally and Co.

Stigler, George. 1946. "The Economics of Minimum Wage Legislation," *American Economic Review* 36 (June), pp. 358–65.

Storey, James R. 1972. *Public Income Transfer Programs: The Incidence of Multiple Benefits and the Issues Raised by Their Receipt* (paper No. 1 in series "Studies in Public Welfare," prepared for use of the Subcommittee on Fiscal Policy, Joint Economic Committee of Congress). Washington: U.S. Government Printing Office.

——— 1974. *Welfare in the Seventies: A National Study of Benefits Available in 100 Local Areas* (paper No. 15 in series "Studies in Public Welfare," prepared for the use of the Subcommittee on Fiscal Policy, Joint Economic Committee of Congress). Washington: U.S. Government Printing Office.

——— Alair A. Townsend, and Irene Cox. 1973. *How Public Welfare Benefits are Distributed in Low-Income Areas* (paper No. 6 in series "Studies in Public Welfare," prepared for use of the Subcommittee on Fiscal Policy, Joint Economic Committee of Congress). Washington: U.S. Government Printing Office.

Thurow, Lester and Robert E. Lucas. 1972. *American Distribution of Income: A Structural Problem* (a study prepared for use of the Joint Economic Committee of Congress). Washington: U.S. Government Printing Office.

Tillmon, Johnnie. 1973. Hearings, Joint Economic Committee of Congress, *Economic Problems of Women*, pt. 2 (July 26), 93d Cong., 1st Sess. Washington: U.S. Government Printing Office.

Tobin, James. 1968. "Raising the Incomes of the Poor," in Kermit Gordon, ed., *Agenda for the Nation*. Washington: Brookings Institution.

U.S. Congress. 1972. *Congressional Record* (October 17), 92d Cong., 2d Sess. Washington: U.S. Government Printing Office.

U.S. Department of Health, Education, and Welfare. October 1966. "Program Analysis: Income and Benefit Programs." Washington: Office of the Assistant Secretary for Program Coordination.

——— 1971a. "Public Assistance Statistics, April 1971." Washington: DHEW Publication No. (SRS) 72–03100.

——— 1971b. "Standards for Basic Needs for Specified Types of Assistance Groups, March 1971." Washington: NCSS Report D–2.

——— 1972. "Findings of the 1971 AFDC Study, Part II, Financial Circumstances."

——— 1973. *Summary Report: New Jersey Graduated Work Incentive Experiment*. (December) Washington: Office of the Assistant Secretary for Planning and Evaluation. Washington: DHEW Publication No. (SRS) 72–03757.

U.S. Department of Labor, Office of Policy Planning and Research. March 1965. "The Negro Family: The Case for National Action." Washington: U.S. Government Printing Office. Reprinted in Rainwater, Lee, and William L. Yancy, 1967. *The Moynihan Report and the Politics of Controversy*. Cambridge, Mass.: M.I.T. Press.

U.S. House of Representatives. Committee on Ways and Means. 1967. Report on H.R. 12080, *Social Security Amendments of 1967*, House Report 544, 90th Cong., 1st Sess. Washington: U.S. Government Printing Office.

U.S. Office of Economic Opportunity. 1973. *National Anti-Poverty Plan, FY 1968–FY 1972*, pt. 9. Program memorandum submitted to Bureau of the Budget, June 30, 1966. Reprinted in U.S. Senate Committee on Government Operations, *A New Federalism: Hearings*, pt. 2 (February and March), 93d Cong., 1st Sess. Washington: U.S. Government Printing Office.

U.S. Office of Management and Budget, Department of Health, Education, and Welfare, Department of Labor, and Domestic Council Staff, 1972. Memorandum to the President, *Option Paper on Welfare Reform Provisions*, H.R. 1. (June 2), 19 pages, text and tables.

U.S. Senate. Committee on Finance. 1967a. Hearings on H.R. 12080, *Social Security Amendments of 1967*, 90th Cong., 1st Sess. Washington: U.S. Government Printing Office.

———— 1967b. Report on H.R. 12080, *Social Security Amendments of 1967*, Senate Report 744, 90th Cong., 1st Sess. Washington: U.S. Government Printing Office.

———— 1970. Hearings on H.R. 16311, *Family Assistance Act of 1970*. 91st Cong., 2d Sess. Washington: U.S. Government Printing Office.

———— 1972. Hearings on H.R. 1, *Social Security Amendment of 1971*, 92d Cong., 1st and 2d Sess. Washington: U.S. Government Printing Office.

Weinberger, Caspar W. 1973. Hearing, U.S. Senate Committee on Finance, *Child Support and the Work Bonus*, S. 1842, S. 2081. (September 25) 93rd Cong., 1st Sess. Washington: U.S. Government Printing Office.

Willie, Charles V. 1967. "The Relative Contribution of Family Status and Economic Status to Juvenile Delinquency," *Social Problems* (Winter) 14, pp. 326–34.

Witte, Edwin E. 1962. *Development of the Social Security Act*. Madison: University of Wisconsin Press.

Wurf, Jerry. 1970. Hearings, U.S. Senate Committee on Finance, *Family Assistance Act of 1970*, H.R. 16311, pt. 3 (August 27), 91st Cong., 2d Sess. Washington: U.S. Government Printing Office.

INDEX